Windows NT, UNIX, NetWare Migration and Coexistence

A Professional's Guide

Windows NT, UNIX, NetWare Migration and Coexistence

A Professional's Guide

Raj Rajagopal
Senior Computer Scientist
IIT Research Institute
Lanham, Maryland

CRC Press
Boca Raton Boston London New York Washington, D.C.

LIMITED WARRANTY

CRC Press LLC warrants the physical diskette(s) enclosed herein to be free of defects in materials and workmanship for a period of thirty days from the date of purchase. If within the warranty period CRC Press LLC receives written notification of defects in materials or workmanship, and such notification is determined by CRC Press LLC to be correct, CRC Press LLC will replace the defective diskette(s).

The entire and exclusive liability and remedy for breach of this Limited Warranty shall be limited to replacement of defective diskette(s) and shall not include or extend to any claim for or right to cover any other damages, including but not limited to, loss of profit, data, or use of the software, or special, incidental, or consequential damages or other similar claims, even if CRC Press LLC has been specifically advised of the possibility of such damages. In no event will the liability of CRC Press LLC for any damages to you or any other person ever exceed the lower suggested list price or actual price paid for the software, regardless of any form of the claim.

CRC Press LLC specifically disclaims all other warranties, express or implied, including but not limited to, any implied warranty of merchantability or fitness for a particular purpose. Specifically, CRC Press LLC makes no representation or warranty that the software is fit for any particular purpose and any implied warranty of merchantability is limited to the thirty-day duration of the Limited Warranty covering the physical diskette(s) only (and not the software) and is otherwise expressly and specifically disclaimed.

Since some states do not allow the exclusion of incidental or consequential damages, or the limitation on how long an implied warranty lasts, some of the above may not apply to you.

Library of Congress Cataloging-in-Publication Data

Rajagopal, Raj.
Windows NT, UNIX, netware migration and coexistence:
a professional's guide/ by Raj Rajagopal.
p. cm.
Includes index..
ISBN 0-8493-1669-3 (alk. paper)
1. Microsoft Windows NT. 2. UNIX (Computer file) 3. NetWare (Computer file) I. Title.
QA76.76.063R343 1997
005.4´469–dc21 97–40478
CIP

International Standard Book Number 0-8493-1669-3
Library of Congress Card Number 97-40478
Printed in the United States of America 1 2 3 4 5 6 7 8 9 0
Printed on acid-free paper

About the Author

Raj Rajagopal has more than 17 years of professional experience in all phases of software development, including requirements, architecture, high-level design, low-level design, coding, testing, maintenance, and project and line management. He is currently Senior Computer Scientist at Illinois Institute of Technology Research Institute (IITRI) involved with technology assessments. Prior to IITRI, he worked at IBM for nearly 10 years.

He speaks at conferences, writes magazine articles and books, and reviews books. He recently presented a paper on simulation methodology at the 1997 Summer Simulation Conference. He has spoken at industry conferences such as SHARE and represented IBM on the AIIM standards committee and acted as the committee's secretary. His articles have been published in *Computer Technology Review* and *Application Development Trends*. He has also written and presented many papers at IBM technical conferences.

He is principal or co-author of more than a dozen technical reports on topics such as UNIX vs. Windows NT, modeling/simulation, imaging, office automation, etc., that have been distributed to IITRI customers. He recently completed technical reviews of *Windows NT Programming from the Ground Up* and *Windows NT Registry Troubleshooting*. He is the co-author of multiple patents in computer software.

He has won many awards from the companies he has worked for and has taught computer science and management courses at the University of Maryland, Johns Hopkins University, and the University of the District of Columbia. He has an M.B.A. and an M.S. (computer science) in addition to undergraduate degrees in electronics, communications, and mathematics. He can be reached at RRajagop@capaccess.org.

Also by Raj Rajagopal
Windows NT 4 Advanced Programming, published by Osborne, McGraw-Hill, 1997.

To my daughter Sheila, who is eager to see her name in print, to my son Venkat, who I hope will one day be just as eager, to my wife Chitra, and to my parents.

Acknowledgments

To make this book practical and useful, I have included brief descriptions of products that support a migration or coexistence approach along with discussions of the approach. These descriptions typically are brief summaries of more descriptive product information available at the Web sites of the different product vendors. The source Web address of a product's vendor is mentioned when a product is described. Vendor contact information is also included in Appendix A.

I would like to thank Digital Equipment Corporation, in particular, for the use of some materials published by DEC as part of its AllConnect for UNIX program.

Table of Contents

Part One
Migrating Current Applications and Developing New Applications

Part Two
Coexistence with Heterogeneous Systems

Part Three
Systems Administration and Other Considerations

Part One

Migrating Current Applications and Developing New Applications

1 Overview

INTRODUCTION

Microsoft's Windows NT is competing for the UNIX stronghold-enterprise applications. UNIX already supports many mission-critical applications developed in-house or as third-party applications. Microsoft has established itself on the desktop with Windows and is trying to extend its success to the whole enterprise with Windows NT for the server, Windows NT Workstation and Windows 95 for the desktop, and WIN32, OLE, and Active X technologies. Microsoft is expected to increase its market share based on the strong server functions of Windows NT; its ability to run on multiple hardware platforms such as Intel x86, RISC, and DEC Alpha; and the predominance of Windows on the desktop. At the same time, the UNIX market share may benefit from the downsizing of mainframe applications and from the expansion of the existing UNIX base to enable additional applications. At this time, neither UNIX nor Windows NT has a clear advantage in the enterprise application area and high-end systems. In fact, by the year 2000, more than 90% of all enterprise installations are expected to include both UNIX and Windows NT.*

Because there are compelling advantages to both operating systems, many firms find themselves supporting both in a heterogeneous environment. Clearly, desktop office tools will continue to be predominantly Windows-based despite the availability of UNIX office tools. In the critical area of APIs, however, vendors are just beginning to use WIN32 or port applications from POSIX to Win32. POSIX has proven itself in mission-critical applications. UNIX 95 (the POSIX follow-on) is the latest attempt by the UNIX vendors at standardization.

In the area of network operating systems, Windows NT is gaining market share from NetWare. Microsoft shipped 732,000 NT licenses (for versions 4.0 and 3.51) in 1996, an 86% increase over 1995. Windows NT is well on its way to selling more than a million Windows NT server licenses in 1997. These numbers compare very favorably with NetWare and UNIX sales.

Even when a firm decides to standardize on either the Windows or the UNIX environment, it must undergo a transition period in which both environments will be supported. Applications written to one API must be migrated to the other, or interfaces must be provided across operating systems. The problems which arise in these heterogeneous environments require special tools and techniques for solution.

This book identifies and classifies the solutions and products available to support migration and coexistence between UNIX, Windows, and NetWare. It discusses porting applications and developing new applications using cross platform development techniques, identifies the factors that go into selecting solutions, and provides guidelines for selecting a solution. Based on this guidance, firms can determine which tools are best suited to help mitigate their problems in the migration/coexistence between UNIX, Windows, and NetWare.

OVERVIEW OF MIGRATION/COEXISTENCE ISSUES AND APPROACHES

The subject of migration/coexistence among the important operating environments today (Windows, UNIX, and NetWare) encompasses a number of questions. Each question may have multiple solution approaches. The following is a list of some of the questions:

* "AllConnect for UNIX" program white paper, Digital Equipment Corporation.

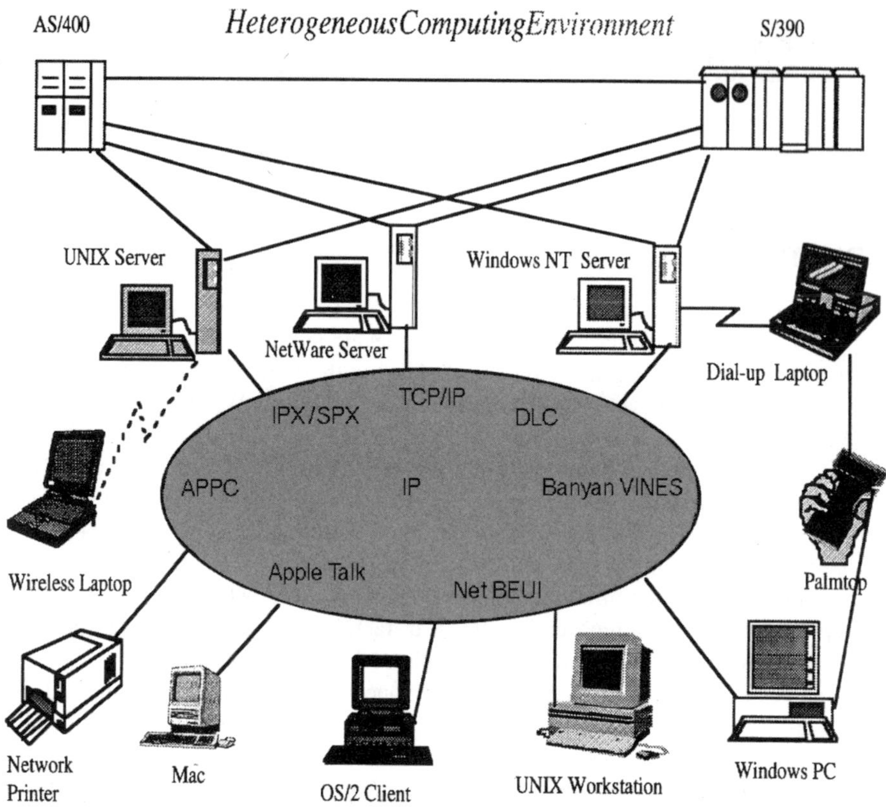

FIGURE 1.1 A heterogeneous computing environment.

- How to port applications from one environment to another?
- How to develop applications that will run in multiple environments without change to the source code?
- How to access applications in one environment from workstations in another environment?
- How to access data in one environment from applications in another environment?
- What are the system administration issues in heterogeneous environments?
- What are the factors to be considered when evaluating migration and coexistence solutions and what guidelines apply in the selection of the solutions?

Let us briefly review the issues raised by the questions, the possible solution approaches, the products that help implement the potential solution, and the chapter reference in the book for that topic.

Porting Applications Between Environments or Rewriting Applications

Whenever you introduce a new environment in an organization, you have an option of porting or rewriting your current applications to the new environment. Table 1.1 summarizes the approaches available to address porting/rewriting applications and the chapter reference in the book where you will find more information.

Developing New Applications in Heterogeneous Environments

If you do not want to be tied to one environment for your applications to execute, you can develop applications so that they can execute in more than one environment. Table 1.2 summarizes the

TABLE 1.1
Porting/Rewriting Applications

Issue	Approach	Products	Book Chapter
	Porting Applications		
Run UNIX applications on Windows NT servers	Port UNIX application to Windows NT using porting products	N*u*TCRACKER, Portage, OpenNT, eXcursion	3
Run Windows applications on UNIX servers	Use products that support Win32 on UNIX	MainWin, Wind/U	3
	Emulate Windows on UNIX	WABI, SoftWindows,	7
Porting database applications	Use multiplatform ODBC drivers	VisiODBC, DataDirect	3
Distributed applications with UNIX and Windows	Supplement NT DCE support with other DCE components	DCE Services for Windows NT	4
	Port ONC RPC to DCE RPC	RhaPC-d	3
	Rewriting Applications		
Capture the business logic in current applications	Use a tool that analyzes source and captures logic	Discover	3

TABLE 1.2
Developing Applications to Work in More than One Environment

Issue	Approach	Products	Book Chapter
Develop applications that will run on both UNIX and Windows NT	Use proprietary APIs — common subset, layered, or emulated	AppWare	4
	Develop for Windows NT and port to UNIX or vice versa	See porting products in Table 1.1	3
	4GL tools	PowerBuilder	4
	Object frameworks	Allegris DSC++ zAPP	4
Develop distributed heterogeneous applications	Develop DCE-based applications and supplement distributed services support in Windows NT	DCE services for Windows NT PC-DCE	4
Access distributed databases	Transparent, seamless access of data across heterogeneous environments	Rdb distributed product suite	4
Interface with legacy mainframe applications and access mainframe data	Use emulation, gateways, and WWW	Microsoft BackOffice, SNA client for UNIX, Novell NetWare for SAA BEA Jolt	4

TABLE 1.3
Application Coexistence in Heterogeneous Environments

Issue	Approach	Products	Book Chapter
Access character-based UNIX applications from Windows desktop	Use Telnet	Many vendors and products	6
Access graphical UNIX applications from NT desktop	Use PC X server software on the Windows NT desktops and access UNIX server	eXceed, XVision, OpenNT X11 server, PC-Xware, X OnNet, N*u*TCRACKER X server, eXalt-X, Reflection, Chameleon, eXpertise	6
Access Windows applications from existing UNIX desktops	Use a Windows NT multi-user server and add Windows to the X station	WinDD, WinTED, Ntrigue, HP 500 WinCenter, NTerprise	5
Access legacy IBM applications from the NT desktop	Use IBM TN3270 & TN5250 emulators on the NT desktop	Many vendors and products	7
Enterprise desktops	Use a desktop designed to support heterogeneous environments	WinTerm, Explora, Network Computer, Personal Workstations, ViewPoint	7
Mac clients in Windows NT	Use built-in Mac client support in Windows NT	Windows NT	7

issues and approaches available to address developing applications that can execute in different environments, and the chapter reference in the book where you will find more information.

Coexistence of Applications in Heterogeneous Environments

Sometimes you may not want to port your application to the new environment, but you would like your applications in one environment to be accessible from workstations in another environment. Table 1.3 summarizes the issues and approaches available to address applications coexistence, products, and the chapter reference in the book where you will find more information.

File Access in a Heterogeneous Environment

When you have heterogeneous environments, one of the most common requirements is for applications and users in one environment to be able to access files in another environment. Table 1.4 summarizes the issues and approaches available to address heterogeneous file and print access and the chapter reference in the book where you will find more information.

Systems Administration in Heterogeneous Environments

Table 1.5 summarizes the approaches available to address system administration issues in heterogeneous environments, approaches, products, and the chapter reference in the book where you will find more information.

Windows NT and NetWare Issues

NetWare is still the dominant network operating system, although as mentioned earlier, Windows NT is gaining market share. When you have both Windows NT and NetWare, then you migrate from one to another or coexist with the two. Table 1.6 summarizes the approaches available to address Windows NT and NetWare issues and the chapter reference in the book where you will find more information.

TABLE 1.4
Networked File and Print Access

Issue	Approach	Products	Book Chapter
Access Windows NT server files from UNIX desktops	Use built-in file access support such as ftp, or use network operating systems or NFS client software on the Windows NT desktop	Windows NT (ftp server), PC-NFS, PATHWORKS, Access NFS, Chameleon NFS, NFS Maestro, InterDrive, Reflection	8
Access UNIX server files from NT desktops	Use built-in file access support such as ftp, or use network operating systems or NFS client software on the Windows NT desktop	Windows NT (ftp, tftp, rcp) PATHWORKS PC-NFS, Access NFS, Chameleon NFS, NFS Maestro, InterDrive, Reflection	8
Print from Windows NT desktops to UNIX controlled printers	Use built-in functions in Windows NT	Windows NT, UNIX operating systems	8
Print from UNIX desktops to Windows NT controlled printers	Use *lpr* in UNIX clients and use *lpdsvc* in Windows NT	Windows NT, UNIX operating systems	8

TABLE 1.5
System Administration Issues in Heterogeneous Environments

Issue	Approach	Products	Book Chapter
UNIX shell on Windows NT	Use shells that simulate UNIX command environment in Windows NT	MKS toolkit, Hamilton C shell, Portage Base	9
System administration functions in heterogeneous environments	Use third-party software for the different aspects of system administration as needed	POLYCENTER, TME 10, Unicenter, others	9

TABLE 1.6
Windows NT and NetWare

Issue	Approach	Products	Book Chapter
Access NetWare server transparently from Windows clients for file and print services	Microsoft built-in support for NetWare in Windows NT and Windows 95	Client Services for NetWare (CSNW)	11
	Novell NetWare client for Windows NT, Windows 95, Windows 3.x, and DOS	Novell NetWare client	11
	Access through Gateway	Gateway Services for NetWare (GSNW)	11
Access Windows NT transparently from NetWare clients for file, print services	Microsoft built-in support for NetWare in Windows NT	File and Print Services for NetWare (FPNW)	11
Migrate system information in NetWare servers to Windows NT	Microsoft built-in support for NetWare in Windows NT	Migration tool from Microsoft	11

TABLE 1.7
Factors and Guidelines

Issue	Approach	Products	Book Chapter
Different factors that affect migration and coexistence solution selection	Look at the different factors and their characteristics	N/A	13
Guidelines for migration and coexistence solution selection	Follow solution selection considerations	N/A	13

FACTORS AFFECTING MIGRATION/COEXISTENCE SOLUTIONS AND SELECTION GUIDELINES

Table 1.7 summarizes the factors that affect migration/coexistence solutions and guidelines for solution selection and the chapter reference in the book where you will find more information.

The tables provide you with a quick overview of the contents of the book. Let us begin our discussions with the basis of migration and coexistence — homogeneous and heterogeneous environments.

HOMOGENEOUS VS. HETEROGENEOUS ENVIRONMENTS

The natural evolution tendency of data processing in many organizations is toward heterogeneous environments. From time to time, organizations develop or buy data processing environments and systems. Even when IBM was a dominant player in the computer industry, many organizations found themselves with a number of products from different vendors in a heterogeneous environment. With the increased number of players and the advent of client/server and the Internet/Intranet, this trend toward heterogeneity is even more pronounced. Nevertheless, many organizations have internal debates on the advantages and disadvantages of having a homogeneous environment vs. a heterogeneous environment. For example, one aspect of the debate centers around whether organizations should standardize on the Windows environment for both production applications and office applications. Another debate centers around adopting the Windows NT workstation as a standard desktop and using Windows NT as the network operating system. There are advantages and disadvantages to both approaches and these are summarized in Table 1.8.

Let us look at some of the basic differences between the operating systems. These differences lead to the need for migration and coexistence solutions between the operating system environments.

OPERATING SYSTEM FEATURES AND COMPARISONS

To get a better understanding of migration and coexistence options, you need to have an overview of operating system features and how the features differ among operating systems. Windows NT and UNIX provide network operating system functions as well as application development and execution functions. NetWare has traditionally been well known for its network operating system functions. Although NetWare provides some facilities such as NetWare Loadable Modules (NLMs) for application support in NetWare environments, you will still find a lot more applications, particularly mission critical applications in UNIX and Windows NT, than NetWare. When we compare the three operating systems, it is worthwhile noting their history.

UNIX started out of a joint Bell Labs/MIT research project in the early 1970s. AT&T, which then owned Bell Labs, could not sell computer-related products due to an antitrust decree and gave the UNIX source away to divisions within AT&T as well as to universities. The University of

TABLE 1.8
Comparing Homogeneous and Heterogeneous Environments

Homogeneous Environments	Heterogeneous Environments
Advantages	**Advantages**
• Improved productivity through interface consistency • Reduced system administration costs • Reduced network administration costs • Exchange of documents and data within the organization is easier	• You can pick the most cost-effective solution at any given point • The natural evolution is toward heterogeneous environments, no additional costs involved in trying to move to another environment • Possibility of lock-in to one or more vendors is reduced
Disadvantages	**Disadvantages**
• Costs of moving to a homogeneous environment • Cost of maintaining a homogeneous environment • Possibility of lock-in to one or more vendors • Extensive retraining of users using different systems	• Interface inconsistency problems • Need to perform system administration for multiple environments • Need to connect and bridge different types of networks • Exchange of documents and data is difficult and often requires format translations and loss of data fidelity

California, Berkeley, in particular did a lot of work on UNIX. Different recipients of the source made their own additions to the operating system and thus came into existence different flavors of UNIX. The incompatibilities between the flavors spawned standardization efforts, the most notable of which is the POSIX APIs.

With the growing popularity of LANs and the need to share expensive peripherals like laser printers, plotters, and so on, Novell came up with the NetWare network operating system to let computers on a network use one or more common file and print servers. Although Novell made some enhancements for supporting applications to NetWare (such as NetWare Loadable Modules [NLMs]), you will find a lot more applications in UNIX than in NetWare.

Windows NT is the most recent of the operating systems and has in many ways built on the strengths of prior operating systems while trying to avoid the drawbacks.

Windows NT is used as the base operating system for feature comparisons. If a feature is mentioned, it is available in Windows NT. The availability of the same or similar feature in other operating systems is mentioned where appropriate. Figure 1.2 shows an overview of the Windows NT operating system and its components.

Although there are still a number of mainframe operating systems in use today, this book will deal with mainframe-based operating systems only in the context of UNIX or Windows NT applications interfacing with mainframe applications or accessing mainframe databases.

Host-Centric and Client/Server Computing

One of the fundamental differences between Windows NT and UNIX is the design assumption about the end user. You may have come across articles mentioning that UNIX is a true multi-user system and Windows NT is not. For the most part, UNIX presumes the user to be a human accessing the UNIX operating system from a dumb terminal. There is a list of authorized users in UNIX who can access the system. Windows NT server (and Windows NT workstation) maintain a list of authorized users, but these are users accessing the server on the same physical computer or domain. Windows NT's concept of a user accessing the operating system is a client computer (which likely has a human interfacing with it). This difference affects many other aspects of the operating systems.

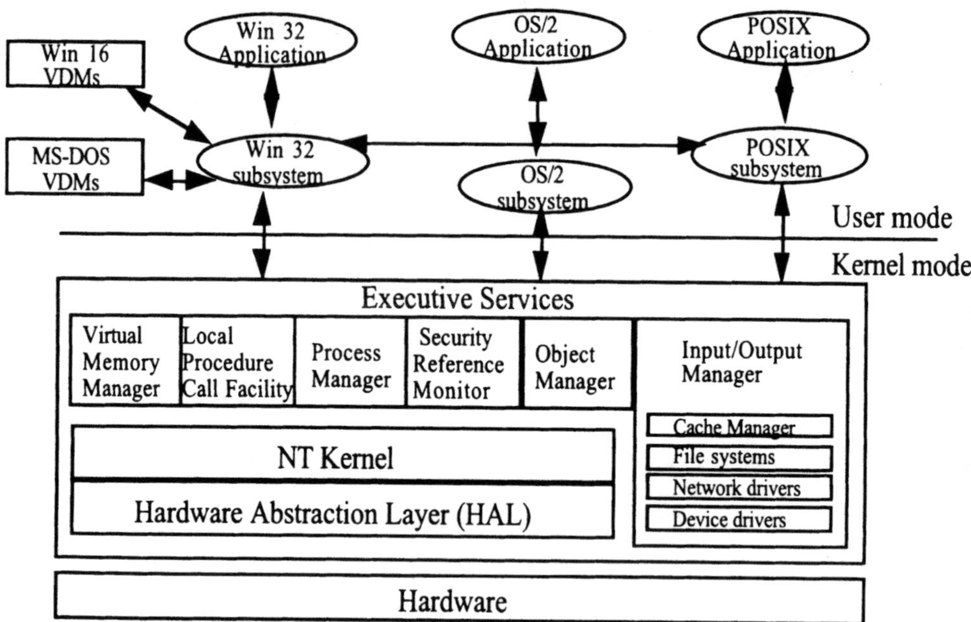

FIGURE 1.2 Windows NT operating system and components. (Reproduced with permission from Microsoft Corporation.)

Operating System Components

Let us take a look at the different components that make up an operating system.

Kernel

The kernel is the layer of Operating System Code that is just above the layer of code that shields the hardware. Operating systems, including Windows NT, are designed to run on more than one hardware platform, and platform-specific details are masked to the rest of the operating system by a *hardware abstraction layer.* Kernel is the nucleus of the operating system. The kernel executes in a privileged mode called the *kernel mode* where it has direct access to the hardware and other system software. The kernel is resident in memory and cannot be preempted (except by some interrupts). Applications, on the other hand, execute in nonprivileged *user mode* and do not have the access that the kernel does. When an application needs to have access to the hardware, for example when an application wants to print or read data from a disk, it invokes the operating system services, usually through a set of well-defined interfaces, called *Application Programming Interfaces (APIs*). Some of the functions performed by the kernel are:

- Handle hardware exceptions and interrupts
- Schedule, prioritize, and dispatch threads (threads are the basic unit of execution)
- Synchronize execution across processors in a multiprocessor environment

Though UNIX and Windows NT are similar in many ways, one of the areas of difference is the kernel. Windows NT uses a *microkernel*-based approach where the core kernel functions are kept as small as possible and the other functions of the operating system are performed in non-privileged portions of the operating system called *protected subsystems.* This is in contrast to UNIX where it is not uncommon for the kernel to be a lot bigger and encompass many more operating system functions. One consequence of the bigger kernel is that it needs to be changed more often compared to Windows NT. UNIX administrators recompile the operating system and reboot the system. Windows NT administrators do not have to modify the Windows NT source. The only significant changes to the operating system itself is when patches are applied.

Executive

The *executive* in Windows NT refers to the operating system code that runs in *kernel mode*. Besides the *kernel* and the *hardware abstraction layer,* the executive includes modules that provide services for applications such as memory management, I/O handling, object handling, process management, security monitoring, and a local procedure call facility. These modules are not implemented as a layered hierarchy, one on top of the other.

Unlike UNIX, this portion of the operating system in Windows NT is not changed locally by a system administrator and is updated only by upgrades issued by Microsoft.

Protected Subsystems

The operating system functions not performed by the kernel are performed by a set of nonprivileged servers known as protected subsystems (Figure 1.1). When your application makes an NT API call, these calls are handled by the protected subsystems. One of the advantages of the protected subsystems approach is that it permits modular development of new protected subsystems without impacting either the base operating system or the other existing protected subsystems. The same is true for enhancements to protected subsystems as well.

For example, if Microsoft wants to drop support for OS/2 or POSIX applications, then essentially all that needs to be done is to drop the code contained in those protected subsystems. Although Windows NT is designed to run POSIX and OS/2 applications, do not expect to be able to pass data or files back and forth between a Windows and POSIX (or OS/2) application. Nor can you expect to see the graphical user interface Windows is famous for. Both POSIX and OS/2 support only character mode applications. This is because the *Win32 Subsystem* is the primary subsystem and supports the programming of text, graphics, networking, and all other functions available in Windows NT.

The *OS/2 and POSIX Subsystems,* on the other hand, are "compatibility mode" subsystems with just text support and without graphics or network support. The lines between the OS/2 or POSIX subsystems and the Win32 subsystem in Figure 1.1 indicate that for many application calls, the OS/2 and POSIX subsystems actually call the Win32 subsystem.

Process Management

A *process* is the execution instance of a program. Each process has its own memory address space (4 GB in Windows NT and many UNIX systems) where the code that makes up the process resides. Each process also owns resources required for the process such as files, threads (see below), etc. The process manager portion of the executive manages the creation and deletion of processes.

Unlike UNIX, processes in Windows NT are not executable by themselves. Also unlike UNIX, Windows NT does not automatically establish a parent/child relationship when one process creates another. For a more detailed list of differences between Windows NT and UNIX, see Chapter 2.

Even though a *process* is an execution instance, the process itself does not execute. A process is made up of one or more *threads. Threads* are the basic units of execution. A process has at least one thread. Multiple threads can be created. Each has its own memory. Threads are a convenient and efficient way to split functions that can be done in the background, while the main thread continues with other processing. In multiprocessor systems, two or more threads of the same process can be executing in parallel, thereby having portions of the same program executing in parallel.

However the price paid for the convenience and efficiency is the need to synchronize threads. If you use a thread to perform a big sort in the background, your main thread has to ensure that the sort input data has not changed, and the main thread must be notified when the sort is done. Refer to Chapter 2 for process/thread differences between UNIX and Windows NT. Both Windows NT and UNIX handle scheduling a process or thread for execution and also handle priority for execution.

Processor Support

Until recently, most computing at the desktop and server level used machines that had only one processor (CPU). *Multiprocessing*, where multiple processors exist on the same physical machine, have been used in the mainframes for some time. With the advent of cheaper processors and operating systems that support multiple processors, *multiprocessing* is becoming more commonplace in desktops and servers.

Asymmetric MultiProcessing (ASMP) is where the operating system uses one or more processors for itself and schedules and runs the application programs in the remaining processors. Operating systems that support *Symmetric MultiProcessing* (SMP) do not impose such restrictions on processors.

The ability to run any program on any processor provides better load balancing (the processor that runs the operating system may be idle while applications are waiting to use the other processor(s)). Fault tolerance is also improved in SMP since the failure of a processor dedicated for the operating system in ASMP means the whole machine is not operational, even though other processor(s) may be operational. The price of improved load-balancing and fault-tolerance is complexity. SMP operating systems are more complex to build and maintain.

Windows NT and many UNIX operating systems support SMP. SMP support is usually transparent to applications.

Memory Management

As mentioned earlier, each process gets its own address space of 4 GB. Most desktops and servers do not have that amount of real memory. Considering that there will be multiple processes at the same time, it is obvious that there must be a mechanism that maps the process address space to real memory. This process is virtual memory management. The "virtual" is to indicate that most (or all) of a process memory is not real memory. Contents of the address space that are not held in real memory are held on the disk.

During the course of execution, programs may need additional memory. This may be because program control gets transferred to part of the code that is not resident in memory or the program asks for more memory. In either case, since real memory is limited, some content of real memory has to be swapped out. The process of swapping memory contents is called *demand paging*. A *page* is the minimum amount of memory that will be swapped in or out. The typical page size is 4K. Both the process address space and the real memory is divided into pages. Each process thus has (4 GB/4K) a million pages. If you have 32 MB real memory, then you have (32 MB/4K) 8000 real memory pages. The technique of selecting which pages will be moved out is called *first-in-first-out* or FIFO. The operating system keeps track of which pages came in first and selects those for swapping out. The idea behind this technique is that the more recent a page the greater are the chances that it will be used and needs to be kept in real memory.

Virtual memory management attempts to strike the proper balance. If too much memory is allocated to processes, fewer processes will run, and real memory occupied by some processes are not being accessed fast enough and are being wasted. Allocating too little memory to processes may cause frequent swapping of pages, resulting in a situation where the operating system is taking up a lot of CPU time which could otherwise have been used by application processes. To compound this, the memory access patterns will vary between processes, and what is optimal for one will not be for another. The operating system monitors the number of pages allocated and used by each process (also called the working set) and automatically fine tunes memory allocation.

Both Windows NT and UNIX systems use 32 bit *linear memory addressing*. This means that the whole memory is considered one big layout, and each memory address is one value in the 32 bit address. Contrast this with the segmented memory model of Windows 3.1, where memory is considered to be composed of 64 KB segments. The 4 GB limit comes from the 32 bit address (2^{32}). Half of the process address space (2 GB) is used by the application process, and the other half for system functions (for the application process).

Both Windows NT and UNIX also use *demand paging*. Both systems also support *memory mapped files,* which is a technique of speeding up file access by keeping files in memory rather than on disk. In addition both systems also use *heaps*, which are unstructured memory.

However there are differences. Windows NT has a richer API set for virtual memory management and for managing heaps. In addition, while UNIX requires that swap space be managed as a separate partition, Windows NT treats swap space as a file and uses the local file system to manage it. Details of differences between memory management are covered in Chapter 2.

Input/Output Management

This part of the NT executive deals with all input and output, including input from and output to displays, disks, CD-ROM drives, etc. The I/O manager uses what is called a uniform driver model. In this model every I/O request to a device is through an I/O *request packet* (IRP) regardless of the specific type of I/O device. The device specifics are handled at a level below the I/O manager. The I/O manager performs the I/O task asynchronously. The process that issued the I/O request is preempted by the operating system, and it waits until it gets a *signal* that the I/O has been completed.

Both Windows NT and UNIX consider all forms of I/O data as a string of bytes or a file. Both systems also implement task preempting for I/O requests.

The I/O manager of Windows NT uses a number of subcomponents such as *Network Redirector/Server (RAS), Cache Manager, File Systems, Network drivers,* and *Device drivers.*

Cache Manager. In both Windows NT and UNIX, cache is used to store frequently accessed data from disk (such as file data) to speed up future requests for data. Unlike some other fixed cache size systems, the cache size in Windows NT varies depending on the amount of available memory.

Device drivers. The need for device drivers is very simple. An operating system can support hundreds of printers, disk drives, CD-ROM drives, and other peripherals attached to it. The low-level code to drive each of these devices is unique to the device. For example, the line feed command for an HP printer would be different from an Epson. It could even be different for different printer models from the same manufacturer. If a word processing application wants to print, it wouldn't make sense for the operating system to format the output including the device unique codes. The job of formatting output for the specific device is taken care of by device drivers.

All operating systems support the concept of device drivers.

Security

Windows NT, many UNIX systems, and NetWare provide security functions to ensure that only authorized users are given the appropriate access. Windows NT includes a Security Reference Monitor. Some UNIX systems support Kerberos, while NetWare has its own set of security functions. Windows NT is C2 certified and so are many UNIX systems.

Application Programming Interfaces

The application programming interfaces for Windows has evolved over the years starting with the Win16 API. The current one is the Win32 API, a 32 bit version supported by Windows NT. The

UNIX systems have supported POSIX. POSIX and Win32 are not compatible. POSIX has evolved over the years, and some common subsets include POSIX.1 and POSIX.2. Recently the X/Open organization has come up with UNIX 95, which is the most recent version of the UNIX standard.

Login Scripts

Windows NT, UNIX, and NetWare support the concept of login scripts. Conceptually the functions provided by the login scripts are the same — to set up a user environment tailored to the user when the user starts using the system. However, the similarity ends there. In UNIX, the script runs on the server and creates an environment at the server for the user. In Windows NT, the scripts run at the client and tailor the client to the user. This is an example of the fundamental difference about the user mentioned earlier in the chapter. The scripting languages (and hence the scripts) are not compatible between the systems. However, there is a way for you to run NetWare login scripts when you access a NetWare server from a Windows machine using a Windows client supplied by Microsoft. See Chapter 11 for details.

Daemons and Services

Operating systems require programs that run in the background (even when no user or client is accessing the operating system) waiting to process requests, such as open connections. These are the programs that are started when an operating system boots up. These programs also handle clean-up related to user or client requests, such as closing connections when the operating system is shut down. In UNIX, these programs are called *daemons*. In Windows NT, these program functions are performed by Windows NT *services*.

Note: There are many vendor products covered throughout this book. The information about the products was gathered from different published sources, but primarily from vendors' published information including online Web pages. The Web addresses and other contact information is included in the description for each vendor and in the Appendix. The products are being updated quickly, and you should check with the product vendor for the latest information. Most vendors also offer free evaluations which are downloadable from their Web sites.

This book is not intended to help you select one vendor over another. You should pick migration/coexistence solutions that meet your requirements and perform an evaluation of vendor products. The inclusion of vendor information is provided to give you an idea of the capabilities of the products and to give you a quick reference to get further information and software.

Conclusion

This chapter summarized the different migration and coexistence issues you can have when you have heterogeneous environments such as UNIX and Windows NT. It also looked at the details of operating system differences that lead to migration and coexistence issues.

In the next chapter, we will take a more detailed look at the differences between the operating systems, and we will also look at coding tips that will help you port applications from one environment to another or develop applications that will execute in multiple environments.

2 Porting Issues Due To Operating System Differences

INTRODUCTION

In the context of this book, heterogeneous applications refers to applications that run on UNIX, Windows NT, and NetWare. Although NetWare has some application facilities, porting applications are a common issue when we try to port applications between UNIX and Windows NT, and that will be the focus of this chapter and the next. The term migration is also used instead of porting.

Both Windows NT and UNIX are preemptive, multitasking, demand-paged virtual memory supporting operating systems that have some common origins. Although they are similar at the upper levels, there are enough differences in the details to make porting applications from one to the other a challenge. One of the major differences is the APIs available for applications.

This chapter covers the differences that cause porting problems, particularly if you are interested in manual porting, and the next chapter discusses some solutions including some commercial products that help in the porting effort. This chapter also includes some tips that show the differences between the environments that will help you in your porting effort.

WHAT IS PORTING?

Let us start with understanding porting. Porting attempts to take current applications in one environment (for example, UNIX) and make them run in another environment (for example, Windows) without significant effort. There are three ways in which porting can be accomplished:

- Manual Porting. One way to port would be to manually replace every language library call, every operating system call, and other functions such as database access or transaction processing calls, with equivalent calls in the environment to be ported to.
- Porting Source Code Using Tools. An alternative to manual porting would be to leave the calls for language libraries and operating system services, etc., in the source and instead "field" the calls and convert them to equivalent calls that the ported-to environment can process.
- Executing Object Code Using Emulation Software. This method bypasses the source altogether. The executable is run under an emulation layer that sits on top of the native (ported-to) environment and emulates the environment that the executable was meant to run in.

Tip: *The term port (or migration) may give you an impression that once you have ported (or migrated) an application, you no longer need the source or the source environment. This is true only if you manually port your application and replace the calls your application makes into equivalent calls in the ported-to environment.*

Manual porting between UNIX and Windows needs to take into account the differences between the UNIX and Windows operating environments, and these are covered in the section titled, *UNIX, Windows NT Differences*, later in this chapter.

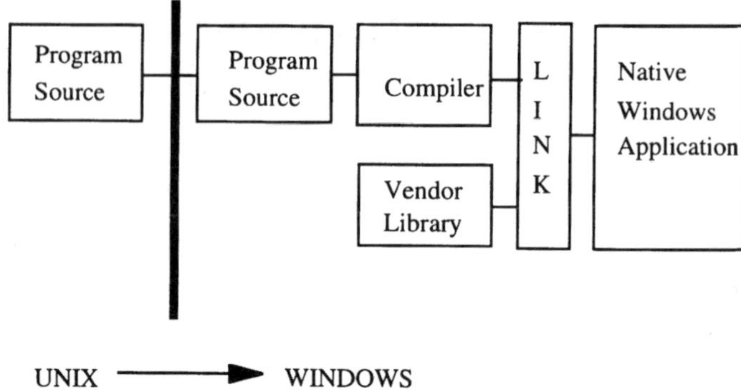

FIGURE 2.1 Porting from UNIX to Windows using source code porting tool.

If you are porting source code using tools, the tools take care of most (not all) of the environment differences. For a list of things you need to take care of even when you use a porting tool, please see Chapter 3.

If you are porting from UNIX to Windows, to make the same calls work in the Windows environment, a layer of "wrapper" code is required to field the calls. This wrapper code lets your application continue to make the calls as it did before, fields the calls, and performs the intended function of the calls using the operating system being ported to. The reverse should happen when the results are sent from the operating system back to the calling application through the wrapper code. One way of providing the wrapper code is through a separate library that is link edited with the program as shown in Figure 2.1.

Both methods have some advantages and disadvantages as summarized in Table 2.1.

Keep in mind however that Windows NT, through its kernel and protected subsystems architecture, supports multiple Application Programming Interfaces (APIs) such as Win32, POSIX, and OS/2, while you normally find support for only one API set (POSIX) in UNIX systems. A natural question at this point is, "If Windows NT has native POSIX support, why should anyone port POSIX applications?" The answer is that the native POSIX support in Windows NT is not adequate for most applications. See "Windows NT Native POSIX Support" for more information.

Porting tool vendors have filled the gap for native POSIX support in Windows NT, and some of the porting products are covered in Chapter 3. If you opt for manual porting, then the detail implementation differences between UNIX and Windows NT have to be addressed. If you have decided to port and you have the skill base to do the porting, then you can address the differences. There are also vendors you can hire to port, such as Digital Equipment and Sector 7 Limited.

UNIX, WINDOWS NT DIFFERENCES

The detailed implementation level differences between UNIX and Windows NT are summarized below.

- Architectural differences
- Signal differences
- Handle differences
- Distributed computing differences
- Memory management differences
- File system differences

TABLE 2.1
Comparing Manual Porting and Tool-Based Porting

Manual Porting	Tool-Based Porting
Can be costly and time consuming, particularly for porting large applications	Can be accomplished more quickly than manual porting
Once ported and tested, original source and development environment are not required	Original source is still in native environment and enhancements need to be made to it
Requires in-depth skills in both (porting-from and ported-to) environments	Skill requirements not as critical as in manual porting
Typically applicable to small applications	You can port larger applications than manual porting since you are not significantly altering the source code

- File input/output differences
- User Interface differences
- Security model differences
- Network support differences
- Multi-user vs. "Single user" differences
- Style differences

Let us look at each of these in some detail.

Architectural Differences

There are some basic differences between the architectures of UNIX and Windows NT in the areas of processes, threads, signals, handles, etc.

Process Differences

Both Windows NT and UNIX allow you to create new processes. In both Windows NT and UNIX, a process has its own protected memory, resources, and priority. You *CreateProcess* in Windows NT what you *fork* in UNIX (actually it is *fork* and *exec*, but it is very common in UNIX to *exec* immediately following a *fork*). However, there are differences in implementation:

- When a UNIX process is forked, a parent-child relationship is automatically established, unlike *CreateProcess* in Windows NT.
- Unlike a UNIX process, a Windows NT process does not execute. Instead, a Windows NT process has one or more executables called *threads*. Windows NT kernel schedules threads for execution (not the process).
- You can pass arguments to *CreateProcess* to control environment, file handling, security, and other attributes, unlike UNIX where the forked process inherits all attributes by default. A process created in Win32 can inherit the handles of the process that created it by setting the *bInherit* flag.
- Win32 does not support terminal process groups, which were meant to support dumb terminals. However, you can bunch applications into groups controlled by a parent process using the *create_new_process_group* flag of the *CreateProcess* API.
- While Windows NT and UNIX systems assume a linear memory space addressable by 32 bits, there are differences in how processes use memory. In UNIX, programmers normally make assumptions about the layout of data in memory, particularly the order and relative locations of data, code, and stack, and sometimes exploit this information

by keeping the data around beyond the life of the process to gain performance at start-up. In Windows you usually cannot make such assumptions, although you can use *OpenProcess* to examine and modify memory, stacks, and threads.

- You can clone a running process together with its memory contents in UNIX, while Win32 does not directly support cloning. But you can use threads and/or pass data using IPC, once you have done *CreateProcess* besides using inheritance options.
- You *pthread_create* in UNIX what you *CreateThread* in Windows NT. However, the concept of threads is much stronger in Windows NT. A thread has its own stack, handle, local storage, unique numerical ID, and there are APIs to use threads as there are for processes. Threads can signal. One of the benefits of this approach is that it permits multiple threads to execute on different processors in a multiprocessor machine, thus having portions of your program executing simultaneously. A thread can be started in a suspended state. There are differences in the way threads are implemented across UNIX systems, and thread usage in UNIX applications is not as common as it is in Windows.
- In Windows NT, when a created process terminates, all data associated with the created process are erased from memory. This implies that there are no zombie processes (processes in UNIX that are no longer executing but that have open handles). If you want any data from the created process, for example the exit code, you have to ensure that you take steps to capture that data before the created process terminates.
- UNIX uses *setuid* to associate a *userid* to a process. There is no direct equivalent in Windows NT. However, you can use named pipes and the *ImpersonateNamedPipeClient* API and a server program that uses the named pipe to communicate to a client to associate the security context of the client. If *setuid* was being used for a daemon, you could use a Windows NT service.

Inter-process Communication

UNIX has many mechanisms for IPC such as sockets, memory mapped files, different variations of pipes, etc. Windows NT supports the above and includes message-oriented pipes as well.

Bits and Bytes Differences

Windows NT is a 32-bit operating system, while UNIX has mostly 32-bit and some 64-bit versions. The order in which the bytes are packed in a Word may be different between Windows NT and some UNIX versions. The byte order difference is also called "little-endian" vs. "big-endian." Most UNIX systems (those that are RISC based), have the most significant byte first (within a word) while Intel-based PCs have the least significant byte first. Windows NT aligns data on boundaries, and so do many UNIX operating systems, but there may still be differences.

Although applications are normally shielded from these bits and byte differences by the operating system as well as the language compilers, you may experience minor hardware-related porting problems, particularly if you have old code and low-level code that attempt to take advantage of the hardware capabilities.

Signal Differences

A signal can be raised by a thread in Windows NT and is processed by the same thread, unlike UNIX. As such, signaling cannot be used for IPC as is done, at times, in UNIX. UNIX programs commonly use signals to indicate completion of asynchronous I/O. Windows NT's preferred method to signal I/O completion would be to use an event object and the OVERLAPPED I/O structure parameter for *Readfile* or *Writefile* call. The C run-time libraries included with Windows NT SDK support the signals: SIGINT, SIGFPE, SIGILL, SIGBREAK, SIGABRT, SIGSEGV, and SIGTERM.

Signals are also commonly used in UNIX to handle exceptions where a programmer writes code to handle exceptions and picks a signal to indicate when the exception occurs. Windows NT provides unlimited user-defined exceptions for the programmer to handle exceptions.

Handle Differences

The use of handles is very common in the Windows environment and just about all objects that get created, such as Processes, Events, Semaphores, etc., return a handle. The returned handle is an index to a process-specific handle table that among other things has the ACL for each handle. As discussed under security, the ACL governs access. Handles are obtained when explicitly creating an object, opening a named object, inherited, or duplicated and can be passed between processes to let processes access resources of other processes. Windows also uses handles while accessing files for which UNIX uses file descriptors. Handles do not have a direct equivalence in UNIX.

Distributed Computing Differences

Distributed computing is still evolving, although many aspects of it are already supported. Both Windows NT and UNIX have domains, although what they stand for is different. In UNIX, a domain is how a computer is named on a TCP/IP network (this is the same as in DNS). In Windows NT, a domain is a server group sharing common security policy and user account databases running on Windows NT servers.

Name Resolution Differences

Typically, a computer on a network is identified with both a name and an address. In TCP/IP systems, computers are identified by unique IP addresses and computer names. The mechanism for converting computer names into their corresponding IP addresses is known as name resolution.

For dynamic name resolution, it is common in UNIX to use the Domain Name Services (DNS). Windows NT includes all the resolver functionality necessary for using DNS on the Internet.

Windows NT can use the following methods for name resolution in TCP/IP networks:

- Windows Internet Name Service (WINS). Provides a dynamic database for registering and querying name-to-IP address mappings in a routed network environment. When a client moves from one subnet to another, the IP address change is updated automatically in the WINS database. WINS can be used in conjunction with Dynamic Host Configuration Protocol (DHCP). DHCP and WINS are covered in Chapter 9.
- Domain Name Services (DNS). DNS uses static configuration for computer Name-to-IP address mapping and allows name resolution for any computer, anywhere in the network. There is a major difference between WINS and DNS. DNS mapping is static, while WINS mapping is dynamic and requires less administration. WINS is practical only for relatively small network segments.
- A HOSTS file. A flat file used to specify the DNS computer name and IP address mapping, comparable to */etc/hosts* on UNIX.
- An LMHOSTS file. A flat file used to specify the NetBIOS computer name and IP address mapping. PATHWORKS for Digital UNIX (Advanced Server) supports an LMHOSTS file for wide area domain support.

Domain names are resolved (mapped to IP addresses) using Windows Internet Naming Service (WINS) in the Windows NT environment, while DNS is used in the UNIX environment. DNS resolves names based on static configuration, while WINS supports dynamic configuration changes.

Memory Management Differences

UNIX applications typically use the *malloc* and *free* C library functions to allocate and free memory. You can use the same C library functions in Windows NT. Both UNIX and Windows NT use the term "heap" for unstructured memory as well. Windows NT has a richer API set for virtual memory management. Windows NT allows you to allocate and manage multiple heaps (unlike UNIX). In Windows NT, memory need not be allocated until actually required. This is accomplished using *VirtualAlloc*, *VirtualLock*, and other virtual memory management APIs. The heap APIs *HeapCreate* and *HeapAlloc* allow you to allocate separate memory structures and manage multiple heaps, which leads to better performance.

The UNIX functions *bzero* and *bcopy* are not available in Windows NT. You can use the equivalent routines *memset()* and *memcpy()*.

Memory Mapped Files

Memory Mapped Files are a fast way to access disk data by keeping files in memory, rather than on disk. This technique avoids using expensive disk input and output. Most UNIX systems support memory mapped files using *mmap* and so does Windows NT using *CreateFileMapping* and *MapViewOfFile*. A memory mapped file can act as shared memory between processes.

File System Differences

Windows NT supports multiple file systems, such as, File Allocation Table (FAT), NT File System (NTFS), and High Performance File System (HPFS), common in OS/2 environments. HPFS was supported up to NT 3.51. The first area of difference to check is whether the specific file system your UNIX application uses is supported by Windows NT in a similar manner. NTFS is the closest to file systems used in UNIX systems, such as NFS, AFS, or Veritas. Windows NT also supports Compact Disc File Systems (CDFS). As such, it can read the CD ROMs readable by UNIX systems supporting CDFS, like Digital UNIX.

Even within the same file system, there are differences. UNIX file hierarchy typically starts with the root (/) while Windows NT supports multiple drives (such as C:, D:, etc.), and each drive has its own root. Windows NT provides some file access structures, just for compatibility, without actual support. For example, the *stat* call will return *st* structure members that do not have valid values. As such, if your program tests for these values and makes decisions, erroneous results would occur. Such a check may need to be rewritten using *GetFileInformationByHandle*.

Tests for symbolic linked files using i-node numbers will not work properly in the Windows environment since Windows NT doesn't use the i-node representation. A POSIX application using the POSIX subsystem can create hard linked file references (required for compliance with the POSIX specification), and this is supported by the NTFS file system. However, this can be done only by a POSIX application, not by a Win32 application.

File access is governed by ACLs in Windows NT, while they are governed by permissions in UNIX. You can set the ACL for a file using the *CreateFile* API. You can check for valid file access using the *AccessCheck* API.

Some special characters that may be allowed in some UNIX file systems are not allowed in Windows NT. Windows NT doesn't allow any of the characters enclosed in the parenthesis- (/,\,<,>,",:,|), and ASCII characters from 0–31. The common hierarchical separator in UNIX is / (for example /pub/bin), while the same in Windows NT would be \ (\pub\bin). While Windows NT is not normally case sensitive, Windows NT will list files with their original case (with the case in which they were first created on the system).

File Input/Output Differences

While Windows NT supports standard C file I/O calls such as *fopen*, these are meant more for compatibility. Windows NT character applications use these calls for console input and output and can be ported without difficulty. Programs that use UNIX system calls (as opposed to standard C calls) may be supported in some cases. However, to use advanced file functions such as asynchronous I/O, you need to use the Win32 APIs such as *CreateFile*.

You cannot mix and match standard C and Win32 calls. For example, you cannot use *ReadFile* to read information from a file opened with *fopen*.

UNIX uses file descriptors 0, 1, and 2 to represent standard input, standard output, and standard error, respectively.

Windows NT implements the equivalent function through handles. You would use the *GetStdHandle* API which will return the handle for standard input, output, or error. You can compare the returned handle with the predefined constants *STD_INPUT_HANDLE, STD_OUTPUT_HANDLE,* and *STD_ERROR_HANDLE*. The UNIX *dupcall* function can be implemented in Windows NT by using the *SetStdHandle* API or by filling in the *StdHandles* element of the *StartupInfo* structure in the *CreateProcess* API, which redirects one of the standard handles to an existing file.

Unlike UNIX, you cannot change the flag values associated with open files. For example, in UNIX, you use the *oflag* in *fcntl* to determine if the file was opened for read-only or read-write and set it if need be. In Windows NT, you can get similar information from the *fdwAttrsAndFlags* parameter of *CreateFile*, but you cannot change it.

UNIX supports long file names. If you are porting a file from UNIX to a Windows system that uses the FAT file system, you may have to come up with a name in the 8-dot-3 format.

UNIX names are case-sensitive and you have to be careful not to overlay files when you port files from UNIX to Windows. For example, the files "Filename" and "filename" are two different files in UNIX, but cannot be two different files in the FAT file system. Even Windows NT (with NTFS) is case-aware, but not fully case-sensitive. NTFS will preserve the case of the filename when it was created and display it in file name lists such as Windows NT Explorer, but ignores the case for other purposes such as searching.

UNIX files use a linefeed (LF) character for line separation, while Windows NT files use carriage return and linefeed (CRLF). Whether this is a problem depends on the type of file you are porting and how you use the file after the port. If you port a text file from UNIX to Windows NT and attempt to print it, this difference could cause a problem. On the other hand, if the file is a program source file and you compile it, then it may not be a problem. Many porting tools, including N*u*TCRACKER, automatically take care of inserting a carriage return (CR) character when required.

User Interface Differences

User interfaces can be classified as text based or graphical depending on content. A typical example of a text-based interface is the command line. Both UNIX and Windows support the command line.

Command Lines, UNIX, and Windows NT

With the popularity of the Windows graphical interface, including icons, drag-and-drop, and mouse clicks, Command Line and Text in Windows NT may seem out of place, but Windows NT does provide facilities to handle Command Lines and Text.

A terminal in UNIX is a console in Windows NT. Thanks to C Standards, C run-time libraries are fairly standard across operating systems, including Windows NT. Thus, if you have a text application that does not use UNIX-specific extensions (such as *termio*), your application should work with just recompilation. There are other instances (such as *curses*) and dumb terminal support that may require third-party add-ons to get the application to work in Windows NT. These are addressed in Chapter 3. Windows NT command line options start with a slash (/), while UNIX command line options start with a dash (–).

Another method of dealing with text requires some more work, but will provide some benefits. The method would be to use Windows graphic functions to create a window and position and display characters, for example by using *Textout*. This gives the user the appearance of a text window, but Windows will treat the text window just the same as any other window on the desktop. This means that the user can interact with the text window and perform functions like cut and paste, scrolling, resizing, etc.

Keep in mind that the supported fonts between UNIX and Windows systems are normally different.

Graphical User Interface (GUI)

Unlike text, the situation is different when it comes to graphical user interfaces. Windows has GDI and other Win32 GUI APIs, and UNIX has Motif/X Windows. While the interfaces may look similar from an end-user perspective, the two are very different from a programming perspective. I said *similar* and not *same* for the end-user perspective because there are differences that may be annoying to the user who has to switch back and forth between the systems often.

For example, the new Windows 95 and Windows NT 4.0 have three icons in the top right-hand corner to indicate minimize, maximize, and close, while Motif/X Window windows normally use only two icons. This is a problem for a user who has to switch back and forth between the two window types. The end-user issues are covered in detail later. There are GUI functions that are present in one environment and not in the other. For example, Windows supports notebook controls, and Motif does not. Besides the font differences mentioned earlier, there are also color palette differences between Windows NT and UNIX. From a programming perspective, there are differences between Windows and X11, and some of these are summarized below. For more details, refer to MainSoft's homepage at http://www.mainsoft.com.

WS_CLIPSIBLING

When the *WS_CLIPSIBLING* style is not set at window creation, painting on the window should also paint on overlapping siblings window. However, this behavior is not configurable and not easily duplicated under X11.

Transparent Windows

In Windows, windows that don't erase their background are visually transparent (the groupbox and combobox controls are good examples). If they respond correctly to the *WM_NCHITTEST* (with *HTTRANSPARENT*), they can also be transparent to mouse events. This is a problem area when using X11 child window management.

Window Scrolling

When *ScrollWindow* is used to scroll windows containing child windows, the code scrolls the bitmap representation of whatever appears on the screen, and then internally updates the position of the child windows. With X11, after scrolling the bitmap representation on the screen, the individual child windows must be moved one by one, and the display area that gets exposed must be repainted.

Message Dispatching

X11 event dispatching is based on a model simpler than Windows and doesn't take into account the *WM_NCHITTEST* result or the fact that windows can be disabled. MainWin, from MainSoft, overcomes the Windows and X11 differences using what it calls "X-ray technology." MainWin uses Microsoft NT code (under license from Microsoft), imported directly, for child windows management, thereby more accurately reproducing Windows user interface behavior. This approach also helps reduce network load by freeing the X11 server from performing child window management. MainWin is covered in more detail in Chapter 3.

If you need to port GUI code from UNIX to Windows, there are four approaches you can take:

- Rewrite the GUI code using a GUI utility and fill in ported non-GUI code. (Of course, you can rewrite completely from scratch too!)
- Run the application on a UNIX client and use an X server program to connect. (This is one area where the UNIX client and server terminology is the exact opposite of the standard usage for client and server.)
- Use a third-party software that will provide run-time support for fielding the Motif calls on Windows NT.
- Maintain a common source base for different environments and conditionally compile for the different environments.

The first and third approaches are discussed in Chapter 3, and the fourth approach is discussed in Chapter 4. The second approach is discussed in Chapter 5.

Security Model Differences

There are fundamental differences in the way security is implemented between Windows NT and UNIX. To Windows NT, just about everything is objects. Each object, at least at the kernel level, and file have an Access Control List (ACL) that determines who is allowed to do what with the object or file. Each access to the object or file, is evaluated for security by comparing the security ID of the access requester (such as processes and threads) with the ACL.

As mentioned in Chapter 1, one of the fundamental differences between Windows NT and UNIX is the definition of a user. A user in UNIX is typically the human who logs onto a terminal that communicates with the UNIX host, while the user for Windows NT could be a client machine. One of the consequences of this difference is that Windows NT doesn't have the equivalent of the */etc/passwd* file that UNIX systems use to store user information such as hashed passwords. Even when Windows NT recognizes multiple users (such as the users of one Windows NT machine), Windows NT, unlike UNIX, doesn't provide direct access to passwords in any format. The system administrator cannot find a lost or forgotten password. Passwords can only be reset.

UNIX has a User/Group/Permission model for security. To port an application, most of the security code is likely to be significantly modified. The concept of grouping users with similar needs and administering the group as an entity is similar between UNIX and Windows NT. However, Windows NT has some group features that do not exist in UNIX. For example, in Windows NT a group can own a file, a group can be a member of another group, and several different groups can be given different permissions on the same file.

Add-on security is available for many UNIX systems such as Kerberos. Kerberos is expected to be included in a future version of Windows NT.

Network Support Differences

As with security, there are some fundamental differences between UNIX and Windows NT for network support. Unlike many UNIX operating systems where network support is an add-on or where the number of network protocols supported is limited, Windows NT integrates network support within the operating system and supports multiple network protocols, such as TCP/IP, Novell's IPX/SPX, NBF (derivation of NetBEUI), AppleTalk, and DLC. Many STREAMS-based transport protocol drivers should work with Windows NT with little or no change. Winsock is compatible with BSD sockets API.

However, compatible does not mean that your UNIX code will work without change. This is because Windows-specific constructs such as WSAStartup need to be used to initialize Windows sockets, and the API returns a handle (unlike an integer in UNIX). Redirector/server subsystems are implemented in Windows NT as file system drivers and are functionally equivalent to file systems in UNIX such as Network File Systems (NFS) and Andrew File Systems (AFS). Windows NT provides transparent access to other networks through provider/redirector pairs.

For example, the add-ons Client Service for NetWare for the Windows NT Workstation and the Gateway Service for NetWare for Windows NT Server enable a computer running Windows NT to connect as a client to a NetWare network. While the Named Pipes facility is similar and is supported by UNIX and Windows NT, the code is not directly compatible.

Windows NT RPC is compatible and interoperable with other OSF DCE-based RPC systems. Again, that does not mean that the code will port without change. This is because the interface definition languages are not the same, and each one supports some features not supported by the other and vice versa. The routine names are also different.

For example, the UNIX routine *rpc_server_use_all_protseqs* has the Windows NT equivalent *RpcServerUseAllProtseqs*. Windows NT RPC does not include naming, security, and time DCE servers. If you are using Windows NT in your DCE environment, these services must be provided by products from other vendors, such as DCE services for Windows NT from Digital. DCE services for Windows NT is covered in Chapter 4. Support for ONC RPC is not built-in, but is supported by third parties such as the RhaPC-d developers' toolkit from Intergraph.

"Multi-User" vs. "Single User" Differences

Windows NT is not a multi-user operating system in the way that UNIX or mainframe operating systems are. But there are functions within Windows NT that keep track of users. On the logon screen of Windows NT, for example, different users can log on, and Windows NT will validate their userid and password. UNIX and mainframe operating systems evolved from the era of dumb terminals and multiple users logging on simultaneously. This multi-user concept is carried forward in the rest of the operating system components as well (such as security, file access, etc.). Windows NT is designed to be a client/server operating system, and the users access Windows NT (server) through clients, which are intelligent devices like PCs and not dumb terminals. So you typically don't have a situation of multiple users logging on simultaneously to Windows NT.

There are some areas in migration/coexistence where this difference needs to be acknowledged and dealt with. Citrix Systems has licensed Windows NT source code and added multi-user support. Many companies that offer different products in the migration/coexistence market have licensed the multi-user technology from Citrix. Microsoft has also licensed Citrix multi-user technology from Citrix.

Style Differences

Besides the technical differences listed above that have to be taken care of for porting to work, there are also some style differences that you should be aware of:

- You probably would type a lot more (and faster too) when using UNIX compared to Windows NT where the mouse rules.
- Unlike POSIX and other UNIX APIs, the Win32 APIs are normally longer. To make the API readable, Win32 normally mixes upper and lower cases in the API name with the upper case used to indicate start of significant words. Win32 APIs also normally support more parameters than the UNIX counterparts.
- Windows NT program file sizes typically are larger than the UNIX equivalent, in part due to the longer names for variables, data types, and APIs (as mentioned above).

CHECKLIST OF LIKELY CHANGES FOR PORTING

Don't be scared by the above list of differences and decide not to port. The above list is meant to help you get an idea of the areas that you need to pay attention to when porting. It will also help you estimate the amount of effort required for porting. The following list identifies the areas that you should look for when you want to port.

- Source code changes. For specific changes to C programs, please see Chapter 3.
- Makefiles. You should have the line include *ntwin32.mak* in your makefile to set up the proper library files, processor variables, etc. Windows NT SDK has a command line *nmake* utility, which is tailored for command line usage like UNIX and includes some common UNIX options such as *-f* or */F*. *nmake* is different from the Windows NT Makefile. Within your makefile itself, you may need to change macros defining source directory paths, header and include file paths, convert command options from UNIX to equivalent NT command options. You may need to change file extensions. If a macro in a UNIX makefile expands a string to a length longer than Windows NT command-line interpreters handle, you can use inline files as a workaround. Refer to the *nmake* online documentation.
- #include statements. Statements dealing with file names in your program code as well as makefiles.

POST PORTING

So far, we have looked at areas that are available under both Windows NT and UNIX and focused on the differences in implementation. Windows also has programming constructs and styles that do not have a direct equivalent in UNIX. If you are a UNIX programmer learning Windows or involved in porting from UNIX to Windows and want to enhance your programs after porting, the following areas are the areas you need to look at:

- Windows low-level programming
  - Windows message loops
  - Inter process communication features, such as shared memory
  - Function callbacks
  - Using handles
  - Clipboard interface
  - Windows resources
- Windows high-level Programming
- Microsoft Foundation Classes (MFC) programming
- Visual Programming Tools — Visual Basic, Visual C++
- Graphics Device Interface (GDI)
- Object Linking and Embedding (OLE) and Enterprise OLE
- Dynamic Data Exchange (DDE)
- C2 (Security)

- Messaging API (MAPI)
- Open Database Connectivity (ODBC) to access databases

WINDOWS NT NATIVE POSIX SUPPORT

So far, we have discussed POSIX in general, presuming that all the POSIX required services are supported by the Operating System, in this case, Windows NT. However, there are some serious limitations with the Windows NT native POSIX support.

Windows NT POSIX support comes in the form of a protected subsystem. Windows NT implementation of POSIX is strictly what is required in the POSIX.1 standard. The subsystem starts automatically when a POSIX application loads and remains active until shutdown. The process name is *psxss*. This is run-time support.

Windows NT has built-in support for TCP/IP commands commonly used in the UNIX environment such as *ftp, ping,* and *rcp,* and the Windows NT Resource kit also includes support for POSIX utilities such as *vi, sh, cat,* etc. The Resource kit also includes the source for the utilities. The utilities can also be downloaded from Microsoft, for free. Besides the run-time support and utilities, there is SDK support for developing POSIX applications. However, quoting from "Microsoft Windows NT from a UNIX Point of View," a white paper from Microsoft:

> "The POSIX and OS/2 subsystems provide 'compatibility-mode' environments for their respective applications and, by definition, are not as feature-rich as the Win32 subsystem."

A more technical quote from the Windows NT resource kit:

> "With this release of Windows NT, POSIX applications have no direct access to any of the facilities and features of the Win32 subsystem, such as memory mapped files, networking, graphics, or dynamic data exchange."

Translated, *no graphics* means that the popular Windows graphical user interface is not natively available for a POSIX application, and you are restricted to Console text applications; and *no networking* means no Winsock, PPP, and the like. I think you get the picture. In providing POSIX support the way it did, Microsoft ensured that Windows NT can be bid on federal and state acquisitions that mandate POSIX compliance, while ensuring that there is enough incentive for users to switch and take advantage of the other Win32 features.

TIPS FOR WRITING PORTABLE SOURCE CODE

Bristol Technology (www.bristol.com) and MainSoft (www.mainsoft.com) provide a number of white papers related to portability and source code considerations. This section contains recommendations from Bristol Technology and MainSoft Corporation as summarized by DEC.* In the following paragraphs, Wind/U refers to the porting product from Bristol Technology, and MainWin refers to the porting product from MainSoft. Both Wind/U and MainWin are covered in more detail in Chapter 3.

COMPILER DIFFERENCES

UNIX C++ compilers are usually based on the AT&T CFront 3.0 implementation, and most Windows C++ compilers are CFront 3.0 compatible. The Microsoft Visual C++ compiler is very compatible with the C++ 3.0 compilers supplied by some of the UNIX vendors. This section lists some minor differences you may encounter.

* Reproduced with permission from DEC.

Semicolons in Class Definitions

Visual C++ allows an extra semicolon at the end of class definitions, as in the following example:

```
DECLARE_DYNAMIC(ClassName);
```

To make this statement portable to UNIX, leave off the trailing semicolon, as follows:

```
DECLARE_DYNAMIC(ClassName)
```

Access to Base Class Private Members

Visual C++ allows derived classes to access base class private members, as in the following example:

```
class base
{
private:
    int some_member
}...
```

To make this code portable to UNIX, allow access to the member by making it protected in the base class, as follows:

```
class base
{
protected:
    int some_member
}...
```

Type Casting

Visual C++ allows type casting using function call syntax, as in the following example:

```
date.d_Day=unsigned char (i)
```

UNIX C++ compilers only support the C syntax for type casting, as in the following example:

```
date.d_Day=(unsigned char)i;
```

Interchanging Types

Visual C++ allows you to interchange int and BOOL types, as in the following example:

```
BOOL WinCalApp::ExitInstance()
```

With UNIX C++ compilers, these are different types, and the return value must match the base class return value type, as follows:

```
int WinCalApp::ExitInstance()
```

Variable Declarations

Visual C++ allows variable declarations in switch statement cases without requiring a new scope, as in the following example:

```
default:
// a real day
int  real_day=d_CellType[cell];
Doit(real_day)
```

To make this code portable, enclose the statements in a pair of braces to explicitly define the scope of the new variable, as follows:

```
default:
{
    // a real day
    int  real_day=d_CellType[cell];
    Doit(real_day)
}
```

Pragmas

Microsoft Foundation Class (MFC) library uses Visual C++ compiler #pragma warning (disable:4xxx) directives to eliminate warning messages during compiles. These pragmas are not portable to UNIX C++ compilers. Therefore, you can ignore warnings such as the following that reference MFC include files:

```
"afxwin.h", line 1694: warning: CStatic::Create() hides virtual
CWnd::Create()
```

Constructor Calls

Visual C++ allows complex statements in constructor calls, as in the following example:

```
//Constructor
CRecorderRecord(RecordID rid=NullRID, WORD monitorID=0, long
counter=0, CProcess &process=CProcess());
```

Make this statement more portable by reducing the functionality and not allowing a default for the CProcess argument. The calling code must create the CProcess object before the constructor call as follows:

```
//Constructor
CRecorderRecord(RecordID rid=NullRID, WORD monitorID=0, long
counter=0, CProcess &process);
```

Inline Functions

Visual C++ allows complex inline functions with multiple return points. For UNIX C++ compilers, you must rewrite inline functions to remove multiple return points, or remove the inline keyword.

New and Delete Operators

As a general rule, if you use [] when you call new, you must use [] when you call delete to make your code more portable and safe. In MFC, if the delete object is not a derived class from CObject, cast the object to a void pointer and make sure you call a global delete operator. For example:

```
struct CRowColInfo {
.
.
.
} *m_pRowInfo;
::delete [] (char *)m_pRowInfo;
```

Anonymous Unions

Visual C++ allows anonymous, or unnamed, unions, as in the following example, which you would access as struct_name.fred:

```
struct{
      union{
            char fred[10].
            struct{
                  }jim
      }
}
```

Many UNIX C and C++ compilers do not allow anonymous unions. Instead, you must name the union, as in the following example. You would then use struct_name.tony.jim.

```
struct{
      union{
                  char fred[10].
                  struct{
                        }jim
      }tony
}
```

Compiler Warnings

Programmers sometimes ignore warning messages when they appear during a compilation. They have learned that the reported problems do not affect either the performance or reliability of their code and do not take the time to isolate them. However, warnings about nonportable code, signed/unsigned mismatches, or data type conversions must be heeded during a port to a new platform. A clean compile in your Windows environment will help to eliminate tedious debugging on the UNIX target.

Using Conditional Compilation

When modifying the source code, try to avoid conditional compilation. If you must, you can write the code modifications in the following way:

```
#ifdef unix (or #ifdef MAINWIN)
 /* Modified code for UNIX compilation...*/
```

TABLE 2.2
C Data Types

C Data Type	16-bit Platform	32-bit Platform
char	8	8
int	16	32
short	16	16
long	32	32 (64 on Alpha)
enum	16	32
float	32	32
double	64	64
long double	64	64 (80 on some machines)
bit field	16	32

```
 ..../...
#else
 /* Original windows code... */
 .../...
#end
```

Pointer Calculation

Any pointer arithmetic based on an assumption of a segmented memory architecture (segment:offset) must be reviewed. When computing offsets to arrays of structures, do not create pointers by combining a computed 16-bit offset with the high-order 16 bits of an address pointer, as this type of computation depends on segment:offset encoded addresses. RISC architectures all have large linear address spaces.

Also, code that uses 16-bit pointer address-wrapping will not work in a linear address architecture and must be rewritten.

C Data Types

Table 2.2 lists common C data types for reference, illustrating how they change when going from 16-bit to 32-bit systems.

Take special note of the following:

- Integer data types such as int and unsigned int may not be portable in the application. Pay special attention to this issue if the Windows compilation already generates signed/unsigned or conversion warnings that have been ignored in the past. Also, because the int data type grows to 32 bits, the sign extension bit moves to bit 31. (Note that Digital UNIX is a 64-bit platform.)
- Any assumptions about the 32768 or 65536 range for an int must be reviewed.
- Loops that depend on a 16-bit int may experience problems when the int grows to 32 bits. (Note that Digital UNIX is a 64-bit platform.)
- Both NEAR and FAR pointers will be 32 bits on UNIX (64 bits on Digital UNIX) and must be managed as such. When recompiling under MainWin, qualifiers such as NEAR and FAR are defined by the C preprocessor.
- You will find, for instance, in Windows.h, #define NEAR. As a result, all pointers will be 32-bit pointers. Your code must not make the assumption that they are 2 bytes long.

TABLE 2.3
C Library Differences Between UNIX and Windows NT

UNIX C Library Function	Windows NT Replacement
strdup()	_strdup()
strcasecmp()	_stricmp()
stricmp()	_stricmp()
iaascii()	_isascii()

- Members of a bit field may not be stored in the same order by different compilers or architectures.
- Be careful about char. ANSI C does not impose a rule that it always be a signed char.

C Library Differences

In most cases, there are minimal or no differences between the UNIX implementation of the C library functions and their counterparts in Windows NT, but there are some.

Some of the Windows NT C library functions are preceded by an underscore; thus the UNIX C library function *strdup()* needs to be replaced by *_strdup()* on Windows NT. Table 2.3 shows the original UNIX C library functions and their replacements in Windows NT.

When opening a binary file for either reading or writing, it is necessary to specify the file type in the *fopen*() call; thus, the UNIX function call:

```
fd = fopen(filename, "w");
```

needs to be replaced by:

```
fd = fopen(filename, "wb");
```

The *fopen*(directory_name, "r") call returns NULL whether directory_name exists or not. In general, Windows NT treats files and directories differently.

The function *bzero*() is not available in Windows NT; thus the UNIX function call:

```
bzero(NamedColors, sizeof(NamedColors);
```

needs to be replaced with:

```
memset(NamedColors, '\0', sizeof(NamedColors);
```

The function *bcopy*() is not available in Windows NT; thus, the UNIX function call:

```
bcopy (ddata, sdata, ndata);
```

needs to be replaced with:

```
memcpy (ddata, sdata, ndata);
```

TABLE 2.4
Windows Data Types

Windows Data Type	Windows 3.1	Windows NT	MainWin
Handle	16	32	32
UINT	16	32	32
Bool	16	32	32
WORD	16	16	16
Byte	8	8	8
DWORD	32	32	32
WPARAM	16	32	32
LPARAM	32	32	32

Windows Data Types

Table 2.4 lists common Windows data types for reference, illustrating how they change when going from 16-bit to 32-bit systems and how they are used in one of the porting tools that let Windows applications run on UNIX, MainWin. MainWin is covered in Chapter 3.

Review the usage of those variables that change, especially WPARAM because it is used so often.

PC-Specific Compiler Directives

To deactivate PC-specific directives, we suggest that you use the C preprocessor. In fact, the MainWin system already removes NEAR, FAR, PASCAL, and many other directives. You will not have to worry about these.

MainWin header files use an #ifdef to deactivate NEAR and FAR directives on UNIX. You can use this method to deactivate other undesirable directives:

```
#ifdef unix
 #define NEAR
 #define FAR
#endif
```

Using New TYPEDEFs to Improve Portability

Your Windows source code can remain the same for both 16-bit and 32-bit versions if you make use of unique typedefs. Using specialized typedefs when defining or casting Windows objects as well as your own application-specific data types and structures will make them easier to modify when porting to different platforms, especially if they are managed by a

```
#ifdef unix..
#endif construct.
```

Microsoft recommends that two new data types be defined to improve portability to 32-bit platforms:

- They recommend that UINT be an unsigned int, which would be 16 bits on a 16-bit machine and 32 bits on a 32-bit machine. The UINT type would be used for objects that naturally widen to 32 bits on the 32-bit target machine. MainSoft also recommends that UINT be used as the type for bitfields.

- The WORD typedef is defined as unsigned short, fixing it at 16 bits, independent of platform architectures. The WORD type is used to specify objects that must remain 16 bits in multiple architectures. You should also try to use the typedefs defined by the Windows API as much as possible.

Redefining Standard Functions

Be careful not to redefine standard UNIX functions (such as *toupper*) because MainWin may rely on them.

Byte Ordering

Byte ordering problems can arise when you use a nonportable construct to pack two shorts into a long or other similar operation. Use the Microsoft macros MAKELONG, HIWORD, and LOWORD, which have appropriate definitions provided by system include files.

For example, to save a short in a byte array (this form is nonportable):

```
short VarData;
unsigned char dlist[2];
*(short *)dlist=VarData;
```

This cast/assignment assumes a specific byte order, a nonportable assumption. The statement should be rewritten as follows (portable form):

```
short VarData;
unsigned char dlist[2];
*dlist = LOBYTE (VarData);
*(dlist+1)= HIBYTE (VarData);
```

This ensures that all byte ordering in byte streams are "little endian."

String Concatenation Differences

Be careful when assuming that methods used in string concatenation on PCs will work the same on 32-bit machines. The C language does not specify that strings will be placed consecutively in memory. Often, on the UNIX side, each string is placed on a word boundary (4 bytes usually).

For example, using the *GetOpenFileName* function, the *lpstrFilter* member should point to something like the following:

```
Text Files\0*.txt\0\0
```

On the PC with the Microsoft compiler, you could get the previous pattern by using the following:

```
char pFilter[] = {"Text Files", "*.txt", ""};
```

This will not work with the UNIX version because the strings do not concatenate seamlessly. A gap is introduced because the compiler starts each string on 4-byte boundaries.

The correct way to do it is as follows:

```
char *pFilter = "Text Files\0*.txt\0";
```

Using MAKEINTRESOURCE

On UNIX, the MAKEINTRESOURCE macro flags the high-order word with a unique bit pattern to distinguish between real strings and an integer resource name. A simple cast to LPSTR, as one might do in Windows, is not enough because it does not flag the high-order word.

Structure Member Alignment

Access to data that are not aligned to proper boundaries can cause problems on most RISC platforms. Arrays of structures can suffer from the same kind of problem.

In some cases, misaligned data elements are illegal in the target architecture and will generate bus error signals. These can introduce a significant performance penalty. Therefore, all data elements should be aligned to their natural boundaries, depending on their type.

When declaring structures and accessing them in a regular way, the compiler will manage the alignment requirements for the target machine, allocating extra space in front of structure items with alignment requirements. However, if you want to access memory directly, using (char*) pointers cast to another data type, then you will need to take into account the alignment requirements of the target system.

Review the technical literature of your target system to ascertain the proper alignments for each data type, and make appropriate changes to your source code.

Example 1:

```
char       szBuffer[10];
short      nIndex;
nIndex = *(short*)szBuffer[1];
```

This last line would cause a problem on RISC machines because a short has to be aligned on an even address boundary. Instead use:

```
nIndex = MAKEWORD(szBuffer[1],szBuffer[2]);
```

Example 2:

```
struct {
 short nX;
 short nY;
} position;
long xy;
xy = *(long*)&position.nX
```

This last statement may cause an alignment error. Instead use:

```
xy = MAKELONG (position.nX,position.nY);
```

It is very important, for example, never to directly assign a Windows POINT structure to a LONG, or vice versa.

Casts

Casts should be scrutinized carefully, especially those dealing with pointers. Add a comment if the purpose of the cast is not obvious. If there are many casts for the same purpose, use a preprocessor macro, activated with #ifdef unix.

File I/O

If sizeof(var) is used in file I/O function calls, data written to a file on a 16-bit machine may not be read correctly by a 32-bit machine.

For example:

```
f/* write data to file, 16-bit */
write(&buf,sizeof(var),1,fp);
/* read data from file, 32-bit */
fread(&buf,sizeof(var),1,fp);
```

If the size of the variable is different on the two machines, the code will not be portable. Examine your source code and evaluate file I/O operations for this kind of problem. In fact, all sizeof(var)-type operations, for file I/O or not, are suspect.

If you want to keep a binary file in the Intel DOS format but still be able to read and write it transparently under UNIX, you may use the DDR facility provided with MainWin.

Buffer Allocations

Hard-coded buffer sizes, especially for path names and environment strings, should be avoided if you want to support the long path and file names found in UNIX environments.

Assembly Language Routines

All assembly language routines must be eliminated or rewritten using ANSI C and the run-time library calls available under UNIX. This includes any inline assembler code within C modules, using inline assembly extensions provided by some C compiler vendors.

To solve this problem, MainWin includes two source files that implement some functionalities of the MS-DOS 21h interrupt:

```
${MWHOME}/doc/InDosCW.c
${MWHOME}/doc/InDosCW.h
```

Eliminate References to DOS ROM-BIOS or the PC/AT Hardware

References to DOS (for instance, INT 21h), the ROM-BIOS (for instance, INT 13h), or motherboard I/O ports or memory addresses must be eliminated because they are intrinsically nonportable.

Keyboard Scan Codes

Avoid using raw keyboard scan codes in your programs. Use virtual key codes only.

Operating System Differences

In DOS and Windows, lines in text files are terminated by a combination of a Line Feed and Carriage Return. UNIX uses just a Line Feed to denote the end of a line. Many applications depend on the Line Feed/Carriage Return combination to work properly. Some applications may have to modify code to work the same in both environments.

Another example of Carriage Return/Line Feed incompatibilities is Edit Controls. The text retrieved from an edit control will not have the Line Feed/Carriage Return, only the UNIX style Line Feed.

Another major difference between Windows files and UNIX files is that UNIX uses the forward slash (/) as a directory separator, while Windows uses backslash (\) characters. UNIX file names are also case sensitive and much larger (256 characters) than Windows file names. You may have to change some applications to handle these differences.

UNIX also does not have any concept of drive letters. Applications should not depend on a:\filename style file names.

To avoid differences between fonts, controls, and focus highlights between Windows and Motif dialog boxes, Wind/U uses the same ratios as Windows. To minimize problems when porting dialogs, follow these guidelines:

- Avoid using Layout->Size to Content. Always create the control about 20% wider than produced by Size to Content, to ensure that the strings fit cleanly inside your controls with the X fonts, which are slightly different than Windows default fonts.
- Always keep controls about 12 dialog units from the dialog edges. Bristol Technology's App Studio (part of Wind/U) partially enforces this guideline because it does not allow you to place a control closer than 10 dialog units to the edge.
- Always leave about 10 dialog units between controls.

ARCHITECTURE DIFFERENCES

Certain architectural differences between UNIX and Windows warrant discussion, because they may impact certain types of applications.

Storage Order and Alignment

Wind/U runs on a variety of architectures, so it is important to make your code as portable as possible.

As a general rule, you should always use the fields of a structure instead of making assumptions about their location or size in the structure.

Shared Memory Model

As with Windows NT, all instance data in UNIX is private to the application and cannot be accessed from other modules (for example, *GetInstanceData* is not supported).

Application Message Queues

Like Windows NT, each Wind/U application has its own message queue that is inaccessible to other applications. A module instance handle is unique only to the modules that comprise the application. Other applications executing on the system may have the same instance handle. Likewise, each application contains its own handle table, so handles are not system unique. For these reasons, interapplication message passing is currently unsupported by Wind/U. However, Wind/U supports interapplication message passing via DDEML.

Preemptive Multitasking

In some instances, the UNIX preemptive multitasking scheduler may require files to be locked (for example, to prevent race conditions between different applications that access common files). An application ported by Wind/U must not assume that it has indefinite control of the CPU until it returns to the message loop (for example, *GetMessage, WaitMessage,* Yield). The application may be time-sliced at any time.

Debugging Tools

In addition to MainWin and Wind/U debugging tools, you may also want to use third-party tools to help you debug your UNIX application. For example, a tool for identifying memory leaks in your application is Purify from Pure Software Corporation. Wind/U has been tested thoroughly with Purify, using many sample programs. Although Purify may still report some problems, Wind/U is relatively free of significant memory access errors or memory leaks. If you use Purify with your application, keep the following in mind:

- Most C library implementations of *malloc()* under UNIX never return memory to the operating system. Thus, the amount of memory used by the program as shown by utilities such as ps will never shrink. An increasing amount of memory consumption as shown by ps does not in and of itself indicate a memory leak.
- Use Purify's Memory In Use (MIU) reporting with care.
- The X, Xt, and Motif libraries on some systems generate a number of Purify warnings. You may wish to suppress some or all of these messages; consult your Purify documentation for details. Another third-party tool you may want to use is XRunner from Mercury Interactive Corporation. Mercury Interactive's WinRunner and Xrunner products are automated testing tools that you can use without any changes to your application. You can use WinRunner to test the Windows version of your application and XRunner to test the UNIX version. To use XRunner, you need only make sure it is included in your LD_LIBRARY_PATH, SHLIB_PATH, or LIBPATH environment variable.

Other Debugging Hints

Here are a few other hints that will help you identify problems unique to the UNIX version of your application.

- Make sure that both the Windows and UNIX versions of your application compile cleanly with the strictest warning level set.
- Use a small sample to isolate problems quickly.
- Vary your configuration. For example, if you are running the OpenLook Window Manager, see if the problem also occurs with the Motif Window Manager. Also try setting your DISPLAY to a different server to see if that server has the same problem (this is particularly helpful for X errors).

Error Handling

UNIX system functions relay errors in a global variable, errno. Applications usually test to see if a function has completed successfully. If not, they get the error from errno, and use the strerror() function to translate the number into a text message. The errno variable is unique for each process, but in a multithreaded environment like Windows NT, this solution is not adequate.

Win32 provides the GetLastError() API, which provides a reliable way for a thread in a multithreaded process to obtain per-thread error information. Use the FormatMessage() API to turn this value into a character string, as shown in the following code example:

```
ErrMsgLen = FormatMessage(FORMAT_MESSAGE_ALLOCATE_BUFFER |
FORMAT_MESSAGE_FROM_SYSTEM,                     NULL,
GetLastError(), MAKELANGID (LANG_ENGLISH,
SUBLANG_ENGLISH_US),        (LPTSTR)&lpvMessage,       0, NULL);

WriteFile(hStderr,      lpvMessage,      ErrMsgLen,      &n_write,
NULL);
```

See the Microsoft SDK online help for the prototypes and more information.

Cross-compiler Support

If you are developing portable applications, you can take advantage of cross-compilation support provided by some vendors. Digital has planned a number of tools that will allow applications to be developed on Windows NT and deployed on Digital UNIX. Digital's C and C++ compilers for UNIX and OpenVMS include a compiler option to enforce Microsoft's syntax (even though the resulting executable will run on Digital UNIX or OpenVMS). This facilitates future porting of these applications to Windows platforms as well as using the same source code to generate applications for different platforms. The Java Development Kit (JDK) for Digital UNIX allows programmers to develop applications on UNIX that will run seamlessly on Windows NT.

Conclusion

In this chapter we looked at some detail differences between UNIX and Windows NT that you need to be aware of if you are porting programs from one environment to another. This chapter also covered some tips that help you port code easily from one environment to another. These tips also help you write common code for multiple environments. Let us now look at some tools that take care of the environment differences.

3 Porting and Rewriting Current Applications

INTRODUCTION

An organization has to look at its current portfolio of applications to determine if the application should be left as is, ported to another environment, or rewritten. This decision depends on a variety of factors such as expected useful life of the current application, size of the application, existing skill base of developers and system administrators, familiarity of users with their user interface, etc. These factors are covered in Chapter 13. This chapter will address porting applications to another operating environment and rewriting applications. Porting can be done either manually or using a tool. Manual porting was covered in Chapter 2. We will discuss tool-based porting in this chapter. To make an application from one environment work in another environment, you can either port the source or emulate the required environment at run time. This chapter deals with porting using source code. Emulation is covered in Chapter 7.

PORTING CONSIDERATIONS

If you have decided to port or rewrite one or more applications to another environment, then there are some business and technical considerations that need to addressed. Porting considerations are addressed in this section. Rewriting applications is addressed later in this chapter.

BUSINESS PORTING CONSIDERATIONS

There are some business benefits that can be derived by porting:

- The biggest benefit of porting is it permits a stepping stone approach to a potentially complex transition.
- Porting permits your system administrators and their custom utilities to immediately transition and be productive in the new environment.
- Porting permits you to continue to use your development and maintenance skills while you transition to the new environment.
- Depending on your applications, you may be able to get the applications working in the new environment with little effort.
- Your end-users can start using your existing applications in the new environment without having to relearn the applications.
- You can take advantage of unique features available in the new environment as a post porting step, but this may introduce divergence in the source between your sources in the old and new environments.

Your business application may have been developed from scratch, purchased as a package, or purchased as a package and modifications made to fit your environment. If you bought a package, then you need to check with the package vendor to see if they offer a version that runs in the environment you are interested in. You should also check if the vendor offers porting assistance, in particular for the custom modifications you may have. An in-house application would be an appropriate porting candidate under the following conditions:

- The application has a long useful expected life.
- The current development and maintenance programmer skill base dealing with the application would require a big learning curve for a new environment.
- The benefits of making the application work in the new environment outweigh the benefits of leaving the application as is or rewriting it.
- The application size is large enough to gain some benefits when ported, but not too large to make porting a long, error-prone, and risky process.

If as a manager you are wondering how serious a porting problem you have, then check your code for the following list of things that make it easy to port:

- Code in which end-user interface handling and business logic handling are isolated.
- Code in which vendor extensions to standards are isolated.
- Code in which dependencies on a specific operating system is isolated (particularly true for UNIX with its many flavors).
- Overall program flow is separated into logical, modular blocks.

The more your code satisfies the above points, the better. However, regardless of how well your code fits, expect some code changes. Be prepared to allocate time and resources for making source code changes when porting to another environment.

Keep in mind that sometimes you may be able to port and make the application work in a limited fashion in the new environment; but to take full advantage of the new environment, you may need to modify the code. For example, let us consider a UNIX program performing file access that is being ported to Windows NT. If the program uses standard C functions such as *fopen*, the program will still work when ported to Windows NT, but it may be unable to take advantage of advanced features like asynchronous I/O unless the *fopen* is replaced by an equivalent Win32 API call.

TECHNICAL PORTING CONSIDERATIONS

Besides the application code itself, there are a few other items that need to be addressed when an application is ported:

- Any shell scripts that are used by the application either during development or execution need to be ported or rewritten.
- UNIX has built-in commands used in application development. If you are using tools to port your code, tool vendors provide most of the commands on Windows NT. If you are manually porting code, you need to write or get the equivalent tools or you need to find the Windows NT equivalent of the tools' function.
- UNIX uses a number of utilities for application development as well as System Administration. Equivalent utilities in the new environment have to be used or the utilities need to be ported or rewritten. Many porting tool vendors include UNIX utilities equivalents with their products. These are covered with the tools later in this chapter. There are also some public domain utilities. Most of these are available from public ftp sites such as ftp.iastate.edu, ftp.cica.indiana.edu, sunsite.unc.edu, and ftp.uu.net. These include *ci, ident, perl, rcsdiff, tic, co, lex, rcs, rcsmerge, yacc, cpp, merge, rcsclean,* and *rlog*.
- Any documentation that may be available such as help files and online manuals that you have may need to be ported.

TABLE 3.1
Equivalent Program Types Between Windows NT and UNIX

UNIX Program Type	Windows NT Program Type
C and C++ programs	C and C++ programs
Shared libraries	Dynamic Linked Libraries (DLLs)
Daemons	Windows NT services
Fortran programs	Fortran programs
Scripts — Shell, login, etc.	Scripts (scripting languages not compatible)
X Windows/Motif programs	Windows GUI programs
UNIX configuration files and programs	Windows NT Registry edit program and APIs
POSIX and other APIs	Win32 APIs

- You may also need to port testing scripts that you may have set up to perform automated and other testing.
- Daemons and other stand-alone utilities that perform some application functions in the background.
- UNIX-shared libraries used by programs must be ported.
- Web-related unique application code using languages such as PERL.

Table 3.1 summarizes some common UNIX types of UNIX programs and the equivalent type in Windows NT.

Let us look at the steps involved in porting application source.

PORTING STEPS

The following steps are involved in porting an application:

- Copy your source code from your UNIX machine to your Windows NT machine (or in some cases, Windows 95). There are a number of different ways to transfer the source and accessory files and these ways are covered later in this chapter.
- Copy compiling accessories to the source such as makefiles, resource files, and scripts.
- Make any changes required to the accessory files. Makefile changes were discussed in Chapter 2. Porting scripts is discussed later in this chapter.
- You can add Windows-specific code, such as Win32 calls, to take advantage of functions not available in UNIX.
- Compile the ported source into object modules using the appropriate language compiler in the new environment.
- Compile required accessories such as resource files.
- Link the object modules with appropriate Windows and tool libraries.
- Test your ported application, identify problem areas in the port, if any.
- Repeat these steps until the ported application works satisfactorily.

Keep in mind that these steps are just a high-level overview. You have to address several details at each stage. While the major steps outlined above are applicable to any porting tool you select, the details will vary depending on the tool you select. The N*u*TCRACKER installation and porting guide included in the CD accompanying this book will give you an idea of the details involved.

Transferring Files from UNIX to Windows NT

You can transfer your source and accessory files from your UNIX machine to a Windows NT machine in a number of different ways. These are listed below.

- Use floppy disks to copy.
- Use the built-in File Transfer Protocol (ftp) function in Windows to transfer files between the UNIX server and the Windows machine.
- Use built-in tftp function in Windows NT.
- Use the built-in rcp function in Windows NT.
- Use a serial link.
- Use a network operating system with built-in support to access UNIX server files.
- Use third-party Network File System (NFS) packages.

Please refer to Chapter 8 for details about these methods.

Porting C Programs

Let us first consider C programs without database or transaction processing calls. At first glance, you may presume that if the C program follows C coding standards, it should compile and execute easily in the other environment. This is seldom the case. There are a number of reasons beyond standards for this:

- Path names are pretty standard in the UNIX world — header files are under */sys*, binary executables are under */bin*, etc. In Windows NT, the user selects most path names.
- Path names are passed as string arguments in many instances. UNIX supports only the forward slash (/), while Windows NT supports both forward and reverse slashes (except for the command prompt).
- UNIX is case sensitive, while NT is, for the most part, not case sensitive. (NTFS preserves case for directory listings. If you see your files in File Manager, for example, you will see the case used when the file was created.)
- It is not uncommon for UNIX applications to hard code directory paths. For example, the code may be looking for a file in */usr/local/bin* presuming a standard UNIX environment. The ported code will almost certainly not be able to find the file in that path and thus fail. These paths have to be identified and taken care of before the ported application would work in the new environment.
- Vendor extension to standards. Where there is a rule, there is an exception. Where there is a standard, there is a vendor extension. In most cases, it is difficult not to use the vendor extension, since the functionality of the standard by itself is limited. The "wrapper code" may provide support for the standard, but may not provide for all vendor extensions of different vendors.

Porting Scripts

Scripts are utilities written in a scripting language that are part of an application in the same manner as programs written in a language like C. Programmers and system administrators typically use scripts to automate routine, repetitive tasks. UNIX operating systems include a shell that supports scripts and so does the Win32 shell. Vendors providing support for porting code provide tools to create and/or port UNIX scripts to Windows NT. These scripts can run the ported UNIX programs as well as native Win32 programs.

PORTING APPLICATIONS FROM UNIX TO WINDOWS

We consider tool-based porting here and take a brief look at some vendor tools. Manual porting is addressed later in this chapter.

Common Porting Products

This section presents an overview of some common porting products available. The information was gathered from different published sources, primarily vendors' online Web pages. The Web addresses and other contact information are included in the description for each vendor and in the Appendix. The tools are getting updated quickly and you should check with the tool vendor for the latest information. Most vendors also offer free evaluations that are downloadable from their Web sites.

This book is not intended to help you select one vendor over another. You should pick migration/coexistence solutions that meet your requirements and perform an evaluation of vendor products. The inclusion of vendor information is provided to give you an idea of the capabilities of the products and to give you a quick reference to get further information and software.

Common products that help in porting applications from Windows to UNIX include N*u*TCRACKER from DataFocus Software and Portage from Consensys Computers.

N*u*TCRACKER

The following is a summary of N*u*TCRACKER from DataFocus Web pages. Additional information on N*u*TCRACKER is available online at http://www.datafocus.com.

N*u*TCRACKER is a product family for developers who want to port their character-based and X/Motif UNIX applications to Windows NT or Windows 95.

Using N*u*TCRACKER, developers can recompile UNIX C, C++, or FORTRAN source code and link it to N*u*TCRACKER DLLs, resulting in native Win32 applications. A schematic of this process is illustrated in Figure 3.1.

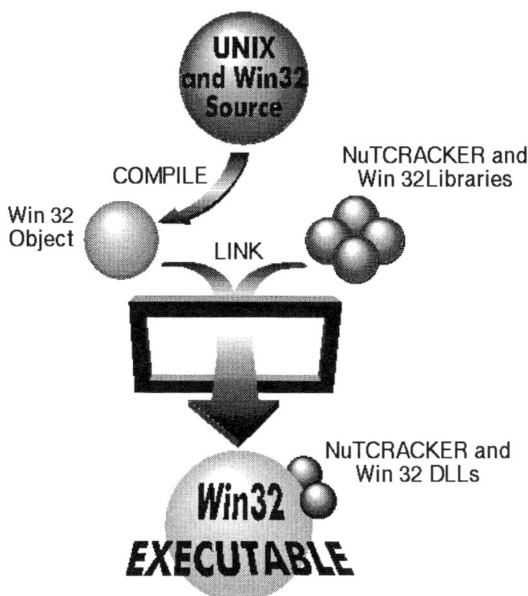

FIGURE 3.1 Porting an application from UNIX to Windows using N*u*TCRACKER.

N*u*TCRACKER supports Intel, Alpha, MIPS, and PowerPC platforms. So if you have source on any of those platforms, you can get Windows NT for that platform along with the corresponding N*u*TCRACKER version and port your source. Please note that IBM recently decided NOT to support Windows NT on the PowerPC.

The N*u*TCRACKER Product Family

The N*u*TCRACKER Product Family currently consists of three products:

- N*u*TCRACKER SDK: N*u*TCRACKER Software Development Kit (SDK) for porting character-based and daemon applications. It consists of the Application Program Interface (API) (which includes system calls and library routines) and a comprehensive set of development utilities. N*u*TCRACKER SDK contains the user interface options, including curses and client-server-designed Win32 enhancements for applications ported using the SDK.
- N*u*TCRACKER: X/Software Development Kit (X/SDK) provides the porting environment you need if your application is designed with an X/Motif user interface. If you are porting with the X/SDK, you may need to purchase N*u*TCRACKER X/Operating Environment (described below) for distribution with your end-user applications. In addition to X11R5 and Motif API support to port X/Motif applications to Win32, N*u*TCRACKER X/SDK also includes the following features for porting X Window applications to Windows NT:
    - Windows NT versions of the X Window System and Motif libraries.
    - OSF/Motif Toolkit and widgets, including the Motif User Interface Language (UIL) compiler and Window Manager.
    - Motif extensions for Toolkit widget creation and manipulation routines, message routines, font routines, and convenience routines that have been added to supplement those provided by the OSF/Motif Toolkit.
    - Motif extensions to the Motif User Interface Language.
    - An X Server that lets you test your X application on a Windows NT computer.
    - A Motif replacement library, Wintif, that lets you present your Motif applications with a Windows "look and feel."
    - The Remote Startup Service, which simulates the *rexec* daemon and lets you start X applications located on a Windows NT computer from the N*u*TCRACKER X Server Control Panel.
- N*u*TCRACKER X/Operating Environment (X/OE) provides a 32-bit X Server environment for your end-user X/Motif applications and the N*u*TCRACKER DLLs necessary to run ported applications. It may also be used to run X applications performing on UNIX platforms.

UNIX Functionality Supported by N*u*TCRACKER

APIs

Process Control. N*u*TCRACKER provides a true UNIX *fork* with proper inheritance of resources, such as handles. Processes and threads are slightly different between UNIX and Windows NT, as mentioned in Chapter 2. This function lets your UNIX programs with *fork* execute as they would in UNIX.

Shared Memory. Your applications can use shared memory consistent with UNIX standards, which supports cross-platform interprocess communication and data access.

Security. N*u*TCRACKER preserves security permissions for User, Group, etc. as set up in your UNIX environment and applications.

Networking. Nu*TCRACKER provides BSD sockets to support networked applications. Sockets are handled as file descriptors, which allow your UNIX code to use other IPC mechanisms without modification. All of Windows NT's supported protocols are available to your applications.

User Interfaces. The N*u*TCRACKER SDK API library includes integrated support for curses user interfaces, while the N*u*TCRACKER X/SDK provides integrated support for X/Motif APIs in the xlib, xt, and other libraries.

As mentioned in Chapter 2, Windows NT and Motif end-user interfaces are similar. While the interfaces look similar from an end-user perspective, similar is not same, and the differences may be annoying to the user who has to switch back and forth between the systems often. To overcome this problem, N*u*TCRACKER provides the Wintif technology, which lets Motif applications be displayed with a Windows look-and-feel. Note that Wintif is optional and if you have users who still want the Motif interface, that is supported as well.

Environment and Utilities

User Environment. As in UNIX, the user environment is fully managed through environment variables you set on either a permanent or temporary basis.

Build Environment. The build environment is set up as it is in UNIX with UNIX *make* environment variables. With N*u*TCRACKER, you also can convert to *nmake* and Windows NT's *make* if you want to.

Utilities. A comprehensive set of UNIX commands and utilities exists (over 140 in all), and this maintains your productivity in the Windows NT environment. The commands and utilities provided address broad areas such as text manipulation, record keeping, the program execution environment, editing, and arithmetic operations.

An exhaustive list of the APIs and Utilities can be found in *NuTCRACKER Installation and Porting Guide*, a 200+ page document. This document is on the CD accompanying this book. It is also available through the DataFocus Web page http://www.datafocus.com. The N*u*TCRACKER X/SDK includes X and Motif APIs in the xlib, xt, and other libraries.

N*u*TCRACKER includes utilities that are part of the MKS Toolkit. MKS toolkit is covered in Chapter 9. Besides the MKS Toolkit utilities, N*u*TCRACKER includes other utilities such as *chmod, whoami, process, sdiff*, etc.

Portage

Information on Portage is available online at http://www.consensys.com. (Be careful when you type in Consensys, as there is another company with the name Consensus and the address http://www.consensus.com.)

Portage is an integration of UNIX SVR4 with Windows NT, including over 125 standard UNIX utilities. It has a base and an SDK. There are four main functions provided by the Portage Base System:

- Lets you use Portage UNIX utilities from the NT Command Prompt.
- Lets you use one of the Portage UNIX shells (*ksh* or *csh*) instead of the NT command prompt.
- Lets you use the Portage Windows Interface to manage UNIX shells.
- Lets you access the Portage online manual pages as Windows Help.

The main components of the Portage SDK are:

- Thirty software development utilities, including *ar, cc, ld, yacc, lex, make*, and *SCCS*
- More than 700 system calls and subroutines

Besides the Portage SDK, you need to use the Windows NT environment and C/C++ compilation tools to port your applications.

Portage makes UNIX an integral part of Windows NT sharing the same hardware. Portage utilities can operate on files and directories created by Windows NT programs, and Windows NT programs can operate on files and directories created by Portage utilities. The Portage shells *ksh* and *csh* can run Windows NT programs, and the Windows NT Command Prompt can run UNIX programs.

Developers can use the Microsoft Windows NT compilers and debuggers directly to develop UNIX programs, or use the standard UNIX *ar, cc, ld,* and make commands included in the Portage SDK. The Portage SDK also enables developers to create hybrid UNIX/Windows NT programs that combine the UNIX API with the Win32 API. Windows NT stores environment variables in the Registry. The Windows NT environment is read by the Portage Kernel when it starts up, and is imported into all Portage programs when they start up.

Portage Base

Portage Base supports the Windows command prompt and provides UNIX command prompt functions.

NT Command Prompt

All Portage utilities can be run from the NT Command Prompt or console. Since the Command Prompt passes command line arguments to programs unchanged (unlike UNIX shells, which perform wild-card expansion and much more), Portage programs are able to provide an overlapping set of UNIX-like and DOS-like syntax. In particular, from the NT Command Prompt, path names can use either UNIX style / or Windows style \ notation. Supported functions include:

- Pattern matching is UNIX style, including '*', '?', single quotes, and double quotes
- Portage environment variables (UNIXROOT, UNIXTMP, SYMLINKS, and CASENAMES) are in effect

Of course, shell-specific features like $X for environment variables and backquotes for subshells are not available from the Command Prompt.

An example of a valid Command Prompt command line is *ls -lrt /bin/b**

There are several name conflicts between NT commands and Portage UNIX utilities. The echo command is built into the Command Prompt (as it is in UNIX shells), so it will always use the NT syntax. Other commands like *more* and *mkdir* are not built in, so you will get whichever one is found first by following your PATH environment variable.

When Portage is installed, the bin directory is added to the end of your PATH, so by default you will get the NT version of these utilities. You can change the PATH environment variable but that may break existing batch and other Windows NT functions using the Path. The simplest solution is to use one of the UNIX shells, where $PORTAGE/bin is added to the front of the PATH environment variable by default.

The UNIX Shells

Portage provides both the Korn Shell (*ksh*) and the C Shell (*csh*). Both of these shells run in the console. This means that you can set a very large buffer size, say 200 lines or more, and keep that much interactive history available for browsing. You can launch a *ksh* or *csh* from icons in the Portage program group. You can also simply type *ksh* or *csh* at an NT command prompt. If you want to run multiple shells (maximum of 20 can be active at any one time), the preferred method is probably to use the Portage Windows Interface to start them.

Once you are running *ksh* or *csh*, you are in a UNIX environment. The shell window provides an emulation of a VT100 terminal (a VT100 subset), and your term environment variable will be set to VT100. The window also provides a limited *tty* line discipline, and you can use *stty(1)* to view the options in effect or to change a subset of them.

In general, you should be unable to tell the difference between the behavior under one of the Portage UNIX shells and a native SVR4 implementation. A list of the few known differences is provided in the Portage documentation.

If you prefer graphical user interfaces, Portage includes the Portage Windows Interface, which serves a number of important functions:

- It allows you to easily start up and manage multiple UNIX shells.
- It allows you to customize the default settings of your shell windows (e.g., size, colors, etc.).
- It provides a dialog box interface to all Portage UNIX commands.
- It provides easy access to online manual pages for every command.

You can start up the Portage Windows Interface by clicking on its icon in the Portage program group. The program's main feature is a set of 140 buttons providing dialog-box access to UNIX utilities. The Portage SDK has an even larger set of buttons (170) than the Base System. Screen shots are available at http://www.consensys.com.

Portage SDK

The Portage SDK includes utilities, system routines, etc.

Portage SDK Utilities

The Portage SDK provides all of the software development tools from standard SVR4 except the basic C/C++ compilation system (compiler, linker, archiver, and debugger). In order to compile and link programs for Portage on Windows NT, you need to install Microsoft Visual C++.

Portage does include SVR4-compatible versions of *ar, cc,* and *ld*, which call the relevant Microsoft utilities to perform the actual work. This means that existing UNIX makefiles can be used with only minor changes.

When you are compiling and linking existing UNIX SVR4 programs with the Portage SDK, you can either use the Portage *make* command or you can use the Microsoft *nmake* command. Using *nmake* may require more effort compared to Portage *make*. Portage includes standard makefile templates for both *make* and *nmake* that you can include at the beginning of your own makefiles. Examples and sample programs are available online at http://www.consensys.com.

Terminal-oriented programs linked with the Portage SDK display their output in a console window within the Win32 subsystem (the same as the NT Command Prompt, and all Portage utilities). The Portage console window provides a (partial) emulation of a VT100 terminal to support full screen functionality, and the Portage SDK includes the complete curses library.

System Calls and Subroutines

The Portage SDK subroutines are supplied in a set of libraries that comes with the Portage product. Individual subroutines can be found in the same libraries as on native UNIX (for example, the math routines are in libm.lib). The standard SVR4 libraries provided are *libc.lib, libcmd.lib, libcurses.lib, libgen.lib, libgenIO.lib, libm.lib*, and *libw.lib.*

There are two cases where Portage does not implement UNIX features so that they are accessible by non-Portage programs — symbolic links and case-sensitive file names. Portage has implemented both of these features in a file system-independent manner, but non-Portage Windows NT programs cannot follow symbolic links, nor create two filenames that differ only in case (e.g., makefile and Makefile). In both instances, Portage provides environment variables (SYMLINKS and CASE-NAMES) that allow each user to decide whether to enable or disable the feature.

Sometimes, Windows NT has greater functionality than UNIX. In those cases, Portage has enhanced the UNIX subroutines and utilities to take advantage of the extended capabilities, while

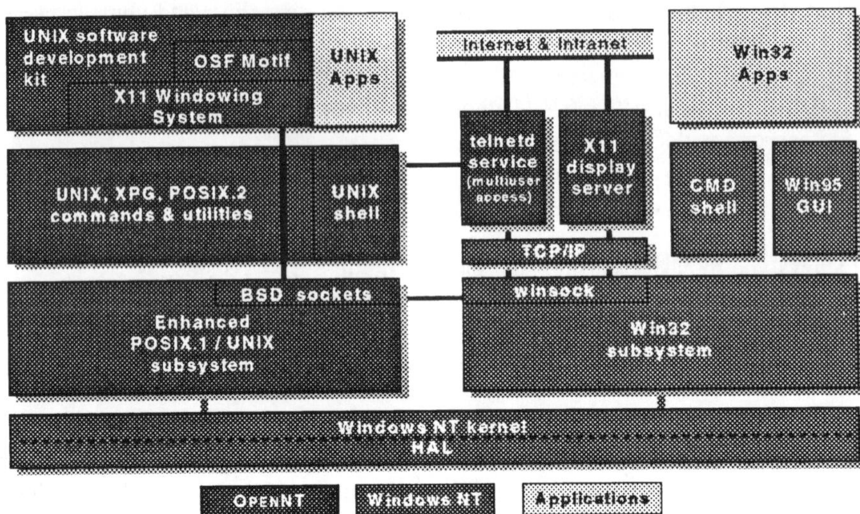

FIGURE 3.2 OpenNT architecture schematic.

maintaining complete backwards compatibility with UNIX SVR4. For example, Portage has extended the *chmod* and *ls* utilities and the related subroutine calls to allow users to view and modify a larger subset of the extended NT file permissions than the standard UNIX read, write, and execute.

There are some differences between Portage and native UNIX SVR4, and this list is included with the Portage documentation. The only significant UNIX SVR4 programs not provided in this release of Portage are the *uucp* family of utilities.

There are a handful of cases where Portage includes new subroutines to implement specific tasks that either must be done differently on Portage than on UNIX, or can be done more efficiently by a different method on Portage than on UNIX.

OpenNT

The following is a brief summary of OpenNT from Softway Systems Web pages. Additional information on OpenNT is available online at http://www.softway.com/OpenNT/.

A schematic of OpenNT Architecture is illustrated in Figure 3.2.

OpenNT is based on a virtual subsystem design allowing for the hosting of a true conforming UNIX environment. By using the POSIX.1 subsystem built into Windows NT, users are given a secure environment that supports many of the features required by POSIX and UNIX systems. Some of the supported features include:

- Proper case-sensitive file names within the NT file system (e.g., files Report and report can coexist in the same directory).
- File links are supported (i.e., one file can have multiple names).
- Background processing and job control via the OpenNT shell.
- Full control over file user ownership, group ownership, and access modes.
- Ability to run both UNIX/POSIX and Windows applications from the OpenNT shell.

Softway Systems is committed to providing complete user and developer products for Microsoft Windows NT that conform to IEEE POSIX and X/Open specifications, and as a demonstration, Softway Systems products will maintain the appropriate National Institute of Standards (NIST) certifications for FIPS 151-2 (POSIX.1) and FIPS 189 (POSIX.2) and the appropriate X/Open brands in future releases.

The OpenNT Product Family

The OpenNT product family includes the following products:

- OpenNT Commands and Utilities
- OpenNT Software Development Kit
- OpenNT X11 Server
- OpenNT Telnet Server

Let us take a brief look at these products.

OpenNT Commands and Utilities

OpenNT Commands and Utilities is a set of utilities that provide functions similar to the UNIX ones, and a POSIX command shell for Windows NT. The product provides conformance to the IEEE POSIX.2 Execution Environment Utilities standard as defined in FIPS 189. (FIPS 189 is the Federal Information Processing Standard required by many federal government agencies and departments for operating system procurements.)

OpenNT also adds a new POSIX.1 subsystem (which is meant as a replacement POSIX.1 subsystem for older Windows NT systems) with increased functionality to provide seamless integration of the POSIX environment with the other components of Windows NT. Additional UNIX utilities supported include *vi, more, uuencode*, etc.

OpenNT Software Development Kit

OpenNT Software Development Kit is a development system for porting and developing POSIX and UNIX applications on Windows NT. In combination with the OpenNT Command and Utilities product mentioned above, this development environment includes the tools necessary for providing a development platform to develop and run UNIX applications. Applications built with the OpenNT environment run as native, 32-bit Windows NT applications.

You can use third-party compilers and tools (e.g., Microsoft Visual C/C++, GNU tools) within the development system. Utilities such as *lex, yacc, make*, and *rcs* are included as standard components in the product.

OpenNT X11 Server

The OpenNT X11 server for Windows NT (and Windows 95) is a PC X Display Server. X servers are covered in detail in Chapter 6. The OpenNT X11 server supports bidirectional copy and paste of text and graphics between X clients and Windows NT/Windows 95 applications. From the same desktop, users can run:

- Win16 (Windows 3.1) applications
- Win32 (Windows 95 and Windows NT) applications
- POSIX and UNIX text-based applications via the OpenNT shell
- X11/Motif applications running natively on Windows NT via the OpenNT X11
- Windowing System and OpenNT Motif (By the time you read this book this function should be available, but check with the vendor on the timing for the availability of Motif support.)
- Remote network-based X Windows and Motif applications

UNIX window managers supported by the OpenNT server include Motif, OpenLook, VUE, and CDE. The OpenNT server also supports XDMCP security through X authority. A full set of X11R6 fonts is provided with automatic font substitution and a choice of full-screen, single-window mode or multiple-window mode.

OpenNT Telnet Server

The OpenNT Telnet Server is a telnet daemon service for Windows NT. Telnet users get full access to the Windows NT Common Command Shell or the OpenNT POSIX/UNIX shell. Multiple users can access one Windows NT server and simultaneously run a variety of Win32, DOS, OS/2, and POSIX character-based applications.

OpenNT telnet server provides a set of configuration options to the Windows NT system administrator, allowing user access and permissions to be defined for individual users and groups of users. OpenNT Telnet Server allows the Windows NT administrator to specify that a user or group of users be dropped directly into a custom application rather than a command line. Windows NT's security features are maintained.

The telnet daemon allows access by telnet clients on any system connected to a TCP/IP network. Clients can be UNIX systems, Macintosh, Windows, DOS, or network terminals connected to the local area network. Dumb terminals connected to a terminal server on the network can also log into the system. Clients can even access the shell from remote sites over the Internet.

The product allows telnet users to log on to the Windows NT server without interfering with the Windows NT console user or file server users.

OpenNT Telnet Server provides ANSI/VT100 terminal emulation to the network client that logs into the system. Certain keystroke sequences map to special PC function keys and can be passed through by terminal emulators and interpreted by applications. This feature allows users to make use of function keys, arrow keys, and ALT key combinations in PC programs while logged into the system. Full-screen applications can be run, and support is provided for character attributes, color, and line-drawing characters.

The product supports the connection of multiple dumb terminals when used with a network terminal server. With OpenNT Telnet Server, users can access the server to perform text mode command-line operations and run any character-based application.

OpenNT Telnet Server can drop a user directly into a custom application or shell after logging in. This allows users on dedicated terminals to see only their application, shielding them from the computer system or a shell.

When the user exits the program, the Telnet client is disconnected from OpenNT Telnet Server. A feature of OpenNT Telnet Server is its integration with the rest of the OpenNT environment. Users can select the OpenNT UNIX shell as their default shell and log in directly to an environment that is consistent with today's UNIX operating systems.

OpenNT Telnet Server uses the security features of Windows NT. OpenNT Telnet Server abides by access restrictions imposed by the server. Each user runs in his own appropriate security context, with all his own permissions in place, just as if he had logged in from the console. OpenNT Telnet Server preserves all of the C2 security features that come with Windows NT.

OpenNT Telnet Server features a graphical user interface application for administration and setup. The system administrator can control:

- User access and permissions
- Maintaining a log of all events and user activities
- Starting, stopping, and pausing the telnet service
- Terminal emulation features and color control
- User shell options and default directory
- Time slice and priority administration
- Program licensing and registration

Now, let us take a look at another porting product, eXcursion from Digital.

eXcursion

The following is a brief summary of eXcursion from DEC Web pages. Additional information on eXcursion is available online at http://www.digital.com.

The eXcursion Software Developer's Kit from Digital contains the libraries and headers you need to port Motif and X applications from the UNIX operating system to Windows NT. The eXcursion SDK includes X Window System and Motif libraries for Windows NT, Motif Toolkit and widgets, the Motif User Interface Language (UIL) compiler and Motif Window Manager (MWM), DECwindows Motif extensions, example X and Motif applications for Windows NT, a platform-independent *imake* utility, and the eXcursion X server.

The eXcursion Software Developer's Kit supports Microsoft's Visual C++ and can operate with Microsoft's TCP/IP (included with Windows NT) and DECnet (included with PATHWORKS for Windows NT).

eXceed XDK

The following is a brief summary of eXceed from Hummingbird Communications Web pages. Additional information on eXceed XDK and other products from Hummingbird is available at http://www.hummingbird.com.

Hummingbird's X Development Kits incorporate all of the X Window System standard libraries and toolkits that are required to develop X applications on the PC, which include Xlib, Xt intrinsics, Xaw, and Xmu.

Also available are the OSF/Motif and UIL compilers, in addition to sample source and sample applications.

PC X server software provides users with a full X Window System implementation typically found on workstations. Available for the Windows, Windows 95, Windows NT (Intel and Alpha), and OS/2 platforms, the Hummingbird eXceed X Development Kits (XDKs) give today's PCs powerful workstation-like functionality by transforming them into a client-host and server, all at the same time.

Local X support permits X clients to be started and displayed locally or remotely on other X servers in the network. Local X support also permits local X clients to run on stand-alone PCs with no network support.

Hummingbird's eXceed 3D for Windows NT includes additional libraries for developing OpenGL X applications on PCs.

PORTING APPLICATIONS FROM WINDOWS TO UNIX

In the previous section, we looked at porting applications from UNIX to Windows. In this section, we look at porting in the opposite direction. We will look at applications written for the Windows environment and look at tools that let the application execute in the UNIX environment.

Windows applications can be run on UNIX in three ways. In one way (which is actually a rewrite and not a port), some vendors saw a market opportunity in providing Windows look-alike native UNIX applications for popular office products. The idea being that customers need not buy any Windows operating environments or software, but still use office applications using the familiar Windows graphical interface on the same desktop with production UNIX applications. Applications ported in this manner have generally not been very successful — for example, Quorum's ports of Microsoft Word and Excel.

A second way is to port the source manually. If you port manually, then you have to take care of the operating system differences between Windows NT and UNIX covered in Chapter 2. You should also take care of the programming language differences such as C language differences covered in Chapter 2 as well as earlier in this chapter. In addition, if you have old Windows sources written for the 16-bit world, you have to take care of the following:

- Direct hardware calls or access to memory space (that would not normally be allowed in 32-bit applications)
- Near and Far pointers
- Compiler options specific to 16 bits, such as NEAR or PASCAL

A third way would be to provide tools that assume the role of Windows in UNIX systems. These tools would provide the function calls, messages, device contexts, and controls on top of the UNIX operating system that Windows provides for application programs executing in the Windows environment. Besides providing support for the Operating System functions, the tools also provide support in the UNIX environment for Windows unique features such as OLE, MFC, etc.

Common Porting Products

Some of the tools that help in the porting from Windows to UNIX include Wind\U from Bristol Technology, MainWin Studio from MainSoft, and the Willows Toolkit from Willows Software.

Wind/U

The following is a brief summary of Wind/U from Bristol Technology Web pages. Additional information on Wind/U is available online at http://www.bristol.com.

Wind/U is an implementation of the Microsoft Windows API under UNIX. Wind/U leverages Microsoft Windows source code, licensed to Bristol Technology as part of the Microsoft WISE program. WISE is covered in Chapter 4. Wind/U supports Win32 with Microsoft Foundation Classes (MFC). Figure 3.3 shows where Wind/U fits in when you develop applications using Visual C++ and MFC in the Microsoft environment and want to run them in the UNIX environment. The Visual C++ and/or MFC application that you have runs on Windows NT and Windows 95 by using the Win32 and MFC libraries. The same applications can also run on UNIX machines such as those from SUN, HP, and DEC using Wind/U libraries.

The following advanced Windows features are supported to make Windows applications using them portable to UNIX:

- GUI features such as Multiple Document Interface (MDI), combo boxes, Common Dialogs, Common Controls, Palettes, and Graphical Device Interface (GDI), including logical coordinate mapping
- Architectural APIs for Dynamically Linked Libraries (DLLs)
- Dynamic Data Exchange Management Library (DDEML)
- Object Linking and Embedding (OLE)
- Windows Sockets
- Kernel Layer APIs for all non-GUI APIs in the Windows environment, including file i/o, memory management, memory mapped files, etc.
- Advanced printing capabilities through Bristol's Xprinter
- PostScript and PCL Language Library; together, Xprinter and the GDI layer provide transparent access to the display and PostScript and PCL printers
- Online help through Bristol's Microsoft Windows-compatible help subsystem, HyperHelp; HyperHelp allows you to use the same rich-text format (RTF) source files from your Windows version to create an equivalent help system in the UNIX environment

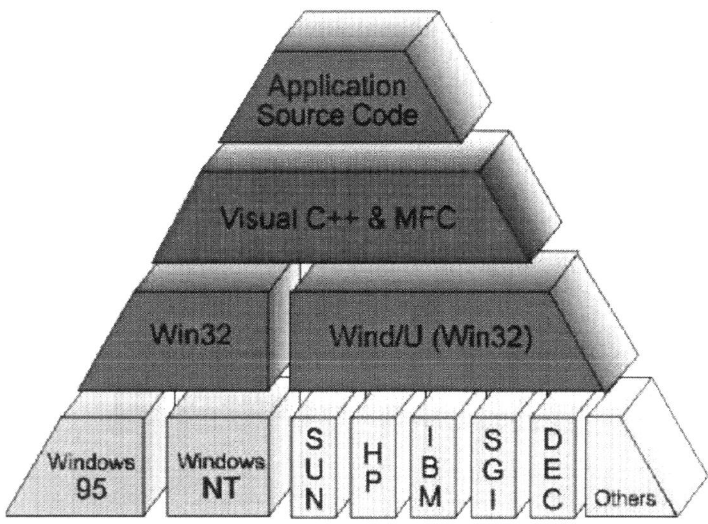

FIGURE 3.3 Using Wind/U to run Windows applications in UNIX.

All of these features are provided as libraries that your application is linked to after recompilation in the native UNIX environment. The result is a truly native application that maintains identical functionality with the Windows version.

The toolkit also includes several tools for the programmer.

- Wind/U Wizard: automatically verifies your installation, checks your environment setup, and contacts Bristol support via e-mail
- Wind/U Documentation Online: provides the complete content of Wind/U printed documentation in a cross-referenced, browsable format
- make_windumakefile: scans the original Windows source code to create an appropriate make file for the UNIX environment
- prepare_source: scans the original Windows source to automatically replace DOS format characters (end-of-line, etc.) with equivalent UNIX or OpenVMS characters
- Resource compiler: a ported version of the Microsoft resource compiler that accepts Windows resources as input
- regedit: a ported version of the Microsoft Registry Editor that enables you to change setting in your system registry
- dllink: creates a dynamic link library from a set of objects and a definition file
- windu_clientd: a color management daemon that enables sharing of Wind/U color resources across Wind/U applications
- windu_registryd: manages communication between applications and the Wind/U registry
- windu_scmd: manages interaction between OLE processes and the Wind/U registry

Wind/U is currently available for the following platforms-HP 900 Series 700 and 800, Sun SPARC (SunOS and Solaris), IBM RS/6000, Silicon Graphics, Digital UNIX, and Digital OpenVMS.

MainWin Studio

The following is a brief summary of MainWin from MainSoft Web pages. Additional information on MainWin Studio is available online from MainSoft at http://www.mainsoft.com.

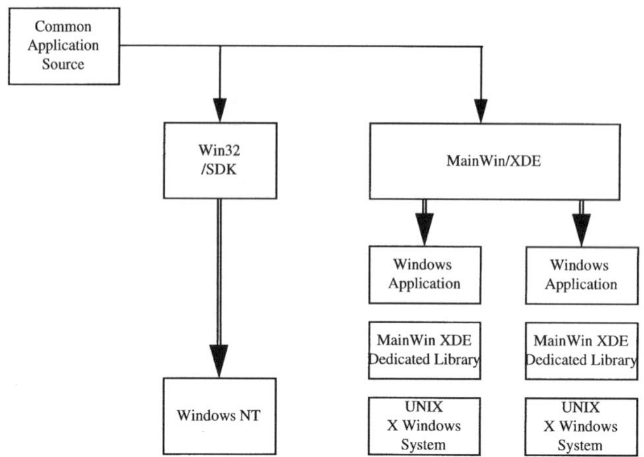

FIGURE 3.4 MainWin XDE environment.

MainWin Studio is a complete set of development components that enable a software developer to port an application written to the Microsoft Windows API onto all major UNIX platforms. Figure 3.4 shows an overview of the MainWin XDE environment.

The components of MainWin Studio are:

- MainWin XDE (eXtended Development Environment), which includes MainWin Help (the Microsoft Help engine on UNIX)
- MainWin Test (testing tool to generate test cases and port test scripts across platforms; equivalent of Microsoft Test)
- Visual SourceSafe for UNIX (source code manager, equivalent of Microsoft Visual SourceSafe for Windows)

MainWin XDE

MainWin XDE provides a complete package of development tools for cross-developing Windows applications to run on multiple UNIX platforms. It includes support for MFC Libraries, Common Controls, resource compiler, help engine, automatic makefile generator, specialized source files to include with application programs, and a set of tools that implement the cross-development environment on the target systems.

The MainWin XDE Dedicated Library is required to enable the Windows Application Programming Interface (API) on each individual UNIX workstation. MainWin supports both a Windows and Motif look, selected "on-the-fly" by the end-user.

The MainWin XDE Dedicated Library is based on Microsoft Windows source code and essentially replaces Motif. MainWin has source code license agreements with Microsoft for Windows, Windows 95, and NT, Microsoft Test, and Microsoft Visual SourceSafe. MainWin XDE Dedicated Library improves performance by directly interfacing to Xlib.

Mainsoft has ported the Microsoft Foundation Class (MFC) library to work on UNIX platforms. MFC is included as part of MainWin XDE. While MFC DLLs can be shared extension DLLs or statically linked USER DLLs, MainWin supports only the extension DLL model.

Extension DLLs are more resource efficient as they link to a single instance of the MFC library. MainWin does not support USER DLLs as many UNIX linkers do not discriminate between the symbols in multiple instances of MFC libraries. Support for MFC DLLs with "state" information (DLLs with AFX_MANAGE_STATE) is planned for a future release of MainWin XDE.

MainWin Test

MainWin Test is an automated testing tool that permits retesting of applications on multiple platforms. MainWin Test leverages the investment in test script development by letting the test scripts be used for different platforms. MainWin Test is compatible with test scripts developed using Microsoft Test on the PC.

MainWin Test has its own scripting language (TestBasic) and Bristol is a Microsoft Test source code licensee. Platforms supported by MainWin Test include DEC, HP, IBM, SCO, SGI, and Sun. An included syntax editor and debugger provides an interactive environment for test script development, and a Trap error handler allows the unattended collection of test results.

Visual SourceSafe for UNIX

Visual SourceSafe for UNIX is a project-oriented version control system that provides a graphical user interface. MainSoft is a Microsoft SourceSafe source code licensee and Visual SourceSafe for UNIX is compatible with Microsoft SourceSafe (both can share a single repository). Visual SourceSafe for UNIX features drag-and-drop file sharing, user-configurable options, visual file difference displays, and a central code repository.

Visual SourceSafe for UNIX supports file sharing, which allows source code modules to be re-used across projects. Changes to shared code checked into one project are automatically propagated. Visual SourceSafe supports UNIX platforms from DEC, HP, IBM, SCO, SGI, and Sun.

Willows Toolkit from Willows Software

Willows Toolkit lets applications to the Win APIs run on UNIX and Macintosh. Additional information on the Willows toolkit is available online at http://www.willows.com.

The 16-bit version of the Willows Toolkit was known as TWIN APIW. Willows Toolkit Version 2.0 added Win32 Support.

PORTING DATABASE APPLICATIONS

If you are porting applications that access a database, then, besides the C language calls, the POSIX or Win32 API calls, or other operating system calls, the calls to the database have to be ported as well.

In the Windows environment, the common method of accessing databases is using Open Data Base Connectivity (ODBC). ODBC is an attempt to shield an application from variations in databases. If you use direct Structured Query Language (SQL), you may need to change your SQL and recompile and relink your application, if you want to change databases. ODBC has two main components — an ODBC driver manager and ODBC drivers.

ODBC lets your application make the same calls, and handles the variations of databases through ODBC drivers, typically one driver for each database. Your application calls the ODBC driver manager, which interacts with the correct ODBC driver and returns the result to your program. ODBC drivers shield the database specifics in much the same way as device drivers (e.g., printer drivers) shield the specifics of the device from the application.

Support for porting database calls depends on the porting vendor. For example, Wind/U provides a stubbed ODBC library that compiles and links successfully but returns failure codes at runtime. Bristol Technology is working with third-party vendors to provide the actual ODBC driver manager and database drivers in future versions of Wind/U.

Third-party vendors that provide ODBC on UNIX include:

- Visigenic Software, Inc.
- Q+E Software/Intersolv

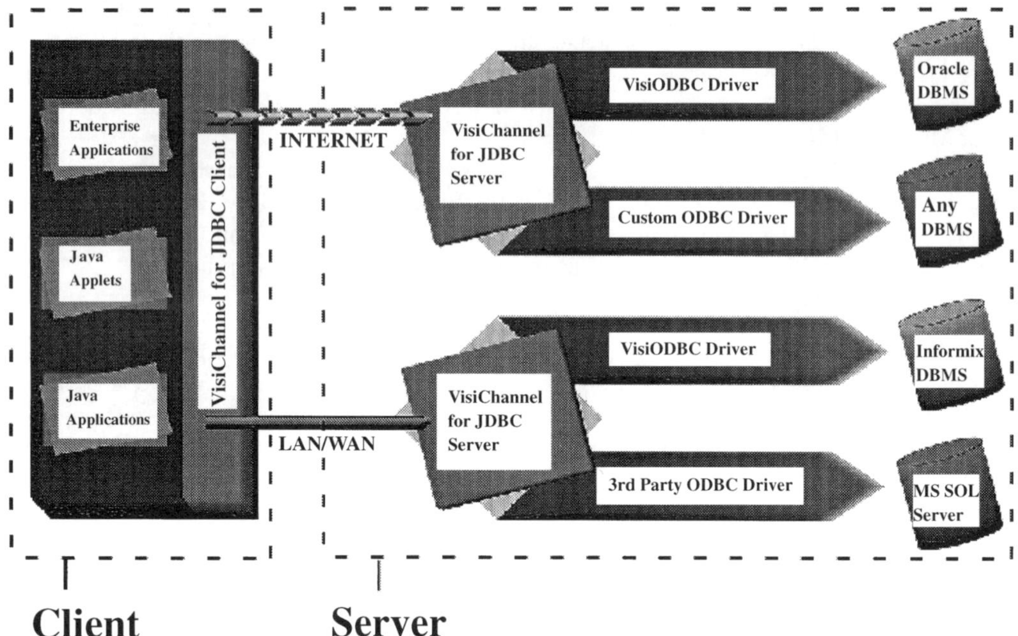

FIGURE 3.5 Visichannel architecture.

Visigenic Database Connectivity Software

The following is a brief summary of Visigenic products from Visigenic Web pages. Additional information about Visigenic is available at http://www.visigenic.com.

Database Connectivity Software from Visigenic Software includes VisiChannel, VisiODBC DriverSets, and VisiODBC SDKs.

VisiODBC Channel

VisiChannel is the overall architecture (see Figure 3.5).

VisiChannel is based on the ODBC standard. VisiChannel is database independent and supports the JDBC API for Java applets and applications.

VisiODBC DriverSets

With the VisiODBC Drivers (formerly Visigenic ODBC Drivers), you can provide cross-platform access to the most popular SQL databases including CA-Ingres, IBM DB2, Informix, Microsoft SQL Server, Oracle, Sybase DBLib, and Sybase SQL Server from any ODBC-enabled application. The VisiODBC drivers are available for Windows, Windows NT, Windows 95, ATT GIS, IBM AIX, HP-UX, SCO, Solaris, Sun OS, Macintosh and Power Macintosh, and OS/2.

VisiODBC SDKs

VisiODBC SDKs (formerly Visigenic ODBC SDKs) are SDKs for developers to develop vendor-independent database applications and ODBC-compliant drivers. Visigenic has an agreement with Microsoft that gives it the right to license and port the Microsoft ODBC Software Development Kit (SDK) to all non-Windows platforms. Visigenic has ported the Microsoft ODBC SDK to ATT GIS, IBM AIX, HP-UX, SCO, Solaris, Sun OS, Macintosh and Power Macintosh, and OS/2.

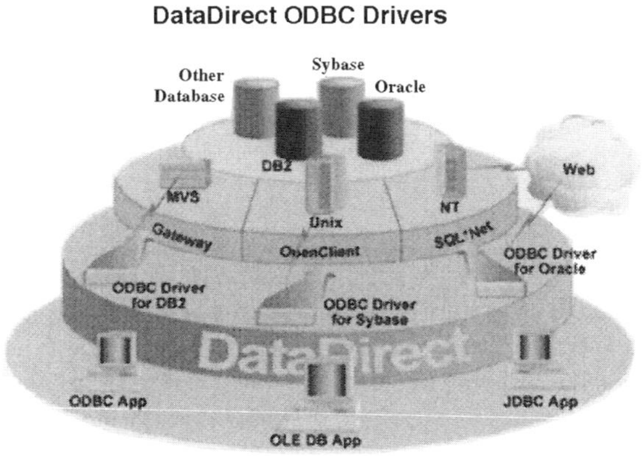

FIGURE 3.6 DataDirect data connectivity.

DataDirect

The following is a brief summary of DataDirect from Intersolv Web pages. Additional information about DataDirect is available at http://www.intersolv.com.

Intersolv's DataDirect includes both client-based and server-based ODBC data access, connecting to most current databases, on most standard server platforms. See Figure 3.6.

DataDirect's client-based connectivity implementation offers ODBC access from clients, including all Microsoft platforms, Mac, OS/2, and many flavors of UNIX through client-based drivers. DataDirect includes connectivity to 35 databases, right out of the box.

Server-based connectivity offers the same functionality of client-based ODBC, without the need for database-specific client middleware. DataDirect server-based connectivity includes direct point-to-point or multi-tier platform data access to different databases and networks, and can be accessed concurrently through DataDirect SequeLink. Server-based connectivity has a single ODBC driver on the client and a thin server listening piece.

Table 3.2 summarizes the criteria to choose between client-based and server-based connectivities.

If you are using databases from database vendors such as Oracle, including some of the advanced versions such as the Oracle parallel server, check with the vendor to see if the same version is available in the ported-to environment (such as Windows NT).

By the time you read this book, Oracle will have announced a parallel version of its database, Oracle Parallel Server, for Microsoft's Windows NT operating system. The Windows NT version makes it possible to divide database workload across multiple servers running Windows NT.

Oracle has already been selling Parallel Server versions for Unix platforms and Digital Equipment's VMS operating system for a few years. Compared to the UNIX versions, which can run across a large number of UNIX servers, the first versions of the NT version of the parallel server will be able to use two to eight servers.

PORTING TRANSACTION PROCESSING APPLICATIONS

Most transaction processing applications are developed using programming interfaces such as X/OPEN organization's X Application to Transaction Manager Interface (XATMI) or the remote procedure call interface-X/Open's TxRPC interface.

TABLE 3.2
Comparing Client-Based and Server-Based Connectivity Options

DataDirect ODBC Drivers	DataDirect SequeLink
Access to one or two relational databases	Concurrent, heterogeneous access to multiple DBMSs
Database vendor's client software already installed on each workstation	Server-based data access for high performance, especially in WAN environments
Enables embedding drivers with application	Enables user to set a corporate standard for enterprise-wide data access
Provides SQL access to flat files (e.g., dBASE, Excel, Paradox)	Provides simplified installation, management and administration through a thin client
Provides the ability to use existing gateways for mainframe access	Supports direct non-gateway access to mainframe databases (e.g., DB2, AS/400)

Porting the transaction processing part of your application should be relatively straightforward if the following conditions are met:

- The transaction processing monitor software you use supports standards such as TxRPC and ATMI.
- Your code is fairly standards compliant.
- Your TP vendor has a version that runs in both your current environment and the environment you want to port to, and supports an (almost) identical programming interface in both.

Most of the major TP products such as Tuxedo, Top End, Encina, etc., come with versions supporting a fairly standard API for Windows and UNIX.

PORTING 3GL/4GL APPLICATIONS

So far, we have been talking about programs written in programming languages with additional database or transaction processing calls embedded in them. If you have applications developed using application development tools like PowerBuilder, then your best bet is to check if your application development tool vendor provides a version that runs in your target environment. Your application source should be portable, but check with the vendor about platform-specific differences and whether they provide support in porting your application's source to the target environment.

PowerBuilder 5.0, for example, has a UNIX and a Mac version. If you are using Tivoli for Application Management, then Tivoli has a UNIX version as well.

PORTING WEB APPLICATIONS

Web applications are similar to other applications with some differences. The languages used to develop Web applications include Hyper Text Markup Language (HTML), PERL, and Java. HTML standards exist, although they are being updated with a frequency quite uncommon for standards.

You should not have a major problem porting HTML source between UNIX and Windows NT environments. Java, by design, is intended to be platform independent but there are differences in Java implementation. Java, being relatively new, does not have a multitude of porting references in the industry. PERL has been used for a while in UNIX Web applications and porting tool manufacturers, such as N*u*TCRACKER support porting PERL applications.

PORTING DISTRIBUTED APPLICATIONS

If you are porting distributed applications, then the area you need to focus on is porting the Remote Procedure Calls (RPC) you have in your distributed applications. While DCE RPC is a very common flavor of RPC, there are some applications that use Sun Microsystems' Open Network Computing (ONC) RPC. Some UNIX systems support ONC RPC. Windows NT provides RPC support that is compatible with DCE RPC. Tools that let you port ONC RPC applications to DCE RPC include RhaPC-d from Intergraph.

RhaPC-d

The following is a brief summary of RhaPC-d from Intergraph Web pages. Additional information on RhaPC-d is available online at http://www.intergraph.com.

RhaPC-d (pronounced "rhapsody"), Intergraph's Remote Procedure Call development toolkit, lets programmers transfer applications across a client/server network without learning network protocols or sockets programming. RhaPC-d operates over both TCP and UDP transport protocols.

On Windows NT, you can link with RhaPC-d's RPC library while compiling your applications. RhaPC-d supplies the protocols needed for exchanging data using ONC RPC and for encoding data using the eXternal Data Representation (xdr) standard.

RhaPC-d provides interoperability with existing RPC-based client/server applications and facilitates their porting to the Windows NT environment. RhaPC-d's port mapper and the Windows NT Service Control Manager combine to allow Windows NT to operate as both a client and a full-function server.

RhaPC-d provides a static library that eliminates the need to deliver additional libraries or DLLs with the application program. RhaPC-d also provides an API interface to create network RPC packets in xdr format. The RhaPC-d RPC protocol compiler generates C code from an RPC protocol description file.

PORTING INTERNATIONAL APPLICATIONS

If you have applications written for international use using different code pages, Multi Byte Character Sets (MBCS) or UNICODE (see box below), Windows NT and many UNIX systems support code pages and MBCS. Windows NT also supports UNICODE, although not all UNIX systems support UNICODE.

The Win32 API and Windows NT support UNICODE. Windows NT uses UNICODE extensively in its internal operations. For example, all text strings in Graphics Device Interface (GDI) APIs are in UNICODE; New Technology File System (NTFS) uses UNICODE for file, path, and directory names, object names; and all system information files are in UNICODE.

The Windows NT subsystems take care of many of the conversions. For example, the Win32 subsystem converts ASCII characters it receives into UNICODE strings and converts them back to ASCII, if necessary, for output. Microsoft Visual C++ and the Microsoft Foundation Class (MFC) library support the most common form of MBCS — DBCS (2 bytes per character).

Digital UNIX supports XPG4-compliant internationalization and includes 22 multibyte versions, primarily for the Asian market.

PORTING OS/2 APPLICATIONS TO WINDOWS NT

If you have OS/2 applications that you want to port to Windows NT, most of the porting considerations we have discussed, such as source code issues and scripts, apply to OS/2 to Windows NT porting as well.

UNICODE
Developed by the UNICODE Consortium, a non-profit consortium sponsored by a number of computer companies, UNICODE is a fixed-width encoding scheme where each character is represented by 16 bits. The number of characters that can be represented by UNICODE is thus 2^{16}, or 65,536.

Using UNICODE, we can represent all the characters from character sets like ANSI, characters from the Cyrillic character set, and special-purpose characters such as publishing characters and mathematical symbols — in short, everything we want to represent (as of now). For a complete description of the UNICODE standard, the characters represented, etc. refer to *The UNICODE Standard: Worldwide Character Encoding*, published by Addison-Wesley Publishing Company: ISBN 0201567881.

If you are doing a manual porting, OS/2 to Windows NT porting may be a little easier than UNIX to Windows NT porting. Earlier versions of OS/2 and Windows were developed with collaboration between IBM and Microsoft, and many concepts between OS/2 and Windows are similar. HPFS and NTFS have many similar features. In addition, unlike the UNIX world, there is only one flavor of OS/2 from one company.

You can also get third-party assistance in your OS/2 to Windows port. Tandem, for one, offers OS/2 to Windows NT porting services. Tandem uses a two-phase approach. The first phase scans OS/2 programs for code that is not compatible with Windows NT and has to be rewritten. The scanning phase gives an idea of the amount of code to be rewritten and also helps create project requirements.

The second phase ports OS/2 source code that can be ported to Windows NT. The second phase also tests and validates the system.

OTHER PORTING CONSIDERATIONS

Object models are at the root of many programming technologies. The object model specifies the rules for object interaction. Examples of object models include the Component Object Model (COM) and Distributed Component Object Model (DCOM) from Microsoft, and System Object Model (SOM) and Distributed System Object Model (DSOM) from IBM. The object models become important because of the technologies the model supports. For example, COM is the basis for Microsoft's ActiveX and OLE technologies.

Microsoft recently announced that Digital Equipment and Hewlett-Packard will support Microsoft's component object model (COM) on their operating systems in a year. HP's support will be in HP-UX, while Digital Equipment will provide COM support in Digital UNIX and OpenVMS.

Once the underlying model is supported in the operating system, you will be able to develop or buy applications using the model-based technologies on these operating systems. Porting OLE and ActiveX applications to UNIX will become easier.

REWRITING APPLICATIONS

As a manager, you may decide that rewriting an application may be better than porting it. Applications that match the following criteria qualify for rewriting:

- Your application is close to its life expectancy.
- You no longer have the source code for some or all of the applications.

- You no longer have the programmers who wrote or have knowledge about the application.
- The application is a maintenance nightmare.
- The application uses obsolete technology (language, architecture, hardware, etc.) that you want to replace.

If you do not have people with knowledge of the application and you do not have the source, then you have a significant rewriting effort. If you have the source, but do not have people knowledgeable in the application, there are some tools, such as Discover, that may help in capturing the business knowledge in your application.

DISCOVER

The following is a brief summary of DISCOVER from Software Emancipation Technology Web pages. Additional information on DISCOVER is available at http://www.setech.com.

DISCOVER scans all C and C++ code and identifies every inter- and intradependency in your software, and then builds a complete Information Model of your entire software system. The Information Model is a highly associative repository that keeps track of every dependency, regardless of the size of your application, allowing all changes to the software to be immediately reflected.

The knowledge stored in the Information Model is leveraged by application sets designed for specific development tasks, providing overall improvements in software process and quality.

There are five major applications sets that make use of the DISCOVER Information Model. Each of these tool sets is a value-added application. The sets include:

- DEVELOP/SET, consisting of PROGRAM/sw, DESIGN/sw, DEBUG/sw, and DEBUG+/sw
- REENGINEER/SET, consisting of PACKAGE/sw, PARTITION/sw, EXTRACT/sw, and SIMPLIFY.H/sw
- CM/SET, consisting of CM/sw.ATRIA, CM/sw.CONTINUUS, CM/sw.CVS, CM/sw.RCS, and CM/sw.SCCS
- ADMIN/SET, consisting of ADMIN/sw
- DOC/SET, consisting of DOC/sw.FRAME and REPORT/sw

PROGRAM/sw provides software comprehension through its browsing, navigation, query, editing, and graphical views. In addition, PROGRAM/sw supplies automated risk assessment and management capabilities through Impact Analysis, which reports on the system-wide impact of any proposed change before the change is submitted. Impact Analysis gives organizations the information necessary for making accurate development decisions, improving software quality during development, not after a release.

Change Propagation, another PROGRAM/sw capability, automatically checks out all needed files from the existing configuration management system and implements the approved change. This unique capability automates a usually tedious and error-prone aspect of development, freeing up time for more creative work, while also increasing the quality of the software produced.

DESIGN/sw provides the ability to create and modify graphical views — data charts, entity relation diagrams, and class inheritance diagrams. Modifying any of these diagrams results in automatic modification (or incremental generation) of the associated code to reflect those changes, speeding development and ensuring accuracy.

DEBUG/sw is an integrated debugger interface to industry-standard debuggers such as GDB, DBX, and DDE. The interface emulates the most popular debuggers and translates familiar commands and conventions to the installed debugger. DEBUG+/sw enhances the chosen debugger by the addition of mixed-mode debugging capability.

CM/SET provides seamless integration with many popular configuration management systems, including Atria's ClearCase, Continuus' Continuus/CM, CVS, RCS, and SCCS.

REENGINEER/SET, used alone or in tandem, breaks large, monolithic applications into smaller, more manageable modules or components that incorporate a subset of the functionality of the original software.

EXTRACT/sw module allows users to create and extract subsystems from existing source code, either manually or automatically. This module also provides dormant code analysis, identifying those functions, variables, structures, and classes not utilized by the software system. Automatic elimination of dead code enables organizations to easily remove software that is no longer called.

PACKAGE/sw subdivides an application into logical components based on the dynamic relationships of the functions and data in the program.

PARTITION/sw performs application restructuring. Teams can physically rearrange software into a new structure that accurately reflects the logical structure. Using this approach, teams can reorganize existing software into more manageable pieces, to delete unnecessary code, or to divide the software into two or more applications.

SIMPLIFY.H/sw uses the information contained in the Information Model to pare down header files to a necessary minimum, resulting in fewer compilations needed after a change. In addition, compilations that are done proceed more quickly since the compiler does not waste time reading and parsing nonessential information.

DOC/SET consists of *DOC/sw.FRAME* and *REPORT/sw. DOC/sw.FRAME* provides multiple methods for establishing direct links between source code and documents, while *REPORT/sw* generates system-wide "as-built" software documentation. Both applications enable organizations to keep software and documentation synchronized.

ADMIN/sw includes software administration utilities for set-up and usage of DISCOVER. These utilities include makefile readers, batch mode support, and a Project Definition File generator and debugger.

Conclusion

We have looked at porting applications from UNIX to Windows NT and vice versa. We also looked at some common porting products available to help with your porting. Porting is not limited to C or C++ programs. We looked at porting applications that access database, Web applications, transaction processing applications, etc.

In the next chapter, we will look at different ways in which you can develop applications that can execute in more than one environment.

4 Developing New Applications

INTRODUCTION

As mentioned in Chapter 1, there are several organizations that have heterogeneous computing environments and will probably continue to have them for the foreseeable future. Developing new applications in these organizations invariably raises a number of environment-related issues that need to be addressed.

If you are responsible for planning or developing new applications, then the following are a few questions that you probably are faced with:

- Should I develop a Windows application or a UNIX application?
- If I decide on one environment for the long term, is there a way to make the application work in another environment in the short term, without too much work?
- Should I use the traditional languages and APIs, or should I use new application development tools?
- Should I use object-oriented frameworks?
- How do I interface with legacy applications, and how do I access the data that resides in the corporate databases?
- What language should I use to develop my application?

This chapter is not intended to be a primer on new application development. It will look at developing new applications from a Windows, UNIX, NetWare coexistence and migration viewpoint. You can develop applications that will execute across platforms in a number of ways:

- You can develop once using a proprietary API and run your application in different environments.
- You can develop APIs for one environment (such as Win32 for Windows NT) and execute in another (such as UNIX) using porting tools. Porting applications are covered in Chapter 3.
- You can develop distributed applications in a heterogeneous environment.
- You can develop applications using 4GL products or object-oriented frameworks.
- You can even use standard 3GL languages such as C/C++ and use compile switches to isolate environment-specific code.

Keep in mind, though, that besides executing in different environments, your applications also need to be able to:

- Interface with legacy applications
- Access the data that resides in the corporate databases
- Perform transaction processing across heterogeneous systems

Let us look at techniques of developing applications that can execute across platforms.

CROSS-PLATFORM APPLICATION DEVELOPMENT

You can develop API-based applications that can run in both Windows NT and UNIX in one of three ways:

- Use proprietary APIs. You can do this in one of three ways:
  - Layered APIs that reside on top of native APIs
  - Layered APIs plus extensions
  - Emulated APIs
- Use Win32 and port to UNIX
- Use POSIX and port to Win32

The API-based approach is covered later in this chapter.

You can move your development a level higher than APIs and use 4GL tools and other application generators, and finally you can use Portable object-oriented Frameworks. 4GL tools such as PowerBuilder are well known in the industry. 4GL products and Portable object-oriented Frameworks are covered later in this chapter.

If you are not using 4GL or other development tools that come with their own language(s) and script(s), then the common development languages, for which many cross-platform toolkits and porting tools are available, are C and C++. Even when you are developing applications using C and C++, you can use some constructs to facilitate the generation of cross-platform applications. A detailed list of C and C++ differences is covered in Chapter 2, and you can include conditionally compilations to generate the executable for the platform of your choice as shown below:

```
#ifdef unix
         int dfile; /* file descriptor */
#endif
#ifdef _MSC_VER HANDLE dfile; /* file handle */
#endif
.
.
.
#ifdef unix
   if ((dfile = open(DataFile, O_RDWR | O_CREAT))== -
1)
#endif
#ifdef _MSC_VER /* using Visual C++ */
   if ((dfile = CreateFile(DataFile, GENERIC_READ |
GENERIC_WRITE, FILE_SHARE_READ, NULL, OPEN_ALWAYS,
FILE_ATTRIBUTE_NORMAL, NULL)) ==
INVALID_HANDLE_VALUE) #endif
```

If you are developing Web-based applications, you would most likely use Java, HTML, etc., which for the most part are portable across platforms. You need to interface with mainframe-based applications or access data from mainframe-based databases.

Even though COBOL is the language most commonly used in mainframe applications, you can still interface with mainframe applications using the language of your choice.

CROSS-PLATFORM DEVELOPMENT USING PROPRIETARY APIS

There are three variations of proprietary APIs: layered APIs supporting the least common subset, layered APIs plus extensions, and emulated APIs.

If you are the manager or architect trying to evaluate the pros and cons of proprietary APIs, here are a few advantages and disadvantages of using proprietary APIs.

The advantages are:

- Applications can be easily ported to different environments, in many cases transparently to the application. Thus, you can switch operating systems with very little change to the applications themselves. If you do not want to standardize on Windows or UNIX, but want the applications you develop run on either, this is one way to do it.
- It is easy to have a common source for developing applications that will eventually run on multiple hardware/software platforms. This is particularly true if your applications eventually need to run in multiple environments.

The disadvantages are:

- Proprietary APIs are tightly linked to the vendors that provide them. If all applications in an organization are written to a proprietary layer, the organization becomes dependent on that API and the API vendor.
- The number of environments the application will work on and the features the application can support depend on the number of environments and features supported by the API vendor.
- If the API vendor discontinues the API or goes out of business, then you may have a problem updating your application to take advantage of enhancements to underlying OS and maintaining your application.
- It is one more layer of software and increases the chances of introducing bugs and interface problems.
- There may be a performance penalty (compared to a native application that does not use the API but uses OS calls directly), but the penalty may vary.
- Programming support usually comes from the software vendor and others using the software through newsgroups, etc. While the vendor support depends on the vendor, support from others using the software depends on how popular the product is.
- Proprietary APIs, as shown, avoid the differences between APIs of different platforms and operating systems by providing the least common subset of the underlying native APIs. The least common subset limitation can be overcome by providing additional proprietary APIs, as discussed below.
- If you are a manager and decide to go with a proprietary API approach, you may want to check if the availability and price of the API vendor's source code (either delivered outright or at least in escrow deliverable to you in case the API vendor goes out of business). While getting the source code may not be the best solution in case the API vendor goes out of business, you at least have an option you can exercise.

LAYERED APIS SUPPORTING LEAST COMMON SUBSET

Proprietary APIs allow for the development of applications that are independent of target systems. As shown in Figure 4.1, the proprietary APIs provide a layer of abstraction and map the APIs

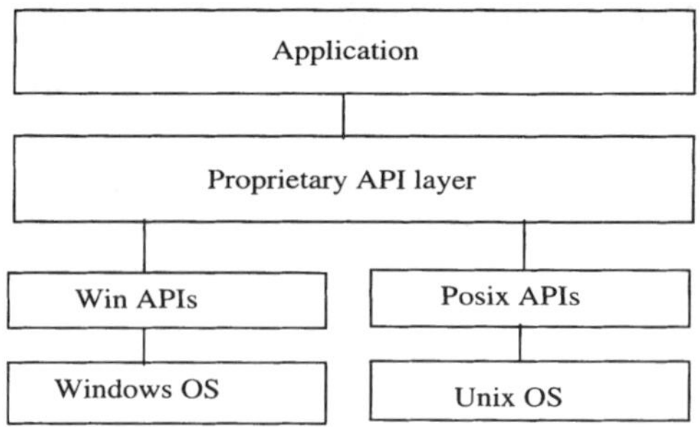

FIGURE 4.1 Layered APIs supporting the least common subset.

invoked by the applications to those provided in the native environment. Thus, your application always makes the same calls regardless of the target operating system.

"Layered APIs" are a reference to the fact that the APIs provide a cross-platform layer on top of a native OS layer. The main problem is that the proprietary APIs as shown above support only functions that are common to the underlying environments, i.e., the APIs support the least common subset of the functions in the underlying environments.

Layered APIs Plus Extensions

The least common subset problem mentioned above can be overcome by the API vendor providing its own APIs for functions not supported in the native APIs. There are two ways in which this can be done. One way is to use the native APIs wherever possible and provide extensions for unsupported functions.

Another method is to avoid using any native APIs, but instead provide a replacement API library for the native APIs. The second method is commonly called "Emulated APIs" and is covered later in this chapter. The layered APIs plus extensions approach is shown in Figure 4.2.

Although the least common subset problem is solved, the proprietary extensions introduce diversity between the proprietary implementation and the Operating System provider's native implementation. An application that uses the vendor's extension will not run natively.

Emulated APIs

Many operating environments include a set of low-level calls and a library of high-level calls that are built on top of the low-level calls. For example, Motif uses xlib calls for performing many user interface functions, such as displaying a window.

When an application needs to display a window, it can call Motif or it can call xlib directly. Now imagine a third-party library that is a replacement for Motif that implements whatever Motif

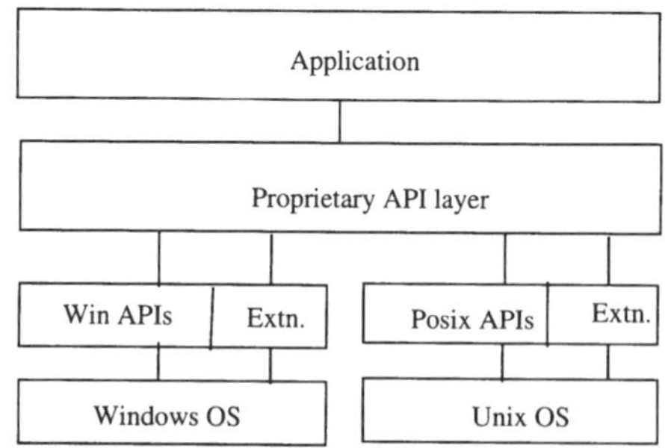

FIGURE 4.2 Layered APIs plus extensions.

supports plus other functions available in other environments such as Windows, but not in Motif (example: Notebook controls). Such a library would be an emulated API library.

There are advantages and disadvantages to the emulated API approach. The advantages are that porting applications across supported platforms tends to be relatively simple, and an emulator can opt to provide a completely consistent look and feel across all platforms since it doesn't use the native functions.

However, since emulated APIs replace all the native high-level functions, the code size tends to be much larger than the layered APIs. And you may not be able to use an enhancement to APIs made by the native OS vendor until an equivalent enhancement is made by the emulated API vendor. An example of Proprietary API would be AppWare from Novell, although Novell is de-emphasizing this product.

CROSS-PLATFORM GUI DEVELOPMENT

Many vendors provide cross-platform development tools that let you develop both GUI and non-GUI code. Regardless of which vendor you choose, it is a good idea to segment your applications into GUI and non-GUI portions. Segmenting applications provides a number of benefits:

- It is easy to extend your application to another GUI environment as well as drop support for a GUI environment, if necessary.
- Developing, testing, and debugging your applications is easier.
- Segmenting provides the option of implementing the GUI portion natively, particularly if performance is an issue.

While segmenting allows you to partition your source, keep in mind that if you opt for native implementation of GUI, you need to maintain separate source libraries for the different GUIs should you decide to go for native implementation. You need to weigh the cost of managing multiple sources for development and maintenance with the performance benefits and potential cost benefits (of not using a porting toolkit). In addition, keep in mind that you need developers familiar with the environments you decide to go native, besides developers familiar with the porting toolkit (if you use one).

DEVELOPING APPLICATIONS USING WIN32 API ON UNIX

Instead of proprietary APIs, there are tools that provide the Win32 API support on UNIX and thus enable Windows applications to run on UNIX. These tools assume the role of Windows in such systems, providing the function calls, messages, device contexts, and controls that Windows provides for application programs. Microsoft offers a licensing program called WISE to facilitate development using the Win32 API and subsequent porting to UNIX.

Examples of companies who have used WISE include MainSoft, Bristol Technology, Insignia Solutions, and Locus Computing. This approach offers cross platform development capabilities starting with the WIN32 API, instead of a proprietary API. This approach also helps in porting current Windows applications (whose source is available) to UNIX as covered in Chapter 3.

MICROSOFT WISE

The Microsoft Windows Interface Source Environment (WISE) is a licensing program from Microsoft to enable customers to integrate Windows-based solutions with UNIX and Macintosh systems. WISE solutions come in two forms: WISE SDKs and WISE emulators.

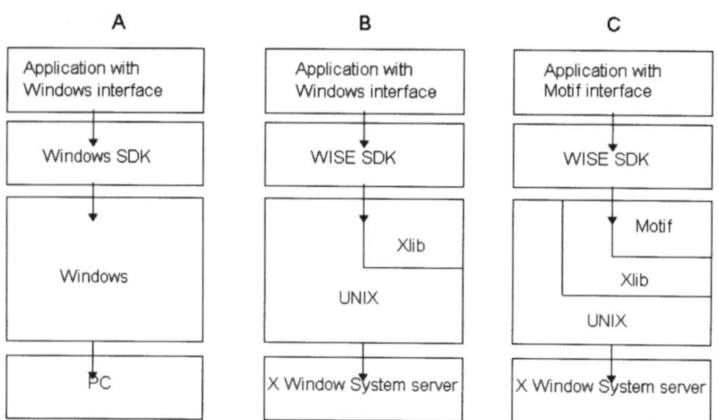

FIGURE 4.3 WISE SDK overview. (Reproduced with permission from Microsoft Corporation.)

WISE SDKs

WISE SDKs provide source code compatibility and the application source code must be recompiled for the different systems the application needs to run on. WISE SDKs are available on Macintosh and UNIX systems. A WISE SDK consists of tools to port code from a PC and libraries to compile Windows code on the Macintosh or UNIX systems.

An overview of WISE SDK is shown in Figure 4.3.

WISE SDKs typically include source code preprocessor, makefile generator, Windows libraries, resource compiler, MFC for UNIX, and online help.

- Source code preprocessor: the source code preprocessor changes PC source code to make it compatible with a UNIX system. For example, the source code preprocessor changes separators in a path name from \ to /. The preprocessor removes the carriage return character from each line to make the file compatible with a UNIX system.
- Makefile generator: to automatically generate makefiles.
- Windows libraries: these libraries provide the same services to applications that Windows provides to Windows applications. Libraries can be built at a low level (using xlib functions) or at a higher level (using Motif functions).
- Resource compiler: the resource compiler is used to compile Windows resource script files (and associated files) that specify details of resources such as menus, dialog boxes, icons, cursors, strings, and bitmaps on the UNIX system and generate a UNIX version of the resource file.
- Microsoft Foundation Classes (MFC) for UNIX: WISE SDKs include support for MFC on UNIX systems.
- Online help: programmers can port rich text format files and help instructions from a PC and use the WISE SDK help compiler to compile and generate a UNIX system help file. The help engine displays the help file to a user.

Examples of WISE SDKs include MainWin from MainSoft and Wind/U from Bristol. MainWin and Wind/U are covered in more detail in Chapter 3.

WISE Emulators

WISE emulators provide object code compatibility and enable shrink-wrapped Windows-based applications to run unmodified on UNIX and Macintosh systems. A WISE emulator intercepts Windows calls from a Windows application and translates the calls into calls that can be satisfied

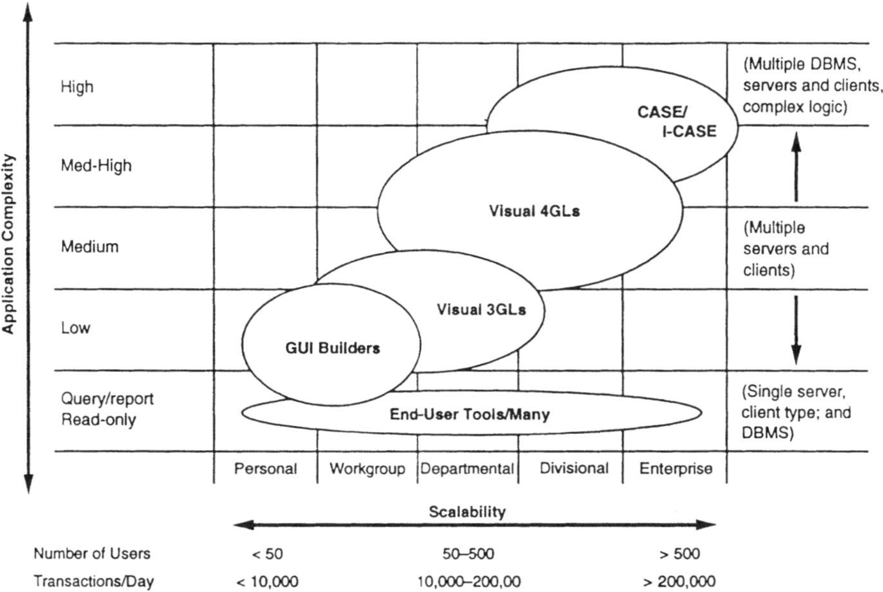

FIGURE 4.4 Categories of 4GL applications. (Reproduced with permission from Digital Equipment Corporation.)

by the host system's services. Examples of WISE emulators include SoftWindows from Insignia and Merge from Locus. SoftWindows and Merge are covered in more detail in Chapter 7.

DEVELOPING APPLICATIONS USING 4GL TOOLS

Rather than adopting an API approach of writing to Win32 or POSIX or a proprietary API, you can develop applications using 4GL tools. 4GL tools come with versions that run on Windows as well as UNIX. Thus, if you develop your applications using a 4GL tool in one environment, you should be able to reuse your 4GL source for the other environments. The advantages and disadvantages mentioned for proprietary APIs apply to 4GL tools as well. One advantage that applies to 4GL tools that does not apply to proprietary APIs is that, in general, it is faster to develop applications using 4GL tools compared to the more traditional programming language/APIs-based approach.

As shown in Figure 4.4, there are several categories of 4GL application development tools. Ranging from GUI builders to CASE and Integrated CASE (ICASE), these categories can be differentiated by their support for application complexity and the scalability of users and transactions.

Table 4.1 summarizes common products and vendors for each of the 4GL categories.

If you are using a 4 GL product for application development, check with your vendor whether the 4 GL application you have developed will execute in other environments that you may be interested in.

PORTABLE OBJECT-ORIENTED FRAMEWORKS

Portable object-oriented application frameworks provide a set of C++ classes that can be reused to build portable applications and functions for print, file, and other application services. Some application frameworks have the same least common subset problem as the proprietary APIs. To avoid this problem, some provide code that emulates the missing functions. Frameworks are

TABLE 4.1
4GL Products and Vendors

4GL Category	Products	Vendor
GUI builders	Galaxy	Visix Software
	Elements Environment	Neuron Data
Visual 3 GLs	InterBase	Borland
	Visual Basic	Microsoft
	VisualWave	ParcPlace-Digitalk Systems
Visual 4 GLs	ApplixWare	Applix
	Sapphire/Web	Bluestone
	Axiant	Cognos
	UNIFACE SIX	Compuware
	DIGITAL Application Generator	Digital Equipment Corp.
	Forte Application Environment	Forte Software
	FOCUS	Information Builders
	APTuser	International Software Group
	Magic	Magic Software
	Elements environment	Neuron Data
	Oracle Designer/Developer	Oracle
	JAM7	Prolifics
	PROGRESS	Progress Software
	Sapiens Ideo	Sapiens USA
	Unify Vision	Unify
	uniVerse	VMark Software
CASE/ICA SE	Foundation Design/I	Andersen Consulting
	Composer by IEF	Texas Instruments

attractive to customers interested in developing new applications using object-oriented techniques and interested in portability. Some object-oriented frameworks are covered below.

DSC++

The following is a brief summary of DSC++ from XVT Web pages. Additional information on DSC++ is available online at http://www.xvt.com.

XVT's Development Solution for C++ (DSC++) helps you in cross-platform development by building applications in one platform, and then porting them easily to other platforms. DSC++ uses C++, which, after compilation, results in native applications.

The core of DSC++ is an application framework that contains a full set of functions common to all GUI-based applications, including documents, windows, scrolling views, visual interface objects, graphical primitives, geometry management, data managers, and inter-object communication. And, DSC++ also includes Rogue Wave Tools.h++ data structures.

The framework's visual tool lets you design and interconnect reusable GUI components with clicks of the mouse. DSC++'s visual tool guides you through the development process, from defining architecture and laying out the interface to writing code and building your final application. You can display and edit project files containing portable GUI application interface information on any XVT-supported platform.

DSC++ generates C++ source code, application resources, and makefiles that you can use with a built-in development library to make your application natively.

Platforms supported by DSC++ include:

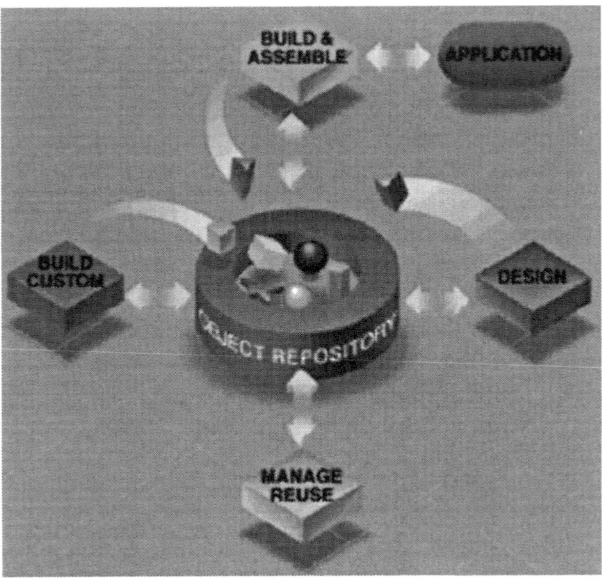

FIGURE 4.5 Allegris product series.

- Microsoft Windows, including Windows NT
- Power Macintosh and Macintosh
- OS/2
- OSF/Motif (on many systems)

Allegris

The following is a brief summary of Allegris from Intersolv Web pages. Additional information on Allegris is available online at http://www.intersolv.com. Intersolv recently announced that it plans to sell Allegris. A knowledge base on Allegris is still available at the Intersolv website.

Allegris includes the following product series:

- Allegris Workshop
- Allegris Constructor
- Allegris Object Repository
- Allegris DataDesigner

The Allegris Series can be deployed on a product-by-product basis or as a complete, integrated development environment, as shown in Figure 4.5.

Allegris Workshop

Allegris Workshop is a complete OO development environment for building reusable components and client/server applications. Allegris Workshop combines a GUI developer offering full Windows 95 controls with Allegris Foundation, a class library of more than 170 cross-platform components.

Windows 95 controls include notebooks, portable fonts and colors, enhanced status bar and flexible, dockable toolbar, multilevel undo/redo, interactive property sheets, menu editor, and online help editor.

The class library includes classes for GUI design, event processing, data management, transparent internationalization, file handling, and OLE 2 support. Allegris Workshop provides double-byte character support (DBCS) across all platforms using UNICODE as a basis. Allegris Workshop is built on a foundation of true object technology and offers the full object-orientation of the Smalltalk Model View Controller.

Allegris Workshop facilitates developing interoperable cross-platform applications using portable resource formats that support multiple languages from a single executable, without recompiling, and geometry management features. Allegris Workshop may be used in conjunction with the Intersolv DataDirect Developer's Toolkit for C++ to provide ODBC access to over 30 relational databases. DataDirect is covered in Chapter 3.

Allegris Workshop provides full ActiveX container support (linking, embedding, activation, and automation). Allegris Webshop, available as an add-on to Allegris Workshop, provides additional C++ classes for building Web-server applications, and the Portable Resource Workshop can generate HTML forms.

Allegris Workshop is currently available for Windows 95, Windows NT, Windows 3.1, OS/2, SunSoft Solaris, IBM AIX, HP-UX, and DEC UNIX.

Allegris Constructor

Allegris Constructor is a component-based development environment that enables developers to build and assemble scalable components from departmental applications to enterprise applications and Internet/intranet applications. Developers use point-and-click, drag-and-drop painters to build application components and control application behavior using scripts written in an object-oriented extension of standard Basic. For example, components are distributed across clients and servers through simple drag-and-drop.

Allegris Constructor delivers applications as compiled C++ applications. Allegris Constructor comes bundled with the command-line version of the Borland C++ compiler, linker, and debugger. Applications created using Allegris Constructor can access data from Oracle, Sybase, Informix, SQL Server, or any other ODBC-compliant data source. Mainframe databases are accessed through DataDirect SequeLink.

ActiveX insertables, controls, and servers can be imported into the Allegris Object Repository for use in developing applications with Allegris Constructor. The capability to deploy components built with Allegris as ActiveX components is planned for the future.

Allegris Constructor can be hosted on either Windows 95 or Windows NT. The Allegris Object Repository (AOR) is supported by Oracle, Sybase System 10 or 11, SQL Server, Informix, or Sybase SQL Anywhere databases. Upon installing Allegris Constructor, a stand-alone, single-user version of the Sybase SQL Anywhere repository is created.

Allegris Object Repository

The Allegris Object Repository (AOR) is a scaleable repository that is tightly integrated with the other products in the Allegris Series and serves as the backbone for the Allegris development environment. It provides a workgroup-management framework to store, manage, and reuse software components.

The AOR leverages Intersolv's DataDirect data connectivity technology and the BLOB (Binary Large Object) storage capability of major relational databases.

The Allegris Object Repository can be hosted on top of many popular databases such as FoxPro 3, Sybase SQL Anywhere, Sybase System 10 or 11, Oracle, SQL Server, Informix, and DB2/2.

Components stored in the AOR, whether built with Allegris Constructor, designed with Allegris DataDesigner, or imported as ActiveX components or DLLs, are assigned categories and given descriptions, and these categories and descriptions, along with component types, may be used as search criteria when attempting to locate components for reuse.

Allegris DataDesigner

Allegris DataDesigner is the analysis and design component of Allegris that enables the design of static object models and relational databases for distributed object applications. Relational models are used in Allegris to automate access to data. Object models in DataDesigner are built using the Unified Modeling Language (UML) notation.

DataDesigner can import existing database definitions from SQL DDL or directly via ODBC.

zApp Developer's Suite 3

The following is a brief summary of zApp from Rogue Wave Software Web pages. Additional information on zApp is available online at http://www.roguewave.com.

zApp Developer's Suite 3 includes the following components:

- zApp Application Framework
- zApp Interface Pack
- zHelp
- zApp Factory

The zApp Application Framework provides a hierarchy of more than 200 classes for standard application objects. The zApp Interface Pack adds components such as bitmap buttons and 3-D controls. The zApp Application Framework also includes a spreadsheet-like table object with a variety of cell types to display any kind of data in matrix format. zHelp is an online help system based on HTML.

zHelp includes a portable help viewer and supports popular features like hypertext links, inline images, and multiple fonts. zApp Factory is a visual development environment for zApp. zApp Factory features a WYSIWYG application generator that allows drag-and-drop construction of complete applications and generates the corresponding zApp source code. zApp factory features an integrated application development environment including the following:

- Project Manager that displays all application components in an organized, hierarchical fashion
- Modeless Object Manager that displays and edits an object's properties
- Window Designer that supports object alignment, sizing, spacing, and positioning, as well as drag-and-drop capability for adding controls, tool buttons, status items, icons, and bitmaps
- Code Generator that produces commented zApp source code, resources, make files, and project files for all supported environments (Code Generator includes incremental and selective code generation and protects user code, so custom routines are preserved on code regeneration)

The zApp factory includes integrated and stand-alone test modes to let programmers run their prototype within the zApp Factory environment, or as a discrete application without compilation. It is possible to execute specific user-written code either through a link to user source code that is triggered as a response to a particular event, or by embedding source code in blocks within the source file in constructs (called protect blocks).

zApp is source-code portable across 12 operating environments, including X/Motif, OS/2, and 16- and 32-bit Windows. zApp provides a method of porting resource files across all supported platforms. zApp supports the current version of all major compilers for each platform and integrates with third party development tools, such as editors, debuggers, and version control systems.

The zApp family of tools is built on Rogue Wave's Tools.h++. zApp's source code is included free of charge.

Systems Toolkit from ObjectSpace

Systems Toolkit is a C++ object library. The following is a brief summary of Systems Toolkit from ObjectSpace Web pages. Additional information on Systems Toolkit is available online from ObjectSpace at http://www.objectspace.com.

Systems Toolkit is not a complete application development system as are the other frameworks. It provides operating system independence for many of the difficult-to-implement subsystems. One of the things it lacks to be a complete application development system is functions for building the user interface.

CROSS-PLATFORM APPLICATION DEVELOPMENT USING JAVA

The most recent trend in business application development is to use Java and intranets. Java provides a way to implement and script components that run on Web browsers. The Web server becomes the application engine, and the browser is the portable user interface.

For Java applications, portability is determined by the browser's ability to provide a Java runtime environment consistent with the Java specification. As with other computer standards, there are differences between Java implementations. Not all browsers implement Java while conforming strictly to the specification.

Besides the Web browsers such as Netscape and Internet Explorer, many operating systems have started providing Java support as well.

DEVELOPING DISTRIBUTED APPLICATIONS IN A HETEROGENEOUS ENVIRONMENT

Some of the application development tools covered earlier in this chapter support the development of distributed applications. These tools permit developing client/server applications where clients and servers are distributed. Developing distributed applications involves the development of an application where portions of the application could reside on heterogeneous systems at different nodes in a network, but work together to fulfill the functions of the application.

To accomplish this, the applications need an environment that will provide distributed services, a mechanism to pass messages between applications, functions to accomplish distributed transaction processing, ability to access data from different databases, and a mechanism to facilitate communication between objects in a distributed environment. This section covers the distributed application environment and services. The other topics are addressed later in this chapter.

Open Software Foundation (OSF)

Information about OSF is available online from its home page at http://www.osf.org.

The Open Software Foundation (OSF) is an industry consortium of hardware and software vendors that aims to advance the cause of distributed computing. The goal of distributed computing is to make the network and other supporting software running on different hardware as transparent as possible to an application. OSF's vision for distributed computing is its Distributed Computing Environment (DCE) specification, produced in 1990. The current DCE version is DCE 1.2.2.

OSF produced an Application Environment Specification (AES). AES consolidated DCE components from different vendors into one standard specification. AES is a reference implementation. AES includes source code and a Validation Test Suite (VTS). Vendors are expected to use AES to come up with their own DCE-compliant product offering. OSF is now part of the Open Group.

DCE

There are six core services that are part of a distributed application and these services are provided by DCE cells (a cell is a unit of one or more computers).

- Remote Procedure Call (RPC) services to let an application access services provided by another computer on the network
- Distributed directory services to locate any named object on the network using a single naming model
- Threads service to be able to execute multiple threads
- Distributed time services to maintain one time across all computers on the network by synchronizing the system clocks of different computers
- Security services to authenticate users, authorize access to resources, and provide user and server account management on a distributed network
- Distributed File Services to access files anywhere on a network

You may not have all the above services when you develop distributed applications. The most important service from the above is the RPC service.

DCE, UNIX, and Windows NT

DCE services have been available on many UNIX environments for a while. If you are interested in porting a UNIX DCE application to run on Windows NT, please refer to Chapter 3.

If you want to develop distributed applications and Windows NT is part of your environment, you should note that Windows NT, natively, includes only full RPC support. Microsoft is working on providing directory services. At this time, you need third-party software to provide the other services.

For example, Digital has a product known as Digital DCE Services for Windows NT that provides RPC services, Cell Directory Services, DCE Threads services, Distributed Time Services, DCE Security Services; and Gradient Technologies has DCE products that provides the core DCE services as well as distributed file services.

Digital DCE Services for Windows NT

The following is a brief summary of DCE Services for Windows NT from DEC Web pages. Additional information on Digital DCE Services for Windows NT is available online at http://www.digital.com.

The Digital DCE for Windows NT is a product family that is an implementation of OSF DCE Release 1.0.3 adapted and enhanced for Windows NT with some additional capabilities from the OSF DCE R1.1 and R1.2 releases.

The Digital DCE for Windows NT product family consists of four separate products, each one of which is supported on both the Intel and Alpha platforms. The products are summarized below.

- Digital DCE Runtime Services for Windows NT
- Digital DCE Application Developer's Kit
- Digital DCE Cell Directory Server for Windows NT
- Digital DCE Security Server for Windows NT

Let us briefly look at these products.

Digital DCE Runtime Services for Windows NT

Every system within a DCE cell must run the DCE Runtime Services. The Digital DCE Runtime Services is a fully integrated set of services that provides applications with the essential capabilities required to use DCE's distributed services. The Digital DCE Runtime Services for Windows NT products makes the following DCE features available to distributed applications:

- OSF DCE RPC including:
  - Transparent mapping to the Microsoft RPC API calls, so that applications that conform to the DCE RPC API can easily be ported to Windows NT
  - Translation of the Microsoft RPC status codes to the standard DCE RPC status codes
  - Use of the DCE Cell Directory Service for location-independent naming of application services
  - Use of the DCE Security Service for authentication, authorization, and secure communication
- Distributed Time Services
- DCE Security Services
- DCE Name Services
- DCE Threads

The Runtime Services kit also includes new Windows-based DCE management tools:

- DCE setup for configuring and managing the DCE services on a system.
- DCE Director for managing DCE cells. It presents an object-oriented view of the DCE environment. The top-level object is the cell. Objects in the cell that a user can manage include users, groups, hosts, CDS directories, and servers. DCE Director makes it easy to perform management tasks, such as creating, deleting, and modifying cell objects.
- In addition, the DCE Director allows you to access the standard DCE control programs (rgy_edit, cdscp, acl_edit, and dtscp), while providing new functions, such as allowing authorized users to preconfigure host machines in a cell and manage user accounts.
- Visual ACL Editor for graphically managing DCE ACLs. It is integrated with the DCE Director or can also be used as a stand-alone tool.

The Digital DCE for Windows NT product supports all the network transports that are supported in Windows NT. In addition, DECnet is supported if PATHWORKS for Windows NT is used. The Digital DCE Runtime Services for Windows NT kit must be installed first and is a prerequisite for installing and using the DCE Application Developer's Kit, the CDS Server kit, and the DCE Security Server kit.

The Digital DCE Application Developer's Kit for Windows NT

The Digital DCE Application Developer's Kit for Windows NT includes the tools and files required for the development of distributed applications. It includes:

- IDL compiler, which generates RPC interface stubs for C and C++ applications
- Standard DCE and additional Windows-based sample applications
- All public DCE application programming interfaces, including the DCE RPC API, DCE Threads API, DCE Security API, DCE name services API, and the DCE Time Services API

Digital DCE Cell Directory Server for Windows NT

Digital DCE Cell Directory Server for Windows NT provides the distributed repository supporting the DCE name services. The kit includes a Cell Directory Services (CDS) server and a Global Directory Agent (GDA) server. The CDS server provides naming services within a DCE cell.

A DCE cell must have one master CDS server and may add any number of read-only replica CDS servers to improve performance and reliability. The optional GDA server provides a means of linking multiple CDS namespaces via either X.500 or the Internet Domain Name Server (DNS BIND).

Digital DCE Security Server for Windows NT

Digital DCE Security Server for Windows NT provides the repository of security information in a cell used to protect resources from illegal access and allow secure communication within and between cells. The DCE Security Server accomplishes this through three services:

- DCE Authentication Service allows users and resources to prove their identity to each other. The DCE Authentication Service is based on Kerberos, which requires that all users and resources possess a secret key.
- DCE Authorization Service verifies operations that users may perform on resources. A DCE Registry Service contains a list of valid users. An Access Control List (ACL) associated with each resource identifies users allowed to access the resource and the types of operations they may perform.
- DCE Data Integrity Service protects network data from tampering. Cryptographic checksums automatically generated by RPC enable DCE to determine whether data has been corrupted in transmission.

There must be one master security server in every DCE cell. Additional read-only security servers, called replicas, can be installed in a cell to improve performance and reliability.

The core DCE functionality provided in the Digital DCE for Windows NT product family can be summarized as:

- DCE Remote Procedure Call (RPC): provides the OSF DCE RPC API used to create and run client/server applications. It allows direct calls to application procedures running on remote systems as if they were local procedure calls. Authenticated (secure) RPC calls are supported through the use of the DCE Security facility provided in the Runtime Services. On Windows NT, the DCE RPC is layered on the native Microsoft Windows NT RPC. The Microsoft RPC is fully interoperable with DCE RPC running on all other DCE platforms.
- DCE Distributed Time Service (DTS): synchronizes time on individual hosts in a distributed network environment.
- DCE Security Service Client: provides access to DCE security services. It enables secure communications and access via authorization and authentication services. This access can be used by either the client or the server side of a DCE application.
- DCE Cell Directory Service (CDS) Client: provides access to CDS name services allowing location-independent naming of resources. This access can be used by either the client or the server side of the user's application.
- The Interface Definition Language (IDL) Compiler: IDL is the language used to define remote procedure calls.
- DCE Threads Service: provides user-context multiprocessing functionality. This provides a simple programming model for building applications that perform many operations

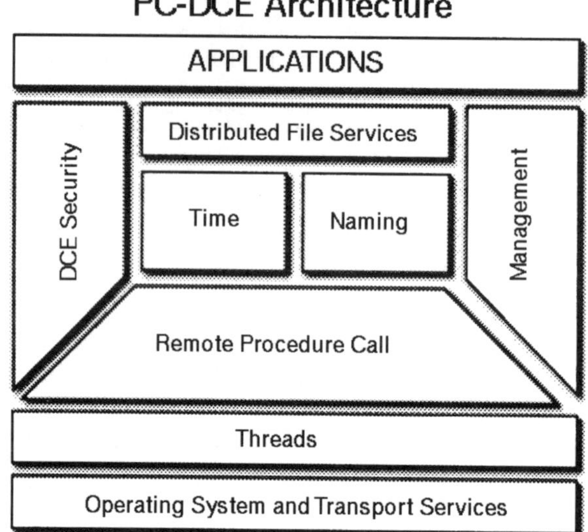

FIGURE 4.6 PC-DCE architecture.

simultaneously. The DCE threads service has been integrated with the Windows NT kernel threads facility.

PC-DCE and DFS for Windows NT

The following is a brief summary of PC-DCE and DFS from Gradient Technologies Web pages. Additional information on PC-DCE and DFS for Windows NT is available online at http://www.gradient.com.

Gradient Technologies produces DCE products for all Windows Operating Systems, many UNIX Operating Systems, Mac, etc. PC-DCE provides the core DCE services such as RPC, Security, etc., and DFS for Windows NT provides distributed file services. The PC-DCE architecture including DFS is shown in Figure 4.6

PC-DCE for Windows NT and Windows 95 product family components are:

- PC-DCE Runtime for Windows NT and Windows 95
- PC-DCE Application Developers Kit (ADK) for Windows 95 and Windows NT
- PC-DCE Cell Directory Server (CDS) for Windows NT
- PC-DCE Security Server for Windows NT
- Regii Remote Configuration Tool for Windows 95 and Windows NT

MIDDLEWARE PRODUCTS FOR DISTRIBUTED APPLICATIONS

Middleware consists of both application programming interfaces (APIs) and protocols that support the mapping of applications to the resources they use in a distributed environment. Also, because middleware works across heterogeneous environments, it enables the integration of applications across those environments. See Figure 4.7.

Message-Oriented Middleware

Message-oriented middleware (MOM) provides reliable communications between the components of a distributed application. MOM allows applications to communicate asynchronously, meaning

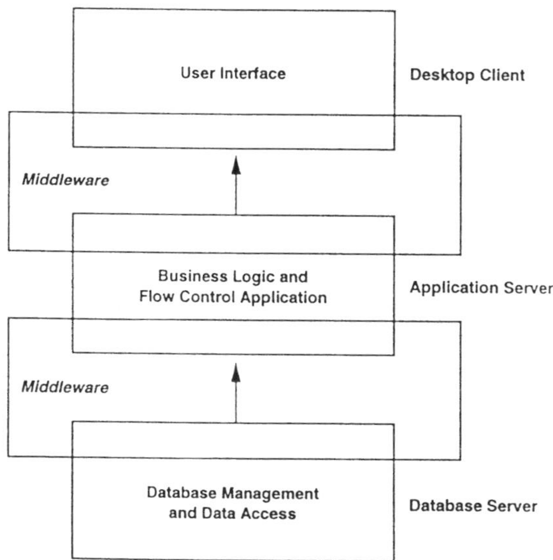

FIGURE 4.7 Middleware facilitates distributed client/server application development. (Reproduced with permission from Digital Equipment Corporation.)

that the sender and receiver do not have to be available on the network at the same time, and that the sending program does not block while waiting for a response. MOM provides guaranteed message delivery even when a process, node, or network fails.

MOM may also provide queue-based semantics to provide other application benefits, such as having multiple writers and multiple readers of a queue. These features allow an application to prioritize messages, to perform publish/subscribe operations, and to do dynamic load balancing. If a queue is backlogged with messages, you can start up additional servers to pull messages off the queue.

MOM has been used to integrate legacy applications with new applications, and is especially effective in dealing with distributed, heterogeneous environments. MOM has achieved great success in manufacturing, telecommunications, health care, and financial services environments.

DECmessageQ (DmQ) is the MOM product based on the message queuing paradigm. DmQ provides application developers with a simple, easy-to-use mechanism to integrate applications across multiple platforms — both Digital and non-Digital. It is primarily used when business solutions require asynchronous communications, high reliability and performance, quick development turnaround, and little or no training of expensive IT staff.

DECmessageQ provides a suite of distributed communication features such as publish and subscribe (message broadcasting), guaranteed delivery, priority selection, global naming, self-describing messages, and flexible configuration (failover and fail-back).

Accessing Distributed Databases

There are products that provide transparent access to distributed heterogeneous databases such as Oracle Rdb Distributed Product Suite from Oracle. The following is a brief summary of Rdb from Oracle Web pages. Additional information can be found at http://www.oracle.com.

The Rdb Distributed Product Suite is data access and integration software that provides transparent, seamless integration of heterogeneous data for applications that run on OpenVMS, UNIX, Windows, and Windows/NT desktop systems. The Rdb Distributed Product Suite tool set includes:

- Rdb Distributed Option (formerly known as DEC DB Integrator or DBI, now included with Oracle Rdb)
- The Rdb Transparent Gateways to Oracle, DB2, Sybase, RMS, CODASYL DBMS, PC Data, and Custom Drivers (all purchased separately)
- Rdb Replication Option (formerly known as DEC Data Distributor, now included with Oracle Rdb).
- The DataBase Integrator (also formerly known as DEC DB Integrator, but purchased separately by customers who do not use Oracle Rdb)

With the Rdb Distributed Option, users transparently read/write data regardless of database management system, data formats, or the data's physical location. For example, you can access legacy RMS files on OpenVMS/VAX, an enterprise Rdb7 database on an OpenVMS Alpha, an Oracle7 on UNIX, and virtually any PC data on Windows or Windows NT like a single relational database. Multiple local and remote Rdb databases appear as a single Rdb database to your application.

The Rdb Distributed Option's unique query optimizes and analyzes both network costs and the capabilities of the source databases to enhance parallel query performance.

You can use the read/write Rdb Transparent Gateways separately or with the Rdb Distributed Option to integrate non-Rdb data sources. The Rdb Transparent Gateways can access Oracle and Sybase data on any platform supported by these database managers. The Rdb Transparent Gateway to PC data can read and write to all popular ODBC data sources, including Microsoft SQL Server, Microsoft Excel, Microsoft Access, dbase, Btrieve, FoxPro, Paradox, and ASCII files. The Rdb Transparent Gateway to Custom Drivers allows fast development of a Transparent Gateway to any custom data source on OpenVMS or Digital UNIX.

You can use the Rdb Replication Option to provide scheduled and on-demand, full or partial database replication on a single system or over the network. You can use the Rdb Replication Option to transfer data between Rdb databases and, with the Rdb Distributed Option and Rdb Transparent Gateways, it can transfer distributed and heterogeneous data. For full replication or incremental transfers, the source database must be Rdb and the target database can be either Rdb, Oracle7, DB2, Sybase, or a relational PC data source. For data transfers (on-demand or scheduled), sources can be Rdb or any database accessible through the Rdb Transparent Gateways. Targets are Rdb, Oracle7, DB2, Sybase, or a relational PC data source.

Distributed Objects

You can develop distributed applications that are object oriented using distributed objects that interact with each other through an object request broker. Distributed objects is a very active topic and the technologies that are relevant here include:

- Common Object Request Broker Architecture (CORBA) from the Object Management Group (OMG)
- ActiveX and the Distributed Component Object Model from the Open Group (Microsoft has provided these technologies to the Open Group to standardize these technologies)
- Java-based applets and applications

Some of the products that are available for developing distributed object-oriented applications in a heterogeneous environment include:

- ObjectBroker from Digital Equipment
- PowerBroker product family from Expersoft
- Orbix from Iona Technologies

Let us now look at mainframe-based applications. There are still a lot of mainframe applications in use today and by some estimates over 80% of corporate data still resides on mainframe-based data storage. Let us look at options that will let you interface with mainframe-based legacy applications and access legacy data.

MAINFRAME LEGACY APPLICATION INTERFACING AND DATA ACCESS

When you are developing new applications, you may often have a situation where your application needs to interface with mainframe-based existing applications as well as retrieve data from mainframe-based databases. We will look at some of the tools for Windows, UNIX, and NetWare environments that provide these functionalities. We are talking about applications access here. If you have users on Windows or UNIX machines needing to access mainframe applications, solutions like terminal emulation are available, and these are covered later in Part II: *Coexistence with Heterogeneous Systems*.

Microsoft BackOffice

Microsoft BackOffice is a suite of products based on Windows NT server for a number of server functions, including interfacing with mainframes. The following is an extract of extensive data available at http://www.microsoft.com/backoffice. The products in the BackOffice family that pertain to mainframe interface include:

- Microsoft SNA Server: integrates existing operational systems with the Internet and intranet for host connectivity.
- Microsoft SQL Server: a database server that supports large Internet and intranet Web databases
- Microsoft Transaction Server: formerly known by its code name, "Viper," is a new product that combines the features of a TP monitor and an object request broker.

We will take a brief look at these products later in this chapter.

SNA GATEWAYS

SNA gateways are used for interfacing with mainframe applications including interactive access from a heterogeneous LAN attached workstation, program to program access, and file and data transfers. Figure 4.8 shows an SNA gateway. The gateway routes all the client traffic to the mainframes and provides protocol and data translation where necessary.

The SNA TCP/IP gateways can be implemented in one of three ways:

- Branch-based deployment: The branch-based deployment is the traditional way to deploy SNA gateways. SNA Servers are placed in the branch and communicate with the host using native SNA protocols either via dedicated SDLC lines or tunneled over DLC/802.2.. Routers may be used to direct the traffic to the central site or MPR support of NT 4.0 may be used in lieu of a router.
- Centralized deployment: Channel-attached or token-ring attached SNA Servers are placed at the data center and connect to the host using native SNA protocols. The centralized

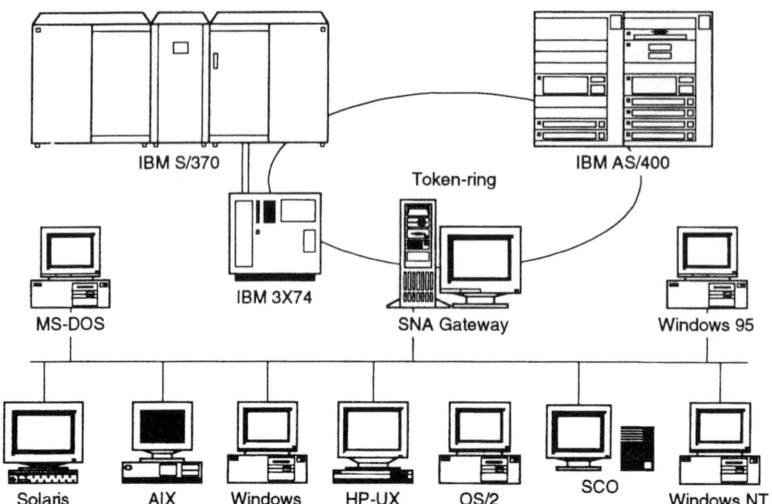

FIGURE 4.8 SNA gateway to interface with mainframes.

SNA servers provide split-stack or TN3270 service for local and remote systems via TCP/IP. Additionally, client-based LU0 or LU6.2 applications can connect anywhere on the TCP/IP WAN.

- Distributed deployment: Combines the two approaches. Branch-based SNA servers funnel TCP/IP-encapsulated traffic to centralized SNA servers. Note that it is not required for each branch to have an SNA server — they may be distributed strategically throughout the network. The most significant advantages of distributed deployment over centralized deployment are improved host response times for users in the branch and reduced traffic load on the WAN.

Distributed deployment of SNA gateways is shown in Figure 4.9.

Microsoft SNA Server

SNA gateways are available from many vendors. Microsoft's SNA server, which runs on top of Windows NT server, has many built-in functions that let it perform as an SNA gateway to allow Windows clients and UNIX clients access to mainframe applications and data.

Figure 4.10 shows an overview of the Microsoft SNA server.

Microsoft SNA server includes a number of built-in or third-party software for SNA gateway functions, as shown in Table 4.2.

The main features of the SNA server are summarized below.

- Shared Folders Gateway: This feature allows PCs with no SNA client software installed to access "shared folders" files on the AS/400. Implemented as a native Windows NT server file system, the Shared Folders Gateway (SFG) service makes AS/400 files appear to users as just another drive on the Windows NT Server.
- Single Signon: The single-signon feature of SNA Server 3.0 automatically provides SNA host account information when starting an SNA application on a client.
- TN5250 Service: This feature enables any TN5250 emulator to connect to the AS/400 via SNA server without installing TCP/IP on the AS/400.
- SNA Server Manager: SNA Server Manager is a graphical console used as the single point of control for configuring and managing all SNA servers, host connections, sessions,

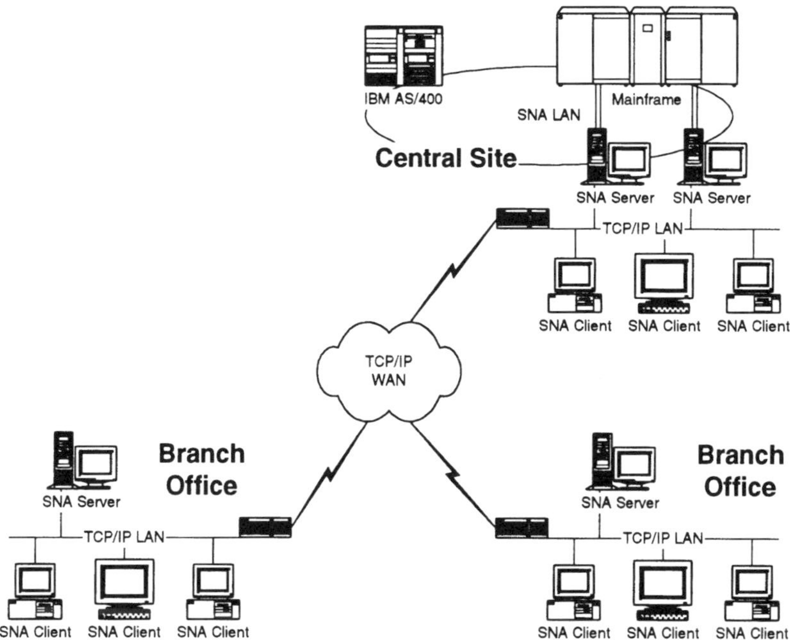

FIGURE 4.9 Distributed deployment of SNA gateways.

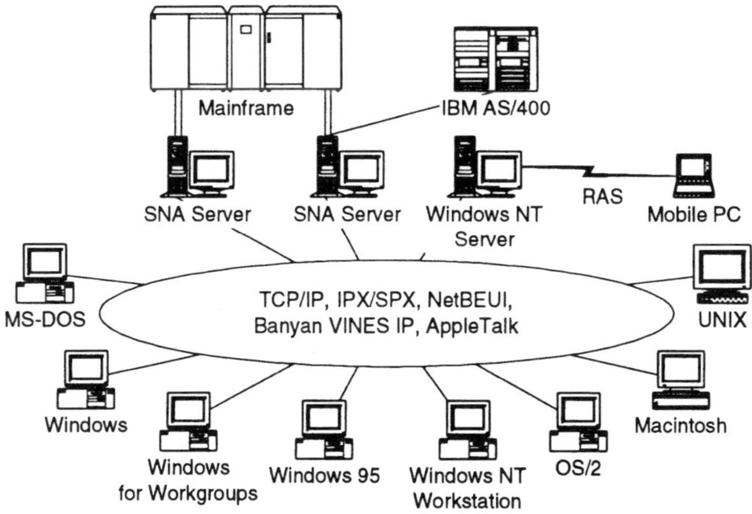

FIGURE 4.10 SNA gateway functions using Windows NT SNA server.

users, security, auditing, and other functions in a Windows NT domain. SNA Server Manager integrates the administration of SNA Server, TN3270 Service, TN5250 Service, SNA Print Service, Shared Folders Gateway, and Host Security into a single interface.

- SNA Print Service: This feature provides server-based 3270 and 5250 printer emulation, allowing mainframe and AS/400 applications to print to any LAN printer supported by Windows NT Server or NetWare. Mainframe printing supports both LU1 and LU3 data streams, including transparent print jobs sent by host-based print preprocessors. AS/400

TABLE 4.2
SNA Gateway Functions in Microsoft SNA Server

Gateway Function	SNA Server 3.0 Solution
3270 emulation	tn3270-server, tn3270E
5250 emulation	tn5250-server
Printing	SNA Print Service
File transfer (m/f)	IND$FILE (from tn3270 client FTP-to-AFTP gateway
File transfer (AS/400)	Shared Folders (i.e., FTP to a shared folder on the NT server) FTP-to-AFTP gateway
Remote administration	SNA Remote Access Server (i.e., TCP-over-SNA), w/MPR
Program-to-program	Parker Software's SNA/APPC Client for UNIX

printing supports standard SCS line printing as well as pass-thru support for host-based 3812 graphics printing emulation by using the IBM Host Print Transform function.
- SNA Client-Server Encryption: This feature provides encryption of all data between the SNA Server and the client using the RSA RC4 data encryption standard.
- Sync-point support for APPC: The SNA server includes support for the APPC Syncpoint API, which is necessary to implement robust, cross-platform distributed transaction processing using host-based databases (such as DB2) and transaction resource managers (such as CICS).

A number of third-party add-ons to the SNA server are available for 3270/5250 Emulation: Channel adapters, Channel Attached Gateways, Coax/Twinax Adapters, Database Replication/Gateways, File Transfer Products, Host Print Servers, SDLC/X.25 Adapters, Web to Host, and other products. More details, including the names of vendors, products, and product descriptions, are included on the Microsoft SNA server Web page http://www.microsoft.com/products/backoffice/sna.

SNA Client for UNIX

Information on SNA Client for UNIX is available online from Parker Software at http://www.parkersoftware.com. SNA Client for UNIX is an implementation of Microsoft's SNA APIs for the UNIX environment, by Parker Software. SNA Client supports the SNA interfaces APPC, CPI-C, LUA/LU0, and CSV for program-to-program communication to IBM mainframes and AS/400s. SNA Client utilizes an NT/SNA Server gateway to provide the underlying SNA transport mechanisms between UNIX and the IBM systems. The architecture of the SNA client is shown in Figure 4.11.

APPC support includes syncpoint support. CPI-C level 1.2 is supported, with many level 2.0 extensions. LUA/LU0 support includes both the low-level RUI and high-level SLI interfaces. CSV includes character-set conversion tables, and an industry-standard programmatic interface to IBM's NetView. The SNA Client utilizes advanced SNA Server features such as load balancing and client/server encryption. Emulation support includes TN3270E, printing, HLLAPI, scripting, and X/Motif.

Versions are available for Solaris, HP-UX, AIX, and SCO. The SNA Client requires Microsoft SNA Server as a gateway (running on NT). SNA Client makes it possible to support Windows, DOS, OS/2, and UNIX clients from the same NT server.

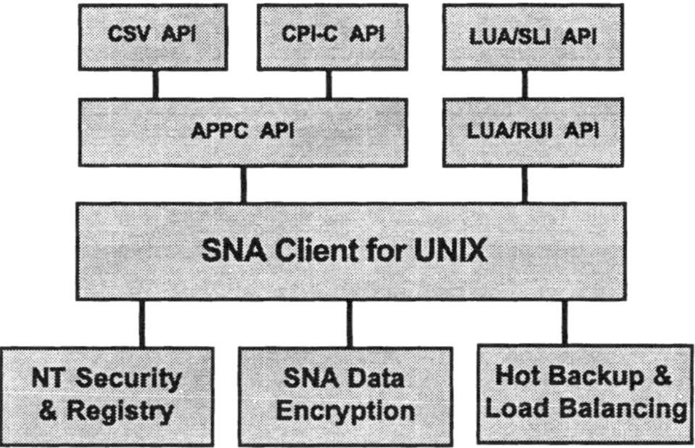

FIGURE 4.11 SNA Client for UNIX architecture. (Reproduced with permission from the White Paper, *Integrating UNIX Systems into an SNA Environment*, by Parker Software and Microsoft.)

As an alternative to using an SNA/APPC client, you can use the IBM ANYNET product. There are significant differences in approach between the two. See the white paper from Microsoft and Parker Software for more details.

Microsoft SQL Server

The Microsoft SQL Server is a database management system featuring support of standards such as ANSI SQL-92, SNMP, and ODBC.

The main features of the SQL server are summarized below.

- Distributed Transaction Coordinator to manage transactions that span two or more SQL Server systems.
- Built-in heterogeneous data replication of text and image data types to enable distribution of data to non-SQL Server systems.
- Dynamic Locking to reduce contention between users trying to insert rows on the same page simultaneously.
- SQL Server systems can send and receive information via the Internet or intranets through tight integration with Microsoft Internet Information Server and other third-party Web servers. A Web Assistant generates HTML pages from SQL Server data on a scheduled or trigger-driven basis.
- SQL Server provides scalability through support for standard symmetric multiprocessing with automatic workload balancing across multiple processors.
- Integrated with C2/E3 security in Windows NT.
- Distributed Data Warehousing.
- Data warehousing functions including OLAP query support, CUBE, ROLLUP, and a new Insert Exec function that allows SQL Server to programmatically retrieve information from multiple sources and populate SQL Server tables with the results.
- Mail Integration to send and receive electronic mail using Microsoft Exchange, or populate Exchange public folders with data from SQL Server. SQL Server can also send optional attachments automatically when the data changes or on a scheduled basis using the built-in scheduling capabilities of SQL Executive.

Microsoft Transaction Server

The Microsoft Transaction Server is a recent addition to the Microsoft BackOffice family. Some of the functions of the transaction server are:

- Developers can build Transaction Server applications as software components using tools that support ActiveX, including Microsoft Visual Basic, Visual C++, and Visual J++.
- Transaction Server includes a component packaging service to facilitate integration, installation, and deployment of many components as a single application.
- Transaction Server manages a pool of ODBC connections to a database.
- Transaction Server automatically provides transparent transaction support to applications running on the server. The application does not need to use low-level transaction control primitives to accomplish this.
- Transaction Server uses DCOM for component-to-component communications across a network. Microsoft is trying to license DCOM as an open-industry standard through the Open Group.
- Transaction Server works with many resource managers, including relational databases, file systems, and image stores, that support a transactional two-phase commit protocol. This enables businesses to leverage existing investments in UNIX and mainframe data stores.
- Win32 "fat" clients and HTML "thin" clients can access Transaction Server applications concurrently.
- Administrators can easily partition an application across multiple servers by deploying an application's components into several packages, with each package running on its own server.

Besides the BackOffice family products that are relevant to interfacing with mainframes, the BackOffice family includes many other products for Mail support (Microsoft Exchange), Internet/intranet support (Internet Information Server and Proxy Server), Systems Management support (Systems Management Server), etc. The BackOffice series runs as an integrated family on the Windows NT server platform. More details on Microsoft BackOffice is available online at http://www.microsoft.com/backoffice/.

Novell NetWare for SAA

Information about Novell NetWare for SAA is available from http://www.novell.com. The following is a brief extract.

NetWare for SAA is a result of a strategic alliance between Novell and IBM. It is a gateway for integrating NetWare and IntranetWare networks with IBM host systems (S/390s and AS/400s). It lets NetWare clients access applications and data on SNA-based IBM hosts via IPX/SPX, TCP/IP and AppleTalk. The clients could be DOS, Mac, Windows 3.1, Windows 95, Windows NT, and OS/2 clients.

NetWare for SAA includes TN3270E emulation support. It provides support for a variety of server-to-host link types and adapters, including SDLC multipoint, Frame Relay, and high-speed FDDI. It includes functions to administer desktops, gateways, and host links from NetWare, remotely or from the host. It includes support for LAN-to-Host and Host-to-LAN printing. It comes in two flavors (NetWare for SAA 2.2 and NetWare for SAA: AS/400 Edition). It uses Novell's directory services-NDS.

More than 100 third-party applications are available supporting NetWare-to-host integration with NetWare for SAA. Applications include host printing, software distribution, database access, centralized data backup, network management, and integrated security. Software development tools are also available for creating custom applications for 32-bit clients and NetWare platforms.

Some of the functions that can be performed using NetWare for SAA include:

- File Transfer: A networked client can download or upload files from and to MVS or AS/400 systems. The client can use IP on the network to communicate with the SAA

gateway. The gateway then communicates with the MVS using APPC, thereby eliminating the requirement for TCP/IP on the mainframe.
- Self Defining Dependent Logical Unit (SDDLU) support: SDDLU support allows a customer to activate a dependent LU without VTAM definitions on the host. By activating the LU only when it is needed, a big list of VTAM definitions need not be predefined and an LU can be added without requiring VTAM generations.

Besides some of the commercial products and add-ons mentioned above, there is public domain software that performs some of the functions provided by the commercial products. Public domain software is typically free and is not guaranteed. Support in many cases is by the author(s) and is on a best-effort basis. Such an approach makes it difficult for public domain software to be used for many business applications.

Heterogeneous Database Access

There are database access products that let an application access data from a database where the database could be any type (PC databases, server databases, or even mainframe-based databases) and located anywhere on the network. Using these heterogeneous database servers, an organization can decide on the optimal data distribution strategy for the enterprise data and pick the optimal combination for the location of the data that satisfies data access and integrity requirements.

Empress

Empress Heterogeneous Database Server from Empress Software is a heterogeneous database server. More details on Empress are available online at http://www.empress.com

The Empress Heterogeneous Database Server is a fully distributed database management system that lets users and applications running Empress and UNIX access data from any database. The database could be PC based, Workstation (Server) based, or even mainframe based.

EDA

EDA, which stands for Electronic Data Access, is a family of client/server products from Information Builders that provide SQL-based access to more than 60 relational and nonrelational databases that reside on 35 different hardware platforms. More details on EDA/SQL are available online at http://www.ibi.com.

The EDA product family includes:

- EDA Client (EDA/Link communications, API/SQL, ODBC driver)
- EDA Server Engines (MVS, VM, Digital, Tandem, UNIX, AS/400, OS/2, and Windows NT) include the following components:
  - EDA Hub Server
  - EDA Transaction Server (CICS, IMS/DC)
  - EDA Relational Gateway (DB/2, Oracle, Informix, Sybase, Rdb, Ingres)
  - EDA Nonrelational Gateway (IMS, VSAM, IDMS, RMS, ISAM, etc.)
  - EDA Stored Procedure Gateway
- Oracle Transparent Gateway to EDA
- EDA Web Client Services
- EDA Open Database Gateway
- EDA Enterprise Copy Manager Overview and White Paper
- EDA Data Extenders (DB2, Oracle, Informix, Lotus DataLens, DDE)
- EDA Communication Gateways (OS/2, Windows NT, Novell NetWare)
- EDA Governing Services

Omni SQL Gateway

Omni SQL Gateway from Sybase offers transparent read/write access to data across many heterogeneous data sources. Omni SQL Gateway is part of Sybase's middleware product family called EnterpriseCONNECT. Additional information on Omni SQL Gateway is available from Sybase at http://www.sybase.com.

HyperStar

The following is a brief summary of HyperStar from VMark Software. Additional information on HyperStar can be found at http://www.vmark.com.

HyperStar from VMark Software provides a set of ODBC driver products that enable transparent read/write access to corporate databases on more than 30 different platforms that include popular database systems. HyperStar works in conjunction with VMark's relational database management system called UniVerse.

The HyperStar Fast Path Server for UniVerse is a middleware product designed specifically to provide fast, reliable, seamless access to data stored in UniVerse from 16- or 32-bit Windows-based third-party tools, programming languages, or an RDBMS running on a UNIX server, using ODBC.

This allows users of Excel, Lotus 1-2-3, Microsoft Word, and many more desktop productivity tools to access UniVerse data more conveniently and transparently, as well as to integrate the data into their applications. The HyperStar Fast Path Server is fully ODBC compliant, providing maximum flexibility in enterprise connectivity tasks. It also features built-in support for many TCP/IP stacks, allowing you to use your existing networks without the need to purchase additional networking or TCP/IP products.

The combination of UniVerse and HyperStar supports the use of UniVerse tables, views, and files with D, S, and A dictionary types. This eliminates the need to make UniVerse data files appear more SQL-like in order to facilitate high-performance ODBC read and write access. The combination also takes full advantage of UniVerse multivalued data structures and extended features, such as select lists and I-types.

With HyperStar Fast Path server, UniVerse users can implement an ODBC solution today, and gradually migrate to using the full UniVerse SQL interface, with its security and declarative integrity features.

Interfacing Legacy Applications with Internet

You can access your legacy applications from the Internet or intranet using middleware such as BEA Jolt.

BEA Jolt

Information on BEA Jolt and BEA TUXEDO is available at http://www.beasys.com.

BEA Jolt, from BEA Systems, Inc., is software for enabling companies to make powerful, secure transaction systems running mission-critical or legacy applications immediately accessible from the Internet or an enterprise intranet, with no additional application programming.

Through BEA Jolt, mission-critical, legacy, or Internet applications can easily share business transactions in the Java environment, which is critical for Java to be used effectively across the enterprise.

BEA Jolt is based on the BEA TUXEDO middleware. BEA Jolt and BEA TUXEDO provide the infrastructure for ensuring that mission-critical and legacy applications can easily interoperate in an environment such as the Java Computing model.

Conclusion

In this chapter we looked at different ways you can develop applications so that the applications will execute in different environments. You can choose low-level API-based approaches or you can choose high-level 4GL or object framework-based approaches. We also covered techniques to interface with legacy applications and data from the applications you will be developing.

Part Two

Coexistence with Heterogeneous Systems

Migrating from one environment to another takes planning, resources, and, most important, time (except in very trivial cases). This implies that even if you are eventually migrating to another environment, you still have to deal with coexistence among environments in the interim. In many companies it would make good business sense not to migrate legacy systems at all. Instead, it may be better to develop new systems in the desired environment and let the legacy applications be phased out. The data created by the legacy applications are important, and you need ways to ensure that you can access that data from your new environment. Coexistence considerations are very important in this case.

Coexistence between Windows NT, UNIX, and NetWare has to deal with a number of related issues. You may have a need to access Windows applications from a UNIX machine. This topic is covered in Chapter 5. You may need to access UNIX applications from Windows desktops. This topic is covered in Chapter 6. You may prefer to have the same type of desktop ("an enterprise desktop") for all users and be able to access different environments. You may also need to emulate one environment within another. Enterprise desktops and emulation is covered in Chapter 7.

You also need to be able to access services such as file and print services in heterogeneous environments. A set of interoperability products exist to enable clients attached to one type of server (e.g., UNIX, NetWare, and Windows NT) to have transparent access to services from other servers and mainframes, as shown in Figure 5.1.

As mentioned earlier, access to the data available in another environment is very important and you need heterogeneous file access. Heterogeneous file and print access among UNIX and Windows NT environments is covered in Chapter 8. In Chapter 11, we will cover how NetWare clients could access Windows NT servers for file and print services and vice versa. Also in Chapter 11, we will cover coexistence between UNIX and NetWare.

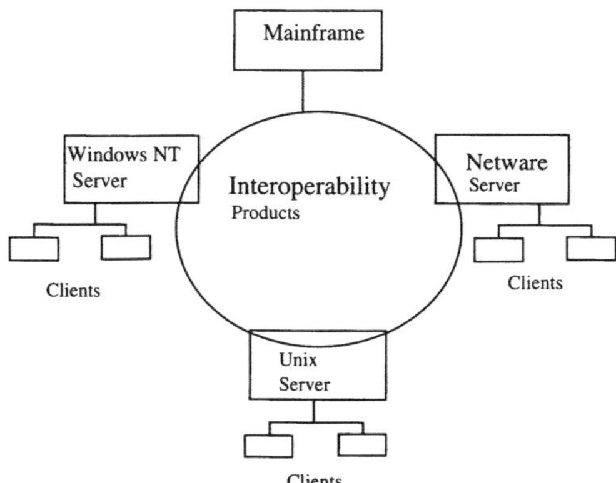

FIGURE 5.1 Heterogeneous client interconnectivity.

5 Accessing Windows Applications from an X-Station

INTRODUCTION

Part One discussed the different options for porting or migrating applications between environments. There are situations where porting would make good business sense. There are other situations where the best business option would be to leave applications running in one environment as they are, and access these applications from other environments. There are many organizations that have existing UNIX applications that work fine. They are also using Windows desktops, primarily for office needs. An important requirement here is to access the Windows office applications from the same X-Stations that are already accessing the UNIX applications. An X-Station includes X-Terminals, UNIX workstations, and any device capable of performing a similar function.

Organizations can provide access to different environments and applications by providing separate systems on users' desks or arrange a shared pool of machines. The advantages and disadvantages of these approaches are discussed in Chapter 13.

There are other options that provide access to applications executing in different environments from the same desktop. These are called coexistence options. Using coexistence options, different applications are accessed in multiple windows on the same desktop, transparently to the user.

Coexistence options may avoid the necessity to port applications, but keep in mind that there are subtle end-user differences between the user interface used in UNIX and that used in Windows. These differences could become an annoying factor for a user to deal with, particularly if the user has to switch back and forth between Windows and UNIX applications often. Another potential problem is the lack of some Windows functionality such as OLE and Clipboard when these functions are not supported by the coexistence solution provider.

COEXISTENCE OPTIONS

There are different ways in which applications in different heterogeneous environments can coexist. These include:

- In an environment where X-Stations or X-terminals are already connected to different applications, Windows applications can be added to the X-Station. Examples of this coexistence approach include WinDD from Tektronix, X Connection from ConnectSoft, and WinCenter from Network Computing Devices. Adding Windows applications to an X-Station is covered in this chapter.
- Just as Windows can be added to an existing X-Station, an X-Server can be added to a PC that may already be running Windows applications to access non-Windows applications. Examples of this coexistence approach include DESQview/X from Quarterdeck, and eXceed from Hummingbird Communications. X-Server on Windows is covered in the next chapter, Chapter 6.

- To cater to the needs of desktops capable of working in heterogeneous environments, some vendors have come up with machines with features useful for operating in heterogeneous environments. Such features include different connectivity options to connect to different networks. Examples of this coexistence approach include Personal Workstations from Digital. Multi-client desktops are covered in Chapter 7.
- There are emulation solutions that permit an executable developed in one environment to run on another through emulation. The emulation solutions interface between the application executable and the operating environment. Examples of emulation solutions include Windows Binary Application Interface (WABI), SoftWindows from Insignia, and MERGE from Locus Computing. Emulation solutions are covered in Chapter 7.
- In some instances, the applications and users access are fine, but you may want to access the data across environments. There are solutions that permit applications to have file access in heterogeneous networked environments. Examples of Networked file access solutions include BW-Connect NFS, Chameleon 32 NFS, PC-Interface, and PC-NFS from Intergraph. Networked file access is covered in Chapter 8.

WINDOWS IN AN X-STATION

An overview of how a Windows application can be added to an existing X-Station is shown in Figure 5.2.

The X-Station may already be attached to an IBM mainframe application using a 3270 emulation window, to a VAX application, and to a UNIX application as an X-Server. The Windows application is enabled as another window on the X-Station and the new window is controlled by an application server running the Windows application.

HOW DO X-STATIONS SUPPORT WINDOWS APPLICATIONS?

A simplified conceptual view of how X-Stations support Windows Applications is shown in Figure 5.3.

The Windows application performs its application processing and invokes the operating system for end-user display services. Typically, the display is physically attached to the same machine the application runs on, but that need not always be the case.

The X-Station vendors provide a server piece and a client piece that comes in between the Windows application and the display and interfaces between the two. The client passes user responses such as keystrokes and mouse clicks to the server, which passes them to the Windows application. The Windows application responds to the user input just as it normally would.

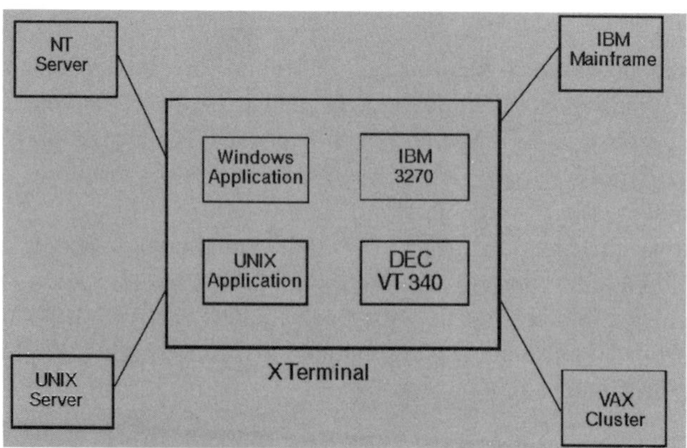

FIGURE 5.2 Windows in an X-Station.

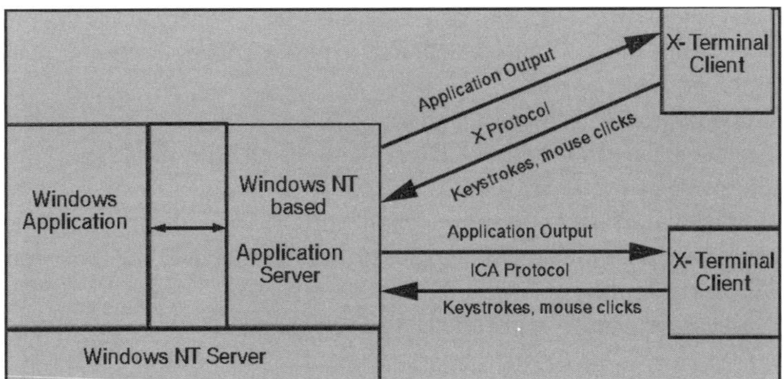

FIGURE 5.3 X-Station support for Windows applications.

The application server sends the output from the Windows application back to the client. The user sees the regular Windows application screens. The protocols used for the exchange between the application server and the client is the X-Windows protocol or the Intelligent Console Architecture (ICA) protocol. The connection between the application server and the client could be LANs (if it is local), intranets, or even the Internet.

Do not confuse the X-Station approach with keeping applications on a file server and loading them locally for execution. With X-Stations, the Windows applications run on an NT server, which has been modified to add multi-user support and not locally.

Note on protocols: The X windows protocol is the industry standard protocol for communication between a client and an X server. Use of X protocol permits the use of any device that follows the protocol. The ICA is similar to the X window protocol. ICA is a proprietary protocol developed by Citrix Systems. Citrix has licensed this protocol to some vendors such as Tektronix and Network Computing Devices.

Microsoft recently announced that it will include ICA support in future versions of Windows 95 and NT, and potentially in Internet Explorer as well. By using the ICA protocol, vendors have been able to provide more functionality and faster responses than the X window protocol. The ICA protocol transmits less data. However some graphics-rich and multimedia applications do not run well with ICA. ICA supports only 256 colors. X-Stations vendors typically offer a choice of protocols that the user can switch between.

Considerations in Using the X-Station Approach

If you are the manager trying to decide if an X-Station approach is right for you, here are some advantages and disadvantages for you to consider.

Advantages of the X-Station Approach

- By using an X-Station approach, you may be able to provide access to Windows applications such as office applications and e-mail without having to buy a PC and Windows for every user.
- It is easier to administer Windows applications usage since the actual Windows application is installed on only one machine (the application server). It is also easier to control usage and availability of the Windows applications. For example, you can easily enforce which users should get DOS sessions or Windows sessions, etc., and you can start or stop the Windows applications, if needed.
- You can improve productivity compared to solutions like having shared PCs (which could be idle for long periods of time). Sharing PCs for occasional use is discussed further in Chapter 13.

- With an X-Window machine that is PC-based, you can actually access Windows 95, Windows NT, and other 32-bit applications using a 486 or even 386 machine, which would not be possible natively.
- An X-Station approach also permits "roving" users to logon from any X-Station. This makes it easier for users to retrieve their Windows-based e-mail from anywhere in the office building(s) or even remotely.
- User customization of how a Windows application works, which is a key design feature of Windows, goes with the user, and the user interface behaves the same way, whichever station the user is logged on.
- You can access Windows applications remotely and, in some cases, even using the Internet.

Disadvantages of the X-Station Approach

- Since the application runs on only one machine, you have to ensure that the machine is capable of handling the load of a number of concurrent users. Typically, you require a certain amount of disk storage and memory on the server for each user, and you also have to use a processor or multiple processors capable of handling the load. You also have a central point of failure, although you can mitigate this by having multiple servers.
- The products that support multiple users have licensed Microsoft source with added multi-user features. This implies that there could be a delay between when Microsoft introduces new features to Windows NT and when they are available to your Windows applications, since you need your X-Station vendor to make corresponding changes to the vendor's extensions.
- You have to be careful when applying NT service packs from Microsoft. Since NT service packs are developed with the NT product (and without regard to how the NT source licensees may have changed the source), there is a chance that the service pack for NT may interfere with some vendor extension to the NT code. You have to ensure with your X-Station vendor that you can apply any service pack, other than the vendor's own service pack.
- It is possible that when an application first becomes available, it may work with Windows NT, but not the Windows application server of your X-Station vendor due to conflicts with the extension code provided by the vendor. Vendors normally fix these types of problems quickly.

Let us take a brief look at some common products that provide Windows with X-Station support.

Common X-Station Products

The information about the products was gathered from different published sources, but primarily from vendor-published information, including online Web pages. The Web addresses and other contact information is included in the description for each vendor and in the Appendix. The products are being updated quickly and you should check with the product vendor for the latest information. Most vendors also offer free evaluations, which are downloadable from their Web sites.

The book is not intended to help you select one vendor over another. You should pick migration/coexistence solutions that meet your requirements and perform an evaluation of vendor products. The inclusion of vendor information is provided to give you an idea of the capabilities of the products and to give you a quick reference to get further information and software.

WinDD Product Family

The following is a brief summary of WinDD from Tektronix Web pages. More details about the WinDD product family are available at Tektronix home page http://www.tek.com.

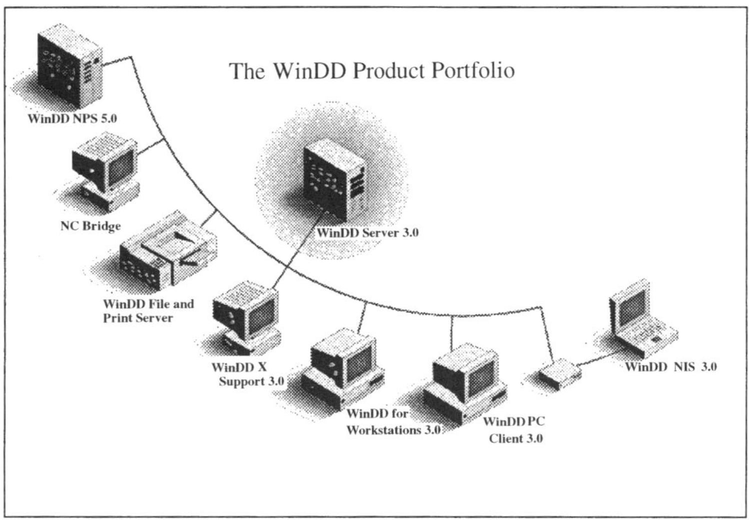

FIGURE 5.4 WinDD product family.

WinDD (Windows Distributed Desktop) is a product family from Tektronix that delivers PC applications running in native mode to multiple users in a mixed desktop computing environment.

WinDD delivers Windows 3.1, Windows 95, and Windows NT applications, including PC-based e-mail and schedulers in native mode to netstations, X-stations, UNIX workstations, and PCs over TCP/IP Ethernet or Token-Ring LANs. Under an agreement with Microsoft, Tektronix has added code to support multiple simultaneous users on Windows NT server. WinDD software can be housed on Intel Pentium or Pentium Pro-based servers with access to TCP/IP Ethernet LANs within the enterprise. The WinDD application server can be scaled using additional processors. WinDD automatically distributes the workload among all processors.

The WinDD Product family is shown in Figure 5.4.

The WinDD product family consists of:

- WinDD Server: Base server software package with the multi-user NT Server software, and simultaneous user licenses.
- WinDD File and Print Server: Optional extension to the base WinDD server, a full print server, file server, and domain controller and can add Macintosh services and remote access services.
- WinDD NFS: Allows bidirectional file sharing between PC and UNIX systems by providing NFS server and client functionality to the WinDD server. Files located on UNIX directories and mapped to Windows drive letters can be accessed, saved, and recalled transparently from the standard file access menus in PC and Windows applications. WinDD NFS is covered in more detail in Chapter 8.
- WinDD NIS: Automates and synchronizes all passwords on all devices and coordinates with NFS dynamically. It allows system administrators to establish a single point of reference for information on user accounts.
- WinDD X-Support: Enables virtually any workstation, netstation, or PC X-Server to connect to the WinDD application server using the X-protocol.
- WinDD for Workstations: Provides ICA client support for major UNIX platforms, including SunOS, Solaris, HP-UX, IBM AIX, SGI IRIX, Digital UNIX, and SCO UNIX. The benefits of ICA include low network traffic, shadowing, connect/disconnect, server broadcast/response, floppy disk support, and keyboard mapping functionality.

- WinDD Xpress for Netstations: Tektronix's first ICA client that runs on netstations.
- WinDD PC Client: Accepts the ICA datastream using a variety of network protocols, including TCP/IP, NetBIOS, and IPX. The PC Client supports Windows 3.1, Windows 95, Windows NT Server, and MS-DOS.

Accessing Windows Applications

WinDD users can access their Windows applications via ICA clients or the X-protocol. WinDD X Support provides Windows application access based on the open system X-protocol to all X11-compliant displays, regardless of platform. The ICA approach provides lower network bandwidth and greater functionality, but does not support as many environments as the X-protocol.

ICA Clients

The features available through ICA clients include:

- Floppy disk support: Netstation users and Sun, HP, IBM, and SGI workstation users can read, write, and format floppy disks with Microsoft's File Manager. The floppy drive shows up as a "networked" A: drive icon in the File Manager.
- Cut-and-paste of text and graphics: WinDD has a configurable clipboard that allows you to cut-and-paste text to and from X, PC, and legacy applications. You can specify which of several X-buffers to copy to and paste from. The WinDD clipboard also allows you to cut-and-paste X-graphics, windows, and screen captures into PC applications and Windows graphics into X/UNIX applications.
- Shadowing: Allows one ICA client user to see and interact with another user's session, whether that user is working on a Tektronix netstation, a UNIX workstation, or a PC. This feature is useful for support staff to debug user problems and for educational purposes.
- If as a WinDD user, you disconnect or accidentally reboot your netstation, or if there is a power outage at your desktop, the WinDD session is suspended on the WinDD server. The screen is restored to the state it was at disconnect time when you reconnect. You can have multiple disconnected WinStations with WinDD and you can select the one you want to get back to when you log on.
- If there are multiple WinDD servers installed, you can choose which Winserver you want to log on. You make your selection from a list of available Winservers. This list also shows the load factor indicating the load on each Winserver. You can also choose whether you want to work with 16 or 256 colors by setting a configuration parameter before you log on to a Winserver. You (or the administrator) can also custom-configure your keyboard.

Windows X-Support

As an alternative to the ICA client, WinDD X-Support provides Windows application access based on the open system X-protocol to all X11-compliant displays, regardless of platform. WinDD X-Support includes features such as support for monochrome workstations and netstations, and connect/disconnect. Connect/disconnect functionality was discussed previously in ICA clients.

For desktops that have an X11R5 or greater X-Server, WinDD can utilize the desktop device's font server by loading the actual Microsoft Windows fonts directly onto the X-desktop. WinDD Server can simultaneously support X-11-compliant displays using Windows X-Support and ICA-connected displays.

WinDD Features

WinDD supports X-, TCP/IP, ICA protocols. WinDD also provides NFS server and client support.

WinDD manages the PC Window on the display and passes only compressed, updated display information in a high-level GDI to the WinDD desktop client. The local client passes back keyboard and mouse events to the WinDD server for processing. Frequently used graphics such as buttons and menus are cached at the desktop.

Any WinDD desktop attached to the WinDD server can run WinDD's centralized administration tools. Helpdesk personnel can shadow a user's session to duplicate what is occurring at the user's station. Both the user and support staff can use the keyboard and the mouse simultaneously. The resulting display is transmitted to both desktops, even over a wide area network.

Even though the Windows application executes on the WinDD server, WinDD supports access to desktop peripherals such as floppy disks and local com ports at the client.

Planned enhancements for WinDD include better integration with UNIX environments using features such as automatic password updates between the Windows and UNIX interfaces and better support for World Wide Web-based environments.

Products that provide similar functionality include WinTerm from Wyse. Besides X-Station support, the WinTerm has a built-in browser, can run Java applets, and includes an e-mail client and audio support. WinTerm is discussed in Chapter 7.

NTRIGUE Product Family

The following is a brief summary of NTRIGUE from Insignia Solutions Web pages. More details about the NTRIGUE product family are available online from Insignia at http://www.insignia.com.

NTRIGUE is a family of products that delivers Windows 95, Windows 3.1, and Windows NT applications to enterprise desktops, including X-Stations, UNIX workstations, PCs, Macintosh, network computers, and Java desktops. Applications run natively on an Intel-based Windows NT server.

The NTRIGUE product family is shown in Figure 5.5.

The family includes the following products:

- NTRIGUE for WinFrame: Application Server is an OEM version of Citrix' Systems WinFrame server. Citrix licensed NT source code from Microsoft and added multi-user extensions.
- WinFrame Clients for PCs: Thin clients that run under Windows 95, Windows 3.1 and Windows NT, and allow connection with NTRIGUE Application server from PCs. WinFrame Clients are optimized for performance over low bandwidth connections.
- NTRIGUE Mac Client: Provides full integration between PowerMac and Windows NT. NTRIGUE Mac Client is Insignia's enhanced version of White Pine Software's eXodus X-Server software, and is best suited for higher-end Power Macs.
- NTRIGUE Net Clients (for Mac and UNIX): A thin client that allows Mac and UNIX users to access Windows applications. NTRIGUE Net Client can also be configured as a helper application to your Internet browser so you can access Windows applications via a Web page. You simply click on a link to a Web page to run the application of your choice.
- NTRIGUE Web Kit.
- NFS for NTRIGUE Server Option Pack: An option pack for NTRIGUE for X (NTRIGUE packaged for the UNIX, X-Station, and network computer environments). The option pack adds functionality to NTRIGUE for X for Remote Access Services, File and Print Services, Domain Services, and Services for Macintosh.
- NTRIGUE Client for Java (in Beta Development at the time of writing this book): A thin client that allows Java-based desktops, such as Sun's JavaStation, to run Windows-based applications on an NTRIGUE server. Users can access Windows 95, Windows 3.x, and Windows NT-based applications from these low-cost, network-based computers. NTRIGUE X-Client for Java is an applet based on the X-Windows System that is implemented in Java and optimized for Java-based desktops.

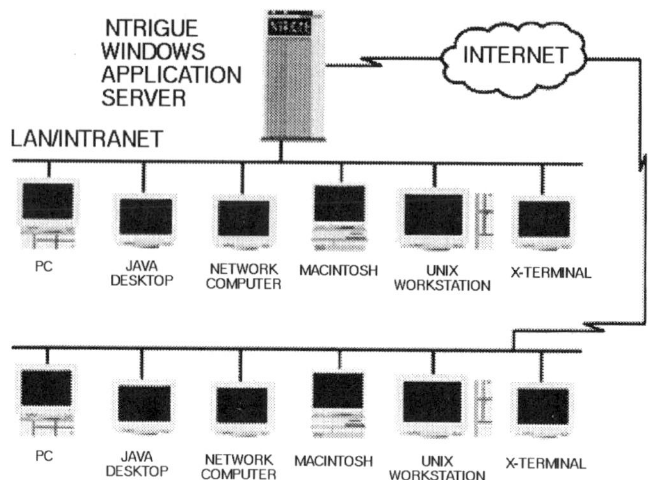

FIGURE 5.5 NTRIGUE product family.

NTRIGUE Features

NTRIGUE supports both X and ICA protocols. NTRIGUE enables users to boot network computers, including computers using the Java OS such as Java station and X-Stations directly from an NTRIGUE server without requiring a UNIX host. NTRIGUE users can access local printers. NTRIGUE lets users access storage mediums on the local machine such as floppy disk, hard disk, and CD-ROM when using the ICA protocol.

Using NTRIGUE, system administrators can control users' access to disk drives. This can help an organization prevent unauthorized copying of data and programs. NTRIGUE includes NIS import features, including directly importing user information. User information can be copied from a NetWare server as well. NetWare users can access using NT's NetWare Gateway services. A disconnect/reconnect feature helps roving users, like system administrators, quit a session on one PC and resume it on any other desktop, including remote access.

An NTRIGUE server can be integrated into an existing network. The NTRIGUE server can be a backup controller, or it can be the primary domain for NTRIGUE /NT servers.

Web Access

One interesting variation that NTRIGUE supports is Web access of Windows applications. You can configure Net Client as a helper application within a Web browser, and then establish connections to the NTRIGUE server over the corporate intranet or the Internet. The server application could be Windows office application, but it could also be a Web browser. Thus, any client can access the Internet and the World Wide Web through the Web browser running on the NTRIGUE server.

WinCenter

The following is a brief summary of WinCenter from National Computing Devices Web pages. More information about WinCenter is available online from National Computing Devices (NCD) at http://www.ncd.com.

WinCenter is a family of products from NCD designed to provide Windows applications over an intranet to heterogeneous desktops. WinCenter server software runs on Intel-compatible servers on a network. WinCenter supports any client capable of communicating with the X-Window protocol (including PCs, Macs, UNIX workstations, etc.) and the clients receive graphics and audio output of the Windows applications. WinCenter supports Windows 3.1, Windows 95, and Windows NT applications.

WinCenter Product Family

The WinCenter Product Family includes the following:

- WinCenter Pro
- WinCenter for Workgroups
- WinCenter Connect
- WinCenter Server Option Pack

Let us take a brief look at these products.

WinCenter Pro

WinCenter Pro is a Windows application server consisting of the Microsoft Windows NT server plus added Microsoft-authorized multi-user support. The added multi-user support enables one server to provide graphical login sessions to many simultaneous users. On top of Windows NT is NCD's WinCenter Graphics Accelerator (WGA), which provides open-systems graphics technology. WGA is covered later in this section.

Some of the key benefits of WinCenter Pro include:

- High-performance graphics from any enterprise desktop in your intranet. The desktop could be UNIX workstations, PCs, Macs, and network computers.
- Dialup connectivity from remote PCs using Citrix Systems' ICA3 protocol.
- Support for multimedia Windows applications, including audio.
- Desktop floppy disk drives supported (as A: drive).
- Desktop printers appear as normal Windows printers.
- Cut-and-paste of text and graphics between Windows, UNIX, and other application environments.
- Supports monochrome, grayscale, 256 color, and 16 million color desktops.
- NT window is resizable to make organizing your desktop easier.
- Native NT international keyboard support.
- Existing files can be accessed using NFS client.
- Less colormap "flashing" between Windows, UNIX, and other types of applications.
- Automatic connect from Network Computers, PCs, and Macs, and automatic startup of Windows applications from remote systems.
- Single UNIX *wincenter* command for starting a WinCenter session.
- Graphical window for finding and selecting WinCenter hosts.

WinCenter for Workgroups

WinCenter for Workgroups is a version of WinCenter Pro tailored to the needs of the smaller business or branch office.

WinCenter Connect

WinCenter Connect is a layered product that adds the WinCenter Graphics Accelerator and other NCD services to an existing multi-user NT system (such as WinFrame, NTRIGUE, or WinDD). With WinCenter Connect, you can provide the benefits of WinCenter Pro without having to reload your multi-user NT operating system or applications.

Server Option Pack

The WinCenter Server Option Pack adds the ability to use your WinCenter host as a network server for Windows PCs. With the WinCenter Server Option Pack, your WinCenter host can be a:

- PC file server, so that this WinCenter host can share its files with desktop PCs, NT workstations, NT servers, or other WinCenter hosts
- PC printer server, so that this WinCenter host can share its printers with desktop PCs, NT workstations, NT servers, or other WinCenter hosts
- NT domain management services, so that this WinCenter host can be a primary or secondary domain controller for other NT machines

WinCenter Graphics Accelerator

WinCenter uses the WinCenter Graphics Accelerator (WGA) technology. WGA is not a hardware graphics accelerator card. WGA is a set of NT device drivers that intercept an application's graphics and audio calls to Windows NT. These graphics and audio calls are redirected to the client for processing at the client using the X Window protocol. This approach is in contrast to transmitting a graphics output (or a compressed graphics output) to the client after the output has been generated at the server.

WinCenter Features

WinCenter also uses what it calls "IntelliCache" technology, which can trade CPU and memory on the NT. WinCenter batches graphics calls together so that they can be sent in a single packet. WinCenter supports different displays for client desktops, including monochrome displays, 256 color displays, and even color displays capable of handling 16 million colors.

WinCenter uses the Font Server standard in X-11 to dynamically distribute font data over networks, when necessary. In addition, font glyph images are cached in the desktop so that text can be sent as strings of characters instead of as bitmaps. To ensure compatibility with all X-11 clients, WinCenter uses an appropriate method of sending font data depending on the capabilities of the client. WinCenter uses the Network Audio System for audio support. Support for a variety of UNIX workstations is available in NCD's WinCenter Workstation+ product. For those who wish to write their own drivers, NCD provides the source code for the Network Audio System. The source is available from its ftp site, ftp.ncd.com.

WinCenter supports cut-and-paste of text and graphics among Windows, UNIX, 3270, and other terminal environments. The standard UNIX *rcp* command copies files to and from Windows NT. The standard UNIX *rsh* command starts Windows applications over the network. This means, for example, that you can click on a spreadsheet attachment in your UNIX e-mail application and have Excel start up automatically (by issuing *rcp* from within the e-mail application to start Excel on the server).

NCD's Colormap Flash Protection makes it possible to switch between Windows applications in full 256-color mode to and from UNIX or other applications that do not support 256 colors. WinCenter Pro includes the NFS client from FTP Software to access UNIX files. WinCenter provides floppy disk drive access at the client machine. The floppy drive appears as the normal "A:" drive. File Manager and other Windows applications using the drive behave as expected.

WinCenter supports printing at a printer attached to the client, shared printers attached to the NT host, and network printers attached to other computers. Administration of printer attachments is handled centrally at the server. WinCenter incorporates services for booting the clients, including Network Computers, X-Stations, printers, and even network routers directly from the NT server using the TFTP standard.

WinCenter also provides the ability for clients to login directly to the NT server without requiring any UNIX (intermediary) host.

HP 500 Windows Application Server

More details about the HP 500 Windows Application Server are available online from Insignia at http://www.hp.com.

The HP 500 Windows Application Server is an Intel processor server that resides on the UNIX network. The server runs Windows and Windows applications in native mode. The X-Window System is used to display the applications over UNIX networks. The client could be any device that supports the X-Window protocol and that includes X-Stations and typical UNIX workstations. Users can cut-and-paste between Windows applications and UNIX applications. The HP 500 includes NFS and TCP/IP support. Users can print to network printers.

HP and Insignia Solutions recently announced a strategic alliance. NTRIGUE would run on HP-UX and complement the HP 500 application server by running Windows 95 and Windows NT applications.

NTerprise

NTerprise from Exodus Technologies lets you run Windows application programs from UNIX workstations and X-Stations. More information about NTerprise is available from Exodus at http://www.exodustech.com. (There is another company with the Web address http://www.exodus.com.) Features of NTerprise include:

- Windows applications are run in an application server and are accessed by users.
- Supports cut-and-paste of data between Windows and UNIX applications.
- Supports execution of different applications in separate windows.
- Windows applications share the X-Station desktop as any other X-client.
- Use the standard version of Windows NT.
- Supports the X-protocols, including the XDM access protocol.
- Supports Intel and Alpha platforms; also includes SMP support.
- Permits X-Station users to boot their own stations from the Windows NT server, without a UNIX host.

Exodus includes a chart comparing NTRIGUE and competing products at its home page on the Web (address mentioned at the beginning of this section).

WinTED

WinTED is an X-Server from TriTeal. More information on WinTED is available online from TriTeal at http://www.triteal.com.

Some of the features of WinTED include:

- Provides auto-discovery of UNIX applications
- Offers an integrated ICA client
- File sharing is implemented on the server instead of the client; this saves the need to update clients

CONCLUSION

We looked at different ways of accessing Windows applications from an existing X-Station environment. Using X-Stations makes business sense when you have existing X-Stations that are working fine and you want to provide access to Windows Office applications at the same X-Stations.

In the next chapter, we will look at accessing UNIX applications from Windows desktops.

6 Accessing UNIX Applications from Windows Desktops

INTRODUCTION

In the last chapter we looked at X-terminals that let Windows applications be accessed from desktops that already have UNIX application access, such as X-terminals, X-stations, and UNIX workstations. Now let us look at options that let a UNIX or another (non-Windows) host application be accessed from Windows desktops.

The application could be a UNIX character-based (older) application or a more recent graphical application. There are two ways in which you can access a UNIX application from Windows desktops. These are:

- Use the Windows desktop as a remote terminal using software such as Telnet
- Use X-Server software to run X-Windows applications from Windows desktops

For the purposes of our discussion here, the UNIX applications are not migrated or ported to the Windows environment. See Chapter 3 if you are interested in accessing UNIX applications in Windows using porting.

TELNET

Telnet is commonly used in the UNIX environment for one UNIX computer to act as a terminal and get the command prompt of another UNIX computer. Windows NT includes Telnet client support, but not Telnet server support.

Tip*: Using Telnet in Windows NT, you can get the UNIX command prompt of a UNIX computer. But you cannot use the Telnet in a UNIX machine and get to the command prompt of a Windows machine. For one thing, Windows NT doesn't keep track of multiple users at different Windows NT machines and so it cannot validate you as a valid user.*

Once you have the command prompt, you can issue all the command prompt commands, including system administration commands, program development commands, etc. The following sequence shows you how to use Telnet to access a UNIX computer from a Windows NT computer. The Windows NT computer is running Windows NT 4.0. The UNIX computer is running Sun OS.

You can start a Telnet session by typing Telnet from **Start**, **MS_DOS Command Prompt** and you get the Windows NT command prompt as shown in Figure 6.1.

Keying in Telnet brings up the Telnet application dialog shown in Figure 6.2.

You connect to the remote system, by clicking on **Connect** and selecting **Remote System**. This brings up the Connect Dialog box shown in Figure 6.3.

Enter the name of the remote system in the host name. You can normally default the port name and terminal type.

If you have used Telnet to access a remote host before, then the computer names will be shown in the pull-down menu. You can click on the host name you want and avoid rekeying the host name.

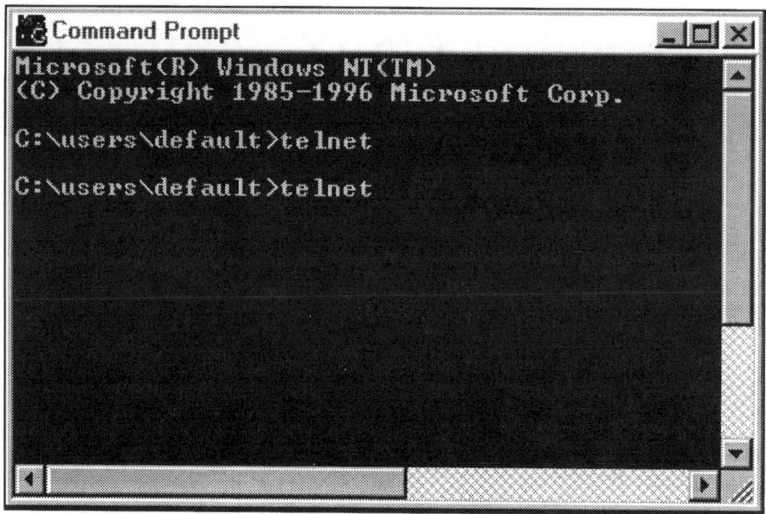

FIGURE 6.1 Starting a Telnet session using Windows NT command prompt.

Windows NT now tries to establish a Telnet session with the remote host and, if successful, will bring up the logon screen or the welcome screen of the remote computer as shown in Figure 6.4.

From now on, until you logoff, the Telnet window is a terminal connected to the remote host, and the contents and user interaction in the Telnet window are controlled by the remote host. But remember, the Telnet window is just another window. You can shift focus to another window and perform other functions while the Telnet session remains connected to the remote host. (Of course, the remote host may log you off if the Telnet session is inactive for a while; the remote host normally logs off inactive terminals.)

You logon to the remote host, which may bring up a main menu as shown in Figure 6.5.

You can now perform functions you normally would on the remote computer. Figure 6.6 shows the read mail function.

FIGURE 6.2 Telnet application dialog.

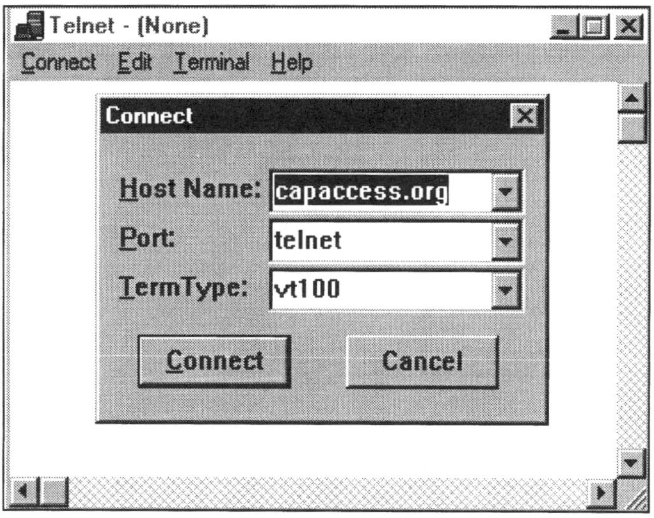

FIGURE 6.3 Connect dialog box of Telnet.

You can change your Telnet session settings such as the emulator type, fonts, terminal options, etc. by clicking from the menu. This brings up the Preferences dialog as shown in Figure 6.7. Using this dialog you can define your terminal type such as VT52 or VT100, whether you want a block or blinking cursor, etc.

X-SERVER

A UNIX graphical application can be accessed from Windows machines using X-Server software. Keep in mind that the terms client/server is used in exactly the opposite way in the X world compared to others. In the X world, the X server is the code that runs in one machine and requests services from another machine, the X Client, on which the application (that provides the services) runs.

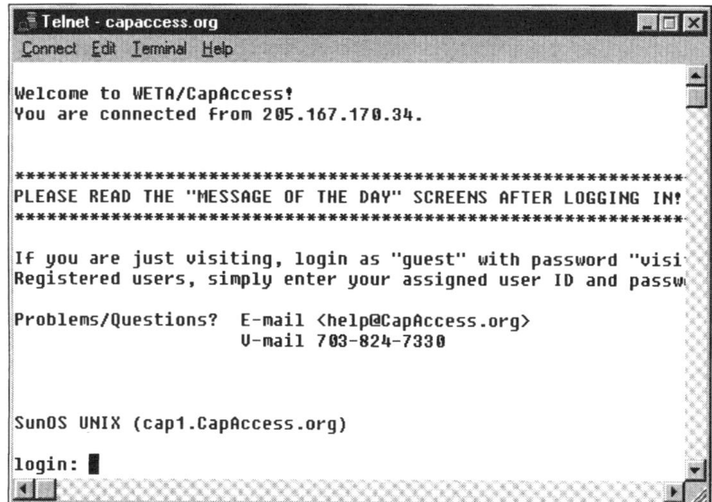

FIGURE 6.4 Logon screen of remote computer.

```
Telnet - capaccess.org
Connect Edit Terminal Help

                    <<< Main Menu >>>

 1 Administration [links directly to WETA/CapAccess Web Site]
 2 Post Office - Email, User Directories
 3 Public Forums
 4 Media Center [links directly to the WETA/CapAccess Web Site]
 5 Government Center [links directly to WETA/CapAccess Web Site]
 6 Education Center [includes link to the WETA/CapAccess Web Site]
 7 Social Services [links directly to the WETA/CapAccess Web Site]
 8 Libraries [includes link to the WETA/CapAccess Web Site]
 9 Health Center [links directly to the WETA/CapAccess Web Site]
10 Community Center [includes link to the WETA/CapAccess Web Site]
11 Sports and Recreation Center [link to WETA/CapAccess Web Site c
12 Arts and Entertainment Center [link to WETA/CapAccess Web Site
13 Business and Professional Center [WETA/CapAccess Web Site link
14 Science and Technology Center [link to WETA/CapAccess Web Site
------------------------------------------------------------------
h = Help, x = Exit CapAccess, m = Main Menu, p = Previous Menu
```

FIGURE 6.5 Main menu of the remote computer after logon.

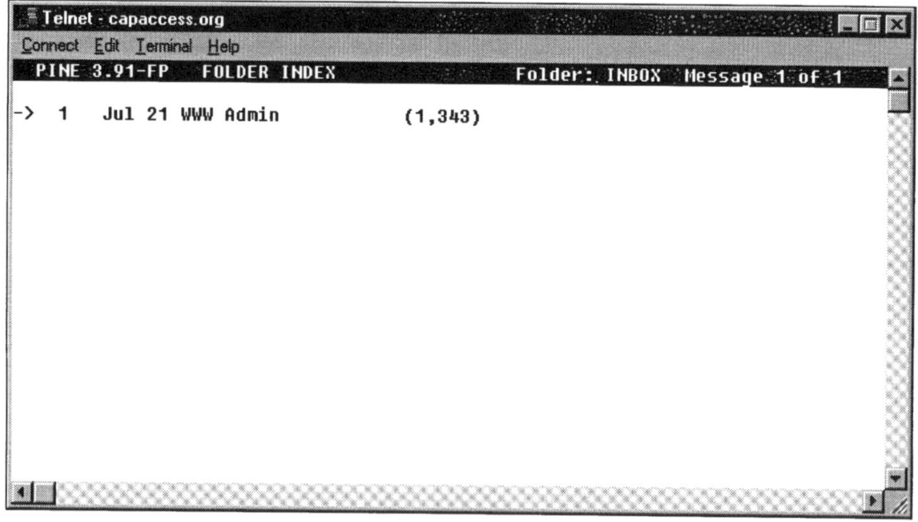

FIGURE 6.6 Reading mail at the remote host.

In a Windows environment, a machine running X-Server software and having suitable connectivity can access a UNIX application running on another machine. The X-Server application is another window on the Windows desktop.

How Does X-Server Work?

Conceptually, the X-Server works in exactly the same way as an X-terminal, as discussed in the previous chapter. An application running on one machine does the processing and displays the results on another machine's (X-Server) window. The application's machine and the machine displaying the results could be connected by a telephone line with modems, LAN, or even the

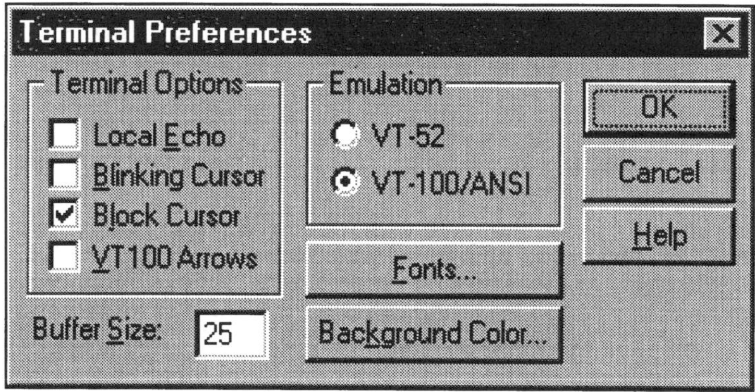

FIGURE 6.7 Setting preferences for Telnet sessions.

Internet/intranet. Keep in mind though that the more graphics you have, the more time it is going to take for transmission. This could be a problem for modem connections (just as you have problems accessing graphics-rich Web pages with slow modem connections). The protocol between an application and an X-Server is typically the X-Windows protocol.

Considerations in Using the X-Server Approach

If you are the manager trying to decide if an X-Server approach is right for you, here are some advantages and disadvantages for you to consider.

Advantages of the X-Server Approach

- By using an X-Server approach, you may be able to provide access to non-Windows applications such as production UNIX applications from existing Windows desktops (without having to buy devices such as X-terminals or UNIX workstations). The alternatives are to provide two machines for each user (with associated footprint problems) or set up a pool of devices for accessing non-Windows applications. The latter approach could save some money, but has its own set of problems. Sharing devices is discussed in Chapter 13.
- As in the case of the X-terminal, the application still resides on a central server. All the advantages of having a central application server — such as ease of upgrades, easier management and control, etc. — are true for the X-Server as well.
- You can improve productivity compared to solutions by having two machines (one of which could be idle for extended periods of time). Having applications like Windows on the same desktop provides for functions such as cut-and-paste between applications.
- With an X-Server that runs on a PC, you can actually run Windows 95 and other 32-bit applications using a 486 or even 386 machine, which would not be possible natively.
- An X-Server approach also permits "roving" users to logon from any X-Server. The state of the application on the server (for the user) could be preserved and the user could continue work from where he/she left off.

Disadvantages of the X-Server Approach

- Since the application runs on only one machine, you have to ensure that the machine is capable of handling the load of a number of concurrent users. Typically, you require a

certain amount of disk storage and memory on the server for each user, and you also have to use a processor or multiple processors capable of handling the load.
- You also have a central point of failure, although you can mitigate this by having multiple servers.

Common X-Server Products

This section presents an overview of some common X-Server products available. The information was gathered from different published sources including vendors' online Web pages. The Web addresses and other contact information are included in the description for each vendor and in the Appendix. The tools are being updated quickly and you should check with the tool vendor for the latest information. Most vendors also offer free evaluations, which are downloadable from their Web sites.

This book is not intended to help you select one vendor over another. You should pick migration/coexistence solutions that meet your requirements and perform an evaluation of vendor products. The inclusion of vendor information is provided to give you an idea of the capabilities of the products and to give you a quick reference to get further information and software.

Common X-Server products include:

- eXceed from Hummingbird Communications
- PC-Xware from NCD Software
- Reflection Suite for X from (WRQ)
- SCO XVision from Santa Cruz Operation
- N*u*TCRACKER X Server from Datafocus
- eXalt-X from Intergraph
- Chameleon from NetManage
- OpenNT X11 server from Softway systems
- X OnNet from FTP Software

A brief overview of some of these products follows.

eXceed

More details on the eXceed product family are available online at http://www.hummingbird.com.

The eXceed family includes a line of X-Servers that run on Windows NT, Windows 95, Windows 3.1.

eXceed for Windows NT

eXceed is a native 32-bit Windows NT application that is X11R6 compliant. It runs in all environments Windows NT runs on. Local Windows and UNIX X-applications run concurrently on the PC screen.

eXceed for Windows NT features

eXceed supports cut-and-paste of text and graphics between Windows applications and UNIX applications. eXceed is fully X11 Release 6 compliant and includes the X11R6.1 extensions Double Buffer, XTEST, SYNC, X input supporting mouse and keyboard, and X Image Extension (XIE) for high-performance image handling.

PC-Xware

More information on PC-Xware is available online from NCD at http://www.ncd.com.

PC-Xware comes in two flavors. The PC-Xware Classic contains exclusively NCD's PC X-Server. The PC-Xware Suite combines the PC X-Server with NFS, terminal emulation, and network utilities.

Features of PC-Xware

PC-Xware is X/Open branded and Windows 95 logo compliant. It features an NFS Client and Server. Its Xremote function allows remote access to X-Windows applications over telephone lines. PC-Xware provides terminal emulation for IBM AS/400, VAX, Wyse, and HP in one program. It includes a graphical FTP client that features drag-and-drop file transfer between PCs and host computers over the network. It also includes a Graphical Keyboard Remapper that gives users a simple tool to customize their keyboards for any application.

N*u*TCRACKER X-Server

Information on N*u*TCRACKER products is available online at http://www.datafocus.com.

N*u*TCRACKER X-Server is a 32-bit PC X-Server that loads automatically with X-based applications, and is transparent to the user. It features seamless shutdown and restart of X-sessions. It includes a virtual desktop manager and supports multiple profiles to run simultaneously.

Reflection Suite for X from WRQ

The following is a brief summary of Reflection Suite from WRQ Web pages. Additional information on Reflection X products by Walker, Richer and Quinn (WRQ) is available online at http://www.wrq.com.

Reflection Suite for X is more than just an X-Server. It also includes terminal emulation and distributed files access (using NFS). To avoid duplication, this product is covered only here and not in terminal emulation or distributed file access. Besides Reflection Suite for X, WRQ also has other products such as Reflection Suite for the enterprise, Reflection Suite for TCP, etc. WRQ also lets you form your own suite by selecting *a la carte* from its products.

Features of Reflection Suite for X

Reflection Suite for X is a 32-bit Windows X-Server that is X11R6.1 compliant. It also includes specific X11R6 extensions, such as XTEST, Multi-Buffering Extension (MBX), and the X-Imaging Extension (XIE). It includes terminal emulation for a variety of terminals, including VT420, VT320, VT220, VT102, VT54, SCO, ANSI, BBS ANSI, TN5250, and TN3270. The Suite also supports TCP/IP and NFS for Windows 95.

Reflection Suite for X includes a set of administrative and diagnostic tools, including ReadyX. ReadyX is designed to simplify PC X connections for both users and system administrators. Reflection Suite for X provides remote X-connections via dialup lines.

Reflection Suite for X provides a full range of Internet/intranet functions, including FTP, e-mail, Web client and server, Newsreader, Finger client and server, etc.

Reflection Suite Administration Functions

Reflection Suite for X includes management and administration functions. It includes a graphical interface that lets administrators control X-Server settings by supplying default values or overriding user selections. Reflection Suite for X lets system administrators define the X-applications available on particular hosts, thereby allowing PC X users to quickly create desktop icons from which to run those applications.

Reflection Suite for X includes a trace and replay utility that lets IS personnel evaluate the interaction between X-applications and the X-Server by capturing the X-protocol for playback on any PC with Reflection X.

Reflection Suite for X support for Microsoft System Management Server (SMS) lets system administrators perform unattended deployment of Reflection X to users' PCs from a network server.

User Interface Features

Reflection Suite for X provides support for remote window managers such as Motif or OpenLook, as well as local window management with Microsoft Windows. You can also use both concurrently.

Reflection Suite for X comes with a full set of X11R5/X11R6 and host-specific fonts compiled into Microsoft Windows format. It also allows you to store fonts locally or use a font server.

Reflection Suite for X can be configured to support displays up to a maximum of 32,000 × 32,000 pixels. Using configurable panning, you can view X-applications that are too large to fit on your screen.

WRQ also sells Reflection for X, which includes the X-Server, the terminal emulation functions, and FTP.

XVision

The following is a brief summary of XVision from SCO Web pages. More information on XVision is available online from Santa Cruz Operations (SCO) at http://www.sco.com.

SCO XVision is part of the Windows to UNIX Integration Vision product series from SCO. The products in the series include:

- SCO SQL-Retriever: ODBC Middleware
- SCO SuperVision: Manage vision family desktops remotely
- SCO TermVision: Extensible terminal emulator
- SCO VisionFS: UNIX file and print services for Windows
- SCO XVision: Transparent PC X-Server
- SCO Wintif: Make UNIX applications Windows friendly

XVision Eclipse

XVision Eclipse is a full 32-bit X-Server that operates on Windows 95 and Windows NT. A version is available for Windows 3.1x as well. It provides access from a PC to character and graphical UNIX applications running on a UNIX Server. It is X11R6 compliant.

Features of XVision Eclipse

Let us look at some of the XVision features such as user interfaces, installation, and so on.

User interface: Eclipse includes a virtual desktop manager, called "Zones." Each zone is a different logical screen to the user. Eclipse lets different Windows managers be selected by configuration options. Support is provided for the Microsoft (local) window manager as well as a local Motif window manager. Eclipse features a UNIX Neighborhood Browser that has an identical interface to the Network Neighborhood on Windows 95 and Windows NT. This allows drag-and-drop file transfer between UNIX and Windows. You can suspend and resume X-sessions using another member of the Vision family, Vision Resume.

Installation: Eclipse includes a Windows 95 style setup wizard. Eclipse eases the task of iterative installations by providing functions to record a "script" detailing which parts of the XVision Eclipse the software are to be installed. The recorded script can then be used for essentially unattended installs. An application wizard provides a list of UNIX servers the X-Server can connect to, as well as a list of applications on that server. Alternately, the user can pick applications by browsing the UNIX file system. Once an application is selected, future access is made easy by using the Windows START or from a Program Group.

Administration: The Vision family includes SuperVision for the central management of Eclipse X-Servers. SuperVision can display snapshots of the users' desktops so that if users encounter problems, the system administrator can see what the user sees.

Graphics optimizer: Eclipse includes a graphics optimizer. The graphics optimizer performs the most commonly used graphics operations using three different methods of drawing and timing each. The fastest method is remembered and used to perform that specific operation in any future XVision Eclipse session.

Embed X-clients in Web documents: Intranet users can start UNIX applications by clicking on embedded application information contained within Web pages.

Terminal emulation support: Eclipse includes terminal emulation support to access character-based legacy applications. Terminals supported include the vt420, vt320, vt200, vt100, vt52, wyse60, wyse50, and SCO ansi.

eXalt-X from Intergraph

eXalt is Intergraph's X11R6-compliant display server for X-based applications. More information on eXalt is available online from Intergraph at http://www.intergraph.com.

eXalt is designed to operate on Intel-based processors running Microsoft Windows 95 and Windows NT. eXalt integrates X-Windows applications over the network with desktop-based, 32-bit Windows applications.

Features of eXalt include:

- Extensive font and digitizer support, including Intergraph's Font Server; supports .PCF and .BDF formats, with network access of fonts through X11R6 Font Server
- Provides choice of window managers, startup modes, and installation levels for administrative flexibility and control
- Allows you to change keyboard language, set bell on/off, and adjust auto-repeat behavior with Keyboard Options
- Controls colors displayed by the eXalt server with the Color Database Options dialog
- Supports all four X Display Manager Control Protocol (XDMCP) startup modes (passive, query, broadcast, and indirect)

Chameleon Xoftware from NetManage

NetManage has a number of products for migration and coexistence between UNIX and Windows NT. The product functionalities include heterogeneous e-mail, terminal emulation, distributed NFS file access, PC X-Server, and Web-enabled access to X-applications. You can get more information online from NetManage at http://www.netmanage.com.

The Chameleon product set includes a PC X-Server that supports the latest release of X Windows (X11R6.3 or "Broadway"). Chameleon UNIXLink 97's PC X-Server (XoftWare) provides seamless integration of X-applications with Web browsers. Users need only start their browsers and click an HTML link to an X-application to get access to the X-application, without needing to know X or UNIX connection commands.

OpenNT X-Server

OpenNT X-Server is an X-Server from Softway Systems. More information on the OpenNT X server is available online from Softway Systems at http://www.softway.com.

OpenNT X server features include:

- X11R6 compliance
- 32-bit architecture
- Concurrent window managers — local Windows and host-based window manager
- Support for UNIX window managers — Motif, OpenLook, VUE, CDE
- Virtual screen size support of 32,767 by 32,767 pixels
- Automatic window panning

- Copy-and-paste of text and graphics to and from Windows NT and Windows 95 clipboard to and from X Windows
- XDMCP security through X-authority
- Backing store and save unders
- Full set of X11R6 fonts are provided with automatic font substitution
- International keyboard support with a choice of 23 international layouts, 3-button mouse emulation for 2-button mouse
- Choice of full-screen, single-window mode or multiple window mode
- Full integration with Windows, providing familiar Windows GUI and ICCCM-compatible operations for editing and window handling

eXpertise

eXpertise is a PC X-Server from Quarterdeck. More information on eXpertise is available online from Quarterdeck at http://www.quarterdeck.com.

Features of eXpertise include:

- 32-bit or 16-bit PC X-Server with integrated Windows manager
- Choice of local or remote windows managers, with support for twm, mwm, and olwm
- 4-, 8-, 16-, and 24-bit display modes
- xdm support
- Font server
- Cut-and-paste capability between Windows applications and X-applications
- Application Manager (users are able to launch the program from the Application Manager, from an icon, or from a menu item)
- Command-line FTP
- Line printer daemon (enables local printing)
- Automated installation
- Serial Xpress(TM) enhanced dial-up connectivity option

EMULATORS

A character-based UNIX application can be accessed using emulators that run on Windows. Emulators are also used for accessing non-UNIX and non-Windows host applications. The most common non-UNIX and non-Windows host applications are the applications that run on IBM mainframes and IBM AS/400s. Emulators for accessing IBM host applications emulate devices such as the 3270 (for mainframes) and the 5250 (for the AS/400).

Emulators are covered in detail in Chapter 7.

Conclusion

We looked at different ways that you can access UNIX applications from Windows desktops. The simplest way would be Telnet from Windows to the UNIX machine, but the capabilities of Telnet are limited. There are a number of vendors who provide X-Server products that run in Windows and let you access UNIX applications, including graphical applications. We looked at some of the products and reviewed the advantages and disadvantages of X-Servers.

In the next chapter, we will take a look at enterprise desktops and emulators.

7 Enterprise Desktops and Emulators

INTRODUCTION

Under applications coexistence, so far, we have looked at two options. Starting with a typical UNIX desktop such as an X-terminal, we looked at solutions that added Windows applications access. We then looked at solutions that add UNIX applications access to a PC desktop. Realizing the requirements of the heterogeneous environments in many organizations, vendors are coming up with devices that are designed for performing as an "enterprise desktop" or a "multi-client desktop." We will take a look at enterprise desktops. We will also take a look at emulators that emulate one environment under another so that applications that execute in one environment can be made to run in another environment. Unlike porting or applications that are written to execute in multiple environments, emulators do not need the source code.

ENTERPRISE DESKTOP

Enterprise desktops are desktops capable of functioning in a heterogeneous computing environment with hardware and software from multiple vendors. If you are a business manager thinking about an enterprise desktop, look for one that is capable of meeting the following business and technical requirements:

TECHNICAL REQUIREMENTS OF ENTERPRISE DESKTOPS

- Provide one stop e-mail access capable of receiving e-mail from multiple e-mail servers.
- Provide legacy application access. Examples of legacy applications include applications that reside on IBM hosts such as a 390 mainframe or an AS/400. This support is primarily accomplished through an emulation function built into the desktop.
- Provide access to file and printer servers attached to different servers across different networks.
- Provide connectivity support, including support for different types of networks and protocols.
- Provide Internet access.
- Provide support for workgroup collaboration.

BUSINESS REQUIREMENTS OF ENTERPRISE DESKTOPS

- Provide functions that enable easy desktop management.
- Provide ease of use functions to minimize training and ongoing support costs.
- Minimize cost of upgrades.
- Provide robust security features.

TABLE 7.1
Enterprise Desktops and Features Comparison

	Desktop Management	Ease of Use	Upgrade Cost	Security	Advanced Function	Offline Working
PCs	L	M[2]	H	M	H	H
Dumb terminals	H	H	L	H	L	L
X-Stations	M[1]	M[2]	M[1]	M[1]	H	M[1]
Network PCs	H	M	L	H	H	M
Laptops	L	M	H	M	H	H

Note: H (high), M (medium), L (low) indicate level of support for a function by the desktop. For example, L for Desktop Management and PCs indicates that support for the desktop management function for PCs is low (L) compared to the other desktops.

[1] Functionality varies greatly as the capabilities of the X-Stations vary substantially. Low-end devices such as X-terminals offer lower functionality compared to high-end workstations.

[2] Depends on the type of usage. A stand-alone word processing usage may be easy compared to accessing multimedia applications across a network.

- Provide functions to perform offline work, including word processing and offline e-mail functions. These offline functions permit users to be productive when the networks or servers (the desktop is attached to) are not available.
- Provide advanced (future) productivity functions such as multimedia support future functions such as desktop videoconferencing and collaboration, computer telephone integration, etc.

There are different types of desktops currently available in many enterprises. They include:

- Personal computers, including Macs
- Dumb terminals
- X-Stations
- Network PCs
- Laptops and other remote access devices

The desktops are capable of meeting the technical requirements with software that resides in the desktop itself or that resides on a server. Table 7.1 illustrates how the different desktops compare in meeting business requirements.

Let us briefly look at some common enterprise desktops. ***Note:*** The information about the products was gathered from different published sources, but primarily from vendor-published information, including online Web pages. The Web addresses and other contact information are included in the description for each vendor and in the Appendix. The products are being updated quickly and you should check with the product vendor for the latest information. Most vendors also offer free evaluations that are downloadable from their Web sites.

This book is not intended to help you select one vendor over another. You should pick migration/coexistence solutions that meet your requirements and perform an evaluation of vendor products. The inclusion of vendor information is provided to give you an idea of the capabilities of the products and to give you a quick reference to get further information and software.

NETWORK COMPUTERS

There are many companies trying to come up with low-cost workstations that have virtually no software installed in them. For this reason, the network computer is sometimes also referred to as a thin-client. (Keep in mind though that the converse is not true. That is, a thin-client does not necessarily mean a network computer. Sometimes thin-clients are used as opposites of fat-clients, and thin vs. fat is more indicative of the amount of functionality in the client). Instead, the software resides on a server and is loaded on demand. Since there is virtually no software that is resident on the network computer, the network computer doesn't need a hard drive. There are many companies working on the network computer, including IBM, Oracle, Microsoft, Intel, etc. The IBM version is called NC (short for Network Computer), while the Microsoft, Intel version is called NetPC. The lack of software on the network computer provides its biggest advantage — lack of any maintenance or upgrade at the network computer level. This significantly reduces administrative costs associated with the network computer compared to a regular personal computer.

WinTerm from Wyse

WinTerm is a family of network computers (also called thin-clients) from Wyse. More information about the WinTerm family is available online from Wyse at http://www.wyse.com.

The features of WinTerm include:

- Based on Java operating system from Javasoft
- Java Virtual Machine
- Embedded HTML 3.2-compliant browser
- Terminal emulation applettes (TNS27O, TN220)
- Citrix ICA3 client
- X-11 client (check with vendor on availability date)
- e-mail client for POPS, SMTP, IMAP4 hosts
- Audio support for .WAV and .AU sound file playback
- Graphics support for JPEG and GIF
- Multilevel security to minimize user access to setup, application, and Web sites
- Support for network printers
- Support for local printers (check with vendor on availability date)

Explora from NCD

More information about Explora is available online from NCD at http://www.ncd.com.

Explora is an enterprise desktop designed to provide seamless, simultaneous access to Windows, legacy, UNIX, applications (any networked applications) from the same desktop. Explora includes a 32-bit PowerPC RISC processor, graphics accelerator, and its own operating system called NCDware. Explora lets you customize your desktop and also supports a range of keyboards.

Heterogeneous application access: Explora provides access to Windows applications using the WinCenter Windows Application Server. WinCenter is covered in Chapter 5. Explora provides terminal emulation functions for a number of terminals, including 3270, VT320, etc. Terminal emulation provides access to IBM and other mainframe-based applications. UNIX graphical applications are supported by the built in X-Server, which is X11 compliant. It also includes Telnet and LAT to access other character-based applications supported by Telnet and LAT.

Heterogeneous network connectivity: Explora comes with built-in support for a number of network protocols, including TCP/IP as well as file server access using NFS.

NCD also has a high-end family of enterprise desktops called HMX. In addition to Explora's functions, HMX features better display resolution, better multimedia support, and support for Java applications (check with vendor for timing of availability).

Personal Workstations from DEC

More information on DEC workstations is available from DEC at http://www.digital.com.

DEC has a line of personal workstations designed to function as enterprise desktops. The personal workstation family includes three series of workstations:

- The i-series
- The a-series
- The au-series

The personal workstations are designed with Windows NT and UNIX migration coexistence features. The Digital Personal Workstation au-series is capable of supporting both Windows NT and Digital UNIX applications on a single workstation. Thus, you can continue using mission-critical technical (UNIX) applications today and seamlessly move to a Windows NT environment tomorrow using a single product family.

The Personal Workstation a-series ships with a Solution Pack CD-ROM containing a suite of enabling software tools designed to boost productivity and connectivity in a technical Windows NT workstation environment. Some of the Windows NT migration and coexistence tools included in the CD-ROM are eXceed and NFS Maestro. eXceed was covered in Chapter 6 and NFS Maestro will be covered in Chapter 8.

DEC also ships the binary emulator and translator software FX!32 free with many personal workstation systems to let Windows applications be run on UNIX. FX!32, the Alpha x86 binary translator, provides fast and transparent execution of x86 Win32 executables on Windows NT V4.0 Alpha. You can load a 32-bit x86 application on Alpha, double-click on its icon, and it runs as if it were running on a Pentium system. According to DEC, a Windows application "in most cases performance matches, and in some cases surpasses, Pentium Pro performance."

ViewPoint from Boundless Technologies

Information on the ViewPoint family of network computers is available at http://www.boundless.com. ViewPoint TC is a family of Intel-based, Windows-oriented network computers from Boundless Technologies. The ViewPoint TC family currently includes models that provide different capabilities but shares the same 133-MHz, x86-compatible hardware architecture. The models include:

- A text-based terminal
- A Windows NT workstation with added multi-user access
- An enhanced workstation that combines Windows and Java support with UNIX and legacy application integration

The multi-user access is based on Citrix System Inc.'s WinFrame, which adds multi-user capabilities to Windows NT. Microsoft recently licensed the multi-user technology from Citrix for use in future versions of the Windows NT server. ViewPoint offerings are comparable to the product offerings from Wyse covered earlier in this chapter.

Network Computer from IBM

IBM is building the network computer, primarily as a replacement for the aging dumb terminals. By the time you read this book, IBM will have announced a version of OS/2 Warp Server to run on Network Computer, called Bluebird. Bluebird is optimized for network computing. Bluebird is a derivative of OS/2 Warp Server.

Bluebird will support up to six different desktop configurations on the server. These configurations are downloaded from the server to network computers when users boot up. The server also stores data files and the user's access to network services.

Bluebird's client systems include 3270 and 5250 mainframe terminal emulation, a WWW browser, and either DOS/Windows 3.x or a slimmed-down version of the Workplace Shell and Presentation Manager. The processing power to run these client systems is the equivalent of a 486-class processor. All client systems also include the Java Virtual Machine to run Java applications. Bluebird will support multiple network cards on a PC and automatically perform load balancing to maximize network throughput.

The first release of Bluebird will run on Intel-based PCs.

APPLICATION EMULATORS

Emulators can be broadly classified as:

- Application emulators
- Terminal emulators

Application emulators are covered here. Terminal emulators are covered in the next section.

Application emulators let the executable in one environment run in another environment by emulating the run-time environment required by the executable. For example, there are emulators that let a Windows application run on a UNIX machine. Application emulators are a layer of software that sit on top of the native environment.

As with other applications-related topics, the focus here will be on Windows NT and UNIX applications. At the time of writing, there are not any application emulators in widespread use that let a UNIX application run on Windows NT. This situation is likely to change soon. There are, however, a number of products that let a Windows application run on different environments. Let us take the instance of Mac clients that need to run Mac applications as well as Windows applications. There are emulator products that let a Mac run Windows applications.

These emulator products can be broadly classified as:

- Hardware-based emulators
- Software-based emulators

Hardware-based emulators essentially have a Mac and a PC in one box. Typically, an add-on board with an Intel processor and memory is added to a Mac, and Windows and Windows Applications use the add-on processor. Peripherals are shared. Since there is no emulation software to execute, hardware-based emulators can run applications at essentially the native speed of the add-on processor.

Software-based emulators do not require the addition of specialized boards or chips. Instead, software-based emulators provide all the emulation functions solely by software. Some of the common software-based emulators include WABI from Sun Microsystems, SoftWindows from Insignia Solutions, and Locus Merge from Locus Computing Corp. Please see the *Note* on vendor products earlier in the chapter.

For running Win32 applications, Insignia Solutions has SoftWindows 95 from Silicon Graphics, which allows users to run Windows 95 applications on UNIX workstations. No other platforms have been announced, but others will follow eventually. SoftWindows is discussed later in this chapter.

Emulation Choices

For 16-bit Windows applications, you have more emulation choices, including SoftWindows 2.0 for UNIX, Merge from Platinum Technology, and WABI from Sun Microsystems. These emulators provide somewhat complete Windows 3.1 and 3.11 environments. However, none of these products do anything for newer Windows 95 and Windows NT applications.

Emulation also has performance costs, and it presents a foreign look and feel to UNIX workstation users. Performance will vary with the hosting platform, but the need to emulate the Intel x86 instruction set hinders application performance when compared to native applications or to running the same application on an Intel platform.

SoftWindows

The following is a brief summary of SoftWindows from Insignia Web pages. Additional information about SoftWindows is available online from Insignia at http://www.insignia.com.

The latest version of SoftWindows lets you run your Windows 95 applications. It comes in two flavors: SoftWindows 95 and 3.0 for the Power Mac, the primary difference being which Microsoft operating system comes pre-installed. SoftWindows 95 includes Windows 95 pre-installed, and SoftWindows 3.0 includes Windows 3.11 and MS-DOS 6.22 pre-installed. Features of SoftWindows include:

- Run Windows 95 applications on your Mac
- Support for local printer connected to your Mac
- Sound Blaster compatibility
- PC SCSI support that lets you access SCSI devices such as SyQuest/Zip drives and scanners

Applications Support

SoftWindows has a feature called "TurboStart" feature that enables the Power Mac to launch Windows 95 applications faster compared to the time it takes a typical PC to launch the same application.

Windows Programs that can run using SoftWindows 95 include Microsoft Office, Lotus SmartSuite, WordPerfect, Encarta, Lotus Notes, and CorelDRAW. Multimedia applications that use MIDI, QuickTime for Windows, or Video for Windows can play both video and audio. SoftWindows95 includes a Windows driver that supports recording and playback of digital sound samples in .WAV format. You can copy and paste text and graphics between a Windows 95 application running under SoftWindows and a native Power Mac application. SoftWindows uses Apple Guide for online help, and you can create scripts to execute PC commands using AppleScript. Windows desktop size is configurable. SoftWindows emulates a 80486 processor.

Peripherals Support

Windows 95 is configured to print on any printer available through the Mac Chooser. Printing can include postscript and non-postscript output. The PC port (LPT1:) is emulated and is linked to the Mac Chooser. You can also print on a PC serial printer using the Mac modem and printer ports.

You can choose to store applications and data in Mac folders (which can be organized as drives E: through Z:) or within the SoftWindows 95 "hard disk" file. The Mac file system is accessible from Windows 95. SoftWindows supports up to two PC floppy drives (as A: and B:), and supports using 3.5-inch PC diskettes in SuperDrive, up to two PC hard disks (as C: and D:) up to 500 MB per hard disk, depending on available Macintosh disk space.

SoftWindows includes Microsoft CD-ROM extensions that enable PC CD-ROMs to be used in Macintosh CD drives. PC serial ports COM1: and COM2: can use Mac modem and printer ports.

Network Support

SoftWindows 95 is preconfigured to attach a SoftWindows-loaded Power Mac to PC networks through the Mac's built-in Ethernet or optional Token Ring connections. SoftWindows 95 also has Novell NetWare and LAN Manager clients pre-installed and connects to Novell NetWare, LAN Manager, TCP/IP, Windows NT Server, Banyan VINES, LAN Server, Windows for Workgroups, and DEC PATHWORKS servers. SoftWindows 95 permits the simultaneous use of either the IPX protocol or the TCP/IP protocol in both Mac and PC environments.

Insignia includes information in its Web pages comparing SoftWindows with a hardware-based emulator.

WABI

More information on WABI is available online from Sun at http://www.sun.com.

Windows Application Binary Interface (WABI) is Sun's solution for Solaris users needing access to desktop Windows office applications. WABI is a software emulator that runs on Solaris and runs popular Windows 3.1x office applications.

Sun maintains a list of Windows applications that are certified to work the same under WABI as they do natively under Windows.

WABI Features

Key features of WABI include the following:

- Support for Windows ODBC applications
- Support for OLE and DDE between Windows applications
- Cut-and-paste between Windows and Solaris applications
- Access from Windows applications to network services such as printers and file servers

Besides the Sun Web pages, information about WABI is available through CompuServe and some Internet sites. Among other things, these sites provide a list of Windows applications known to run under WABI. (Keep in mind, though, that these applications are not certified.)

Windows NT Built-In 486 Emulator for RISC Systems

Starting with version 4.0, Windows NT versions that run on RISC (Reduced Instruction Set Computing) systems have a new software emulator. This emulator helps run DOS and Windows applications on the RISC systems without requiring other hardware or software. Applications requiring 386 enhanced mode or a 486 processor are supported. The performance problem common to emulators applies to this emulator as well.

WINDOWS NT AND MACINTOSH CLIENTS

Besides supporting clients that run different Windows operating systems, the Windows NT server also supports a Mac client in a Windows NT network. Windows NT includes Services for Macintosh (SfM) for this purpose. The Mac version should be 6.0.7 or above.

Setup for Macintosh Client on Windows NT Server

If you are adding services for Macintosh for the first time, follow the steps listed below. If you are not sure if services for Macintosh have already been installed, then select the services icon from the control panel that shows a list of services that have already been installed.

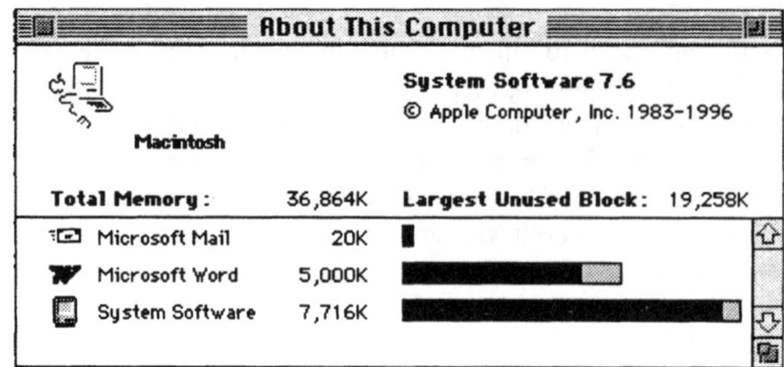

FIGURE 7.1 Checking the version level of MacOS.

- From **Start** menu, select **Settings**, then select **Control Panel**, then double-click the Network icon from the Control Panel.
- From the Network property sheet that comes up, select the **Services** tab.
- From this screen, click the **Add** button, which brings up the Select Network Service dialog.
- Scroll down the list of services (if needed) and select ***Services for Macintosh* entry**.
- Windows NT may prompt you for the Windows NT 4.0 server install CD if necessary and copies the necessary files.
- Windows NT automatically starts the AppleTalk protocol and finds the Macintosh clients that may be connected to your network adapter. If you have multiple network adapters, you can enable routing using the Microsoft AppleTalk Protocol Properties dialog. After configuration completion, you are prompted to restart the system. When the system restarts, you can verify that the new file and print services for Macintosh clients have been installed and are active by checking the Services icon in Control Panel.

Setting Up the Mac Side of the Macintosh Client

The Mac client must run MacOS version 6.0.7 or above. You can check the version by clicking on the desktop and selecting *About this computer* under the Apple menu, as shown in Figure 7.1.

You can use the same built-in support in MacOS to access network files and printers to access the Windows NT network, and no add-on products are necessary. The typical sequence of accessing a file server is as follows:

Click on the *Apple menu* and Select *Chooser*. This brings up the screen shown in Figure 7.2. The AppleTalk zones are listed in the lower left corner. Each zone contains file servers, printers, mail servers, etc. Select the zone you are interested in (by clicking the zone entry) and then select AppleShare to select file servers in the selected zone. The right portion of the screen now shows the available file servers in the selected zone.

Accessing Windows NT Network Files from the Macintosh Client

Select the file server you want by double-clicking it. This brings up the logon screen shown in Figure 7.3.

Entry of a valid password logs you to the file server and shows a list of valid drives you can access. The drives also appear on your Mac desktop. Double-clicking the icon shows the list of folders and files. This list is the same as what you would see with another file server such as a NetWare file server.

Tip: *You may be familiar with Associations for a file in the Windows environment. Associations are what lets Windows invoke an associated program when you double-click on a file. For example,*

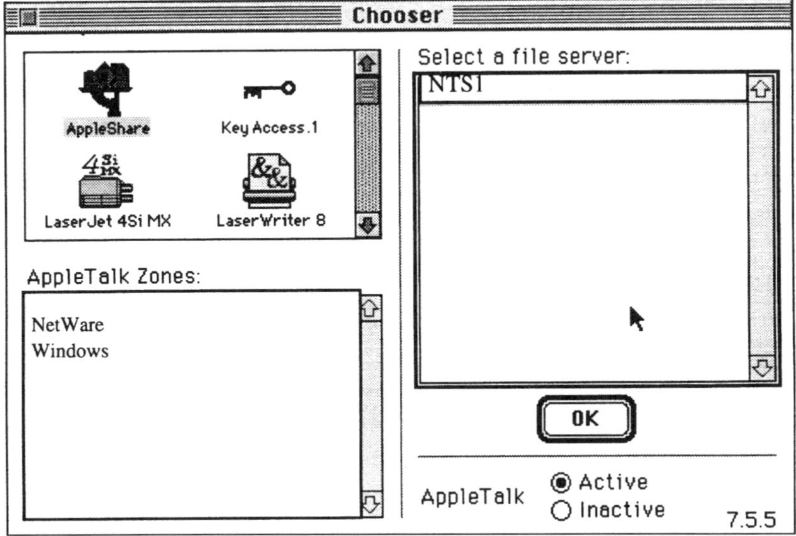

FIGURE 7.2 Selecting a file server.

PowerPoint gets automatically invoked when you double-click on a file with .ppt extension. Similarly, you can associate a Macintosh program to be invoked when a Macintosh file stored on your Windows NT server is double-clicked.

Accessing Windows NT Printers from the Macintosh Client

You can print to a printer on the Windows NT network from a Macintosh client in two ways:

- You can use a printer that is directly connected to the Windows NT server. This can be any printer that can be attached to the Windows NT server.
- You can use an AppleTalk-compatible printer that is directly connected to the network using a network adapter card.

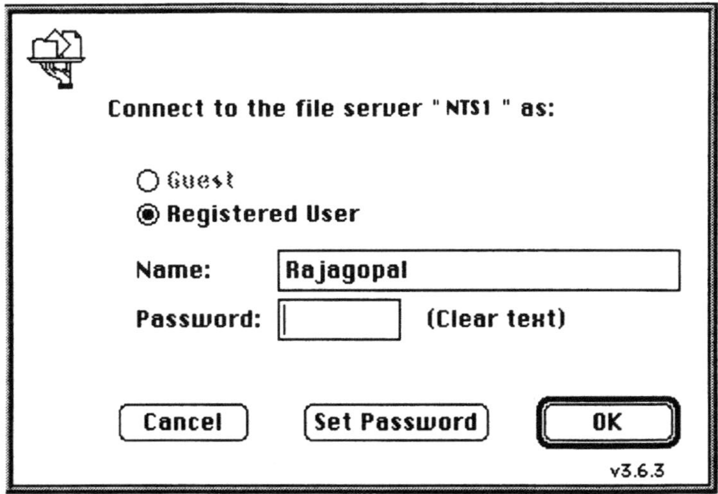

FIGURE 7.3 Logging to a Windows NT file server from a Mac client.

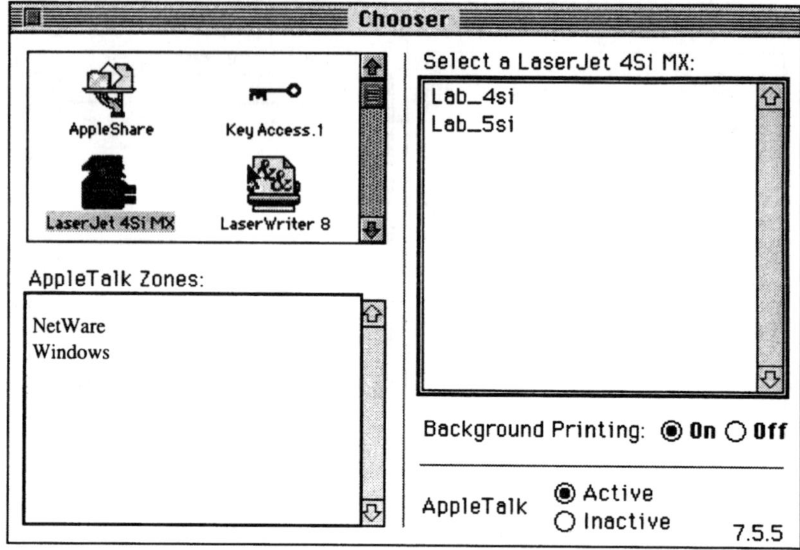

FIGURE 7.4 Selecting a printer from the Mac client.

You select the printer by following these steps in your Macintosh client.

Select *Chooser* from the *Apple menu* and the screen shown in Figure 7.4 will appear. From this screen, choose one of the printers (instead of choosing AppleShare for file server).

Tip: *As shown in Figure 7.4, Macintosh supports local print spooling at the client level using the Background Printing On/Off toggle switch. If you are using the Mac client to print to Windows NT network printers, disable spooling at the client by turning off Background Printing.*

Administering Macintosh Clients from Windows NT

When you install file and print services for Macintosh as described earlier, a MacFile icon gets added to the Control Panel. Double-clicking the MacFile icon brings up a dialog that lets you administer the Macintosh clients. The buttons on the MacFile Properties dialog and the functions are summarized in Table 7.2.

TABLE 7.2
MacFile Properties

MacFile Properties Dialog Button	Function
Users	View, disconnect, and send messages to Macintosh client users.
Volumes	This Volumes dialog has two parts. The top part lists Macintosh-accessible volumes defined on the server. For each volume, the total number of users accessing the volume is also shown. You select a volume from the list by clicking on the volume entry in the list. The bottom part lists the users for the volume selected in the top part. Using this dialog, you can disconnect individual users or all users accessing a volume.
Files	Displays a dialog that lists the open files on the server, the users of the files, and if the files are locked.
Attributes	Displays a dialog that lets you control the attributes of services for Macintosh. You can control if guest logins are allowed, specify whether the clients have to use Microsoft Authentication, specify whether the number of sessions is unlimited, and so on.

While the volumes button showed you the list of Macintosh accessible volumes, you can create new Macintosh accessible volumes using the Server manager dialog (which has a MacFile menu option when Services for Macintosh is installed).

Tip*: When you have Macintosh clients on a network with both NetWare servers and Windows NT servers, be consistent in the configuration setup between the servers for segments, zones, AppleTalk network numbers, etc.*

TERMINAL EMULATORS

Terminal emulators let mainframe applications be accessed from devices like PCs. To mainframe applications, PCs with terminal emulators appear like dumb terminals. Terminal emulators are commonly available to emulate the 3270 attached to an IBM mainframe, a 5250 attached to an IBM AS/400, or a VT 100/220 attached to Digital environments such as VAX.

There are a number of terminal emulators available on the market. Most of the migration and coexistence solution vendors mentioned in this book have the terminal emulation built into their products.

HARDWARE EMULATION SOLUTIONS

You can buy chips and motherboards with an Intel processor and install them in a machine running UNIX or MacOS. Thus, the machine has two CPUs. Using system software, Windows applications are executed using the Intel processor, while the native processor is used as it is normally used.

There are other possible chips and combinations to run a variety of applications on machines not normally supported, but the basic idea is the same. There are some advantages and disadvantages to this approach.

The primary advantage the hardware approach has over other alternatives (such as emulation) is the speed of execution. Since a dedicated processor designed for the application is used, no emulation or translation is necessary. This translates into faster execution speeds.

There are some disadvantages as well. The card is physically installed on one machine, which requires assistance in installing and it takes up a card slot on the machine. The card also typically requires its own physical memory, which may not be sharable with the existing memory on the machine where the card is installed. There may be some problems with Windows applications that require network access, since the application running using the special processor may not have access to network facilities.

PUBLIC DOMAIN EMULATORS

There are public domain emulators available to emulate one environment in another. For the purposes of this book, the one of interest is WINE.

WINE is both a program loader and an emulation library that will allow UNIX users to run MS Windows applications on an x86 hardware platform running under some UNIXes. The program loader will load and execute an MS Windows application binary, while the emulation library will take calls to MS Windows functions and translate these into calls to UNIX/X, so that equivalent functionality is achieved.

WINE is being developed specifically to run on the Intel x86 class of CPUs under certain UNIXes that run on the x86 platform. UNIXes currently being tested for WINE compatibility include Linux, NetBSD, FreeBSD, UnixWare, and SCO OpenServer 5.

Of course, the biggest problem with any public domain software is that, at best, the software is only voluntarily supported.

The newsgroup comp.emulators.ms-windows.wine discusses WINE and WINE-related Web sites include http://www.thepoint.com/unix/emulate/wine and http://www.linpro.no/wine/.

8 Heterogeneous Network File and Print Access

INTRODUCTION

In this chapter, we will look into a very common requirement within a heterogeneous environment — accessing a file server or a networked printer in one environment from a client in another environment. Networked file and print access between Windows and NetWare is relatively easy and is discussed in Chapter 11. We will consider file access between UNIX and Windows NT environments in this chapter.

ACCESSING UNIX SERVER FILES FROM WINDOWS NT CLIENTS

For occasional file transfers between a UNIX machine and a Windows NT machine, you can use floppy disks. UNIX systems normally include the ability to read and write DOS-compatible floppy disks (pcfs, for example). However, watch for problems when you transfer files. The problems you can encounter are listed under problems in file transfers section later in this chapter.

If you want to access Files and Printers that are on your UNIX server from your Windows machine without floppies, there are several ways in which you can do this:

- Use the built-in Telnet function, logon to the UNIX server and your Windows workstation becomes a terminal to the UNIX server. You can do file-related functions available for terminals such as viewing and editing files, executing program files, etc.
- Use the built-in File Transfer Protocol (FTP) function in Windows and exchange files between the UNIX server and the Windows machine. Windows NT also includes two other similar functions.
- Use the built-in rcp function in Windows NT.
- Use built-in tftp function in Windows NT.
- Use a serial link between the UNIX machine and the Windows NT machine.
- Use a network operating system with built-in support to access UNIX server files.
- Use third-party Network File System (NFS) packages.

Let us look at these options in detail.

TELNET

Telnet is a communication protocol for terminal emulation. Windows has built-in Telnet client support. Besides the built-in support, there are a number of communication packages that include Telnet client support. All UNIX operating systems support Telnet. Typically, a Telnet daemon keeps running in background, awaiting requests from Telnet clients.

```
Command Prompt - ftp ftp.microsoft.com

C:\users\default>ftp ftp.microsoft.com
Connected to ftp.microsoft.com.
220 ftp Microsoft FTP Service (Version 3.0).
User (ftp.microsoft.com:(none)): anonymous
331 Anonymous access allowed, send identity (e-mail name) as password.
Password:
230-This is FTP.MICROSOFT.COM.  Please see the
 dirmap.txt file for more information.

 An alternate location for Windows NT
 Service Packs is located at:

 ftp://198.105.232.37/fixes/
230 Anonymous user logged in.
ftp> cd bussys
250 CWD command successful.
ftp>
ftp>
ftp>
ftp>
ftp>
ftp>
ftp>
ftp>
```

FIGURE 8.1 Nongraphical ftp using command line.

Once connectivity is established, the Telnet client can perform the same functions as a directly attached terminal. Functions for file and print access include browsing and editing files, executing programs, and submitting print requests.

Telnet is covered in detail in Chapter 6.

File Transfer Protocol (ftp)

If you have used the Internet, then you are likely to have downloaded (and maybe even uploaded) files using the ftp protocol. File transfers are typically accomplished using the File Transfer Protocol. Windows NT comes with built-in support for ftp and the Internet Information Server (IIS), an add-on product to Windows NT server for Internet functions, includes an advanced version of FTP.

Besides the built-in support, there are a number of third-party communication packages that include ftp support and many of the third-party ftp programs provide graphical user interfaces.

To run the ftp client in the Windows machine and access the UNIX server files, the UNIX server should be running the ftp daemon called *ftpd*.

Windows NT includes a command line version of ftp as well as a graphical version of ftp. The command line version is started by keying in ftp and the name of the remote host (ftp.microsoft.com in this example) at the command prompt as shown in Figure 8.1. The figure shows the connection from the ftp client to the server ftp.microsoft.com. The logon was an anonymous login (the userid was *anonymous* and the password was the e-mail address of the person requesting file access). Once connected, the figure shows a change directory command to change to a specific directory. You can use the *get* command to retrieve files and the *put* command to send files to the server.

Windows NT also includes a graphical version of ftp; it is called WS_FTP32. You typically would find the ftp icon under network or you can search for "ftp" and double-click on the WS_FTP32 entry. The opening dialog of WS_FTP32 is shown in Figure 8.2.

You specify the remote host name, your userid, and your password, and WS_FTP32 attempts to establish an ftp connection. If successful, you get the dialog shown in Figure 8.3.

The dialog shows the highest level directory on the remote system and the subdirectories and files underneath the highest level directory. Clicking on a directory entry shows the list of directories and files underneath the directory. In this example, the directory *softlib* was chosen and the bottom half of the right pane shows the files and directories under *softlib*. The file README.TXT was selected. You can choose the destination on the left pane where a similar hierarchical file structure

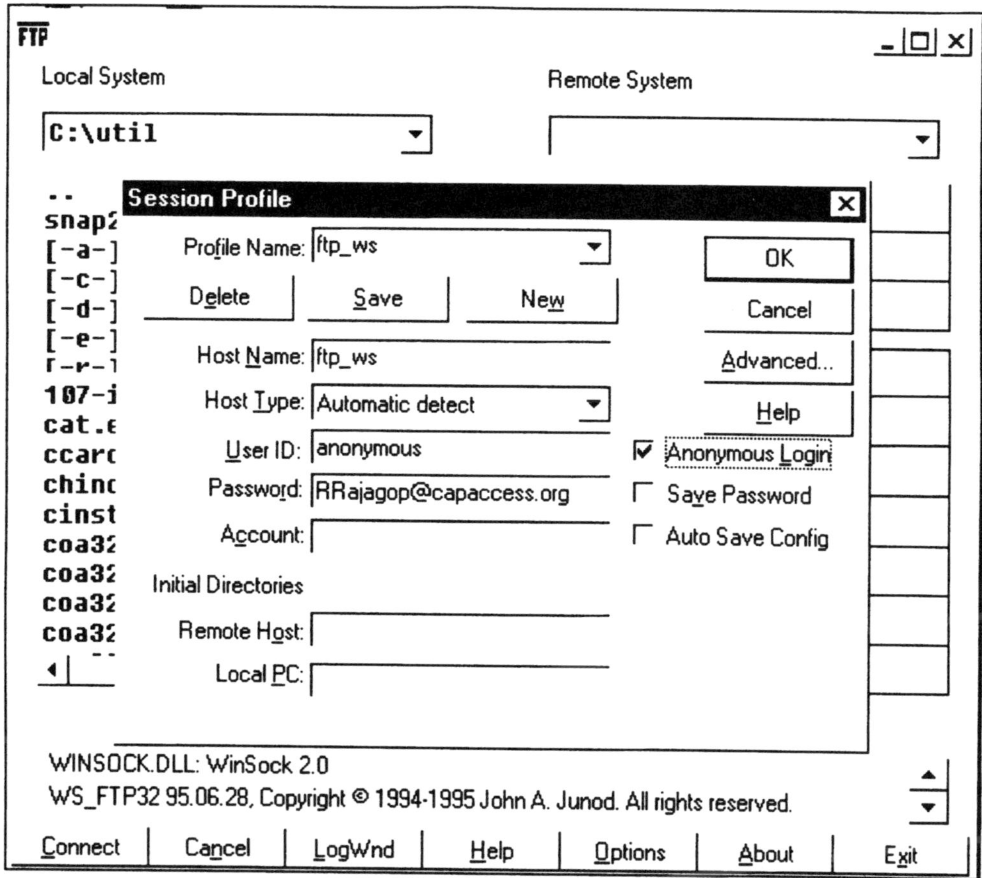

FIGURE 8.2 Graphical version of ftp.

of the local system is shown. Once you have selected the source and the destination, clicking on the arrow that goes from remote to local (right to left) downloads the file. You can upload files using the other arrow. Figure 8.4 shows that the README.TXT file has been downloaded.

Remote Copy Program (rcp)

rcp is similar to ftp. To run the rcp client in the Windows machine and access the UNIX server files, the UNIX server should be running the rcp daemon called *rshd* (Remote Shell Daemon). *rshd* supports other commands besides rcp and hence has a more generic daemon name (other than rcpd). You can specify a source and a destination (which means your computer does not have to be either, and you can copy remotely from one computer to another from a third computer). rcp supports specifying security parameters as well as recursive copying of all files (including subdirectories) between source and destination. The name of the Windows computer should be present in the *.rmhosts* file in the UNIX machine.

You can invoke rcp by keying in rcp from the command prompt, and keying in rcp without parameters shows the help message shown in Figure 8.5.

Trivial File Transfer Protocol (tftp)

tftp, as the name implies, is a trivial (or less functional) version of ftp. One of the functions missing in tftp compared to ftp is security. You cannot specify user information and, hence, no user

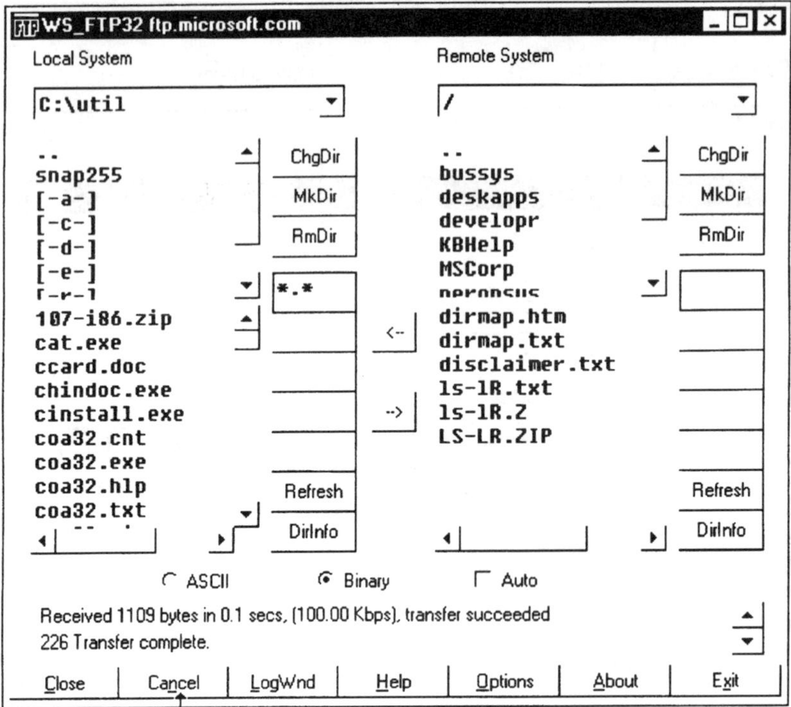

FIGURE 8.3 FTP connection with a remote host.

authentication takes place. (In ftp, you may have come across hosts that do not support Anonymous ftp, and your access will be denied if you tried being an Anonymous user). Another function missing is file browsing capability. Windows NT comes only with a built-in tftp client and not a tftp server. This means that you can use tftp to transfer UNIX files from your Windows NT machine, but not vice versa.

You can invoke tftp by keying in **tftp** from the command prompt, and keying in tftp without parameters shows the help message shown in Figure 8.6.

Using a Serial Link

Files can also be transferred between UNIX and Windows machines using serial links between the computers. There are third-party tools available to facilitate this type of file transfer. You can also use the Terminal function contained within Accessories under Programs, under Start in conjunction with third-party tools to connect to a UNIX machine and download files.

NETWORK OPERATING SYSTEMS WITH BUILT-IN FILE SERVER ACCESS

Network operating systems such as PATHWORKS from Digital and NetWare provide file and print services in heterogeneous environments.

Pathworks

The following is a brief summary of PATHWORKS from DEC Web pages. Additional information can be found at http://www.digital.com.

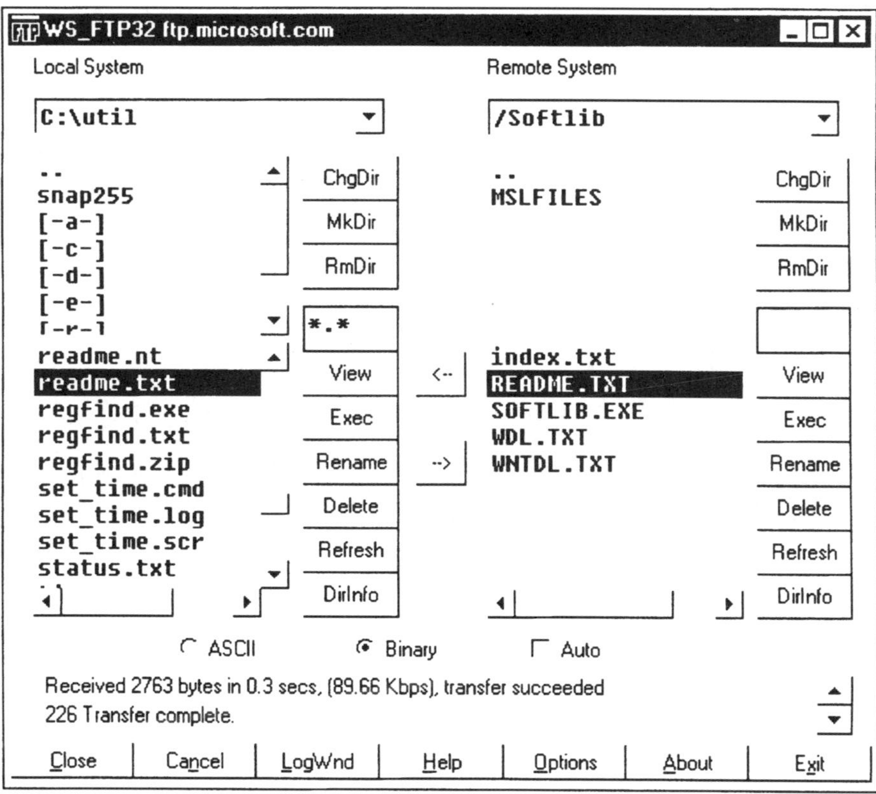

FIGURE 8.4 Downloading a file using ftp.

```
Command Prompt

RCP [-a | -b] [-h] [-r] [host][.user:]source [host][.user:] path\destination

  -a                     Specifies ASCII transfer mode. This mode converts
                         the EOL characters to a carriage return for UNIX
                         and a carriage
                         return/line feed for personal computers. This is
                         the default transfer mode.
  -b                     Specifies binary image transfer mode.
  -h                     Transfers hidden files.
  -r                     Copies the contents of all subdirectories;
                         destination must be a directory.
  host                   Specifies the local or remote host. If host is
                         specified as an IP address, you must specify the
                         user.
  .user:                 Specifies a user name to use, rather than the
                         current user name.
  source                 Specifes the files to copy.
  path\destination       Specifies the path relative to the logon directory
                         on the remote host. Use the escape characters
                         (\ , ", or ') in remote paths to use wildcard
                         characters on the remote host.

C:\users\default>
```

FIGURE 8.5 Invoking rcp from the command prompt.

```
Command Prompt

C:\users\default>tftp

Transfers files to and from a remote computer running the TFTP service.

TFTP [-i] host [GET | PUT] source [destination]

  -i              Specifies binary image transfer mode (also called
                  octet). In binary image mode the file is moved
                  literally, byte by byte. Use this mode when
                  transferring binary files.
  host            Specifies the local or remote host.
  GET             Transfers the file destination on the remote host to
                  the file source on the local host.
  PUT             Transfers the file source on the local host to
                  the file destination on the remote host.
  source          Specifies the file to transfer.
  destination     Specifies where to transfer the file.

C:\users\default>
C:\users\default>
C:\users\default>
C:\users\default>
C:\users\default>
```

FIGURE 8.6 Invoking tftp from the command prompt.

PATHWORKS from Digital provides built-in access to heterogeneous file servers. Using PATHWORKS, for example, a Windows NT client can access files from a Digital UNIX server. PATHWORKS makes NFS exported files automatically available to PCs, where the files can be accessed if the files are local to the PC. PATHWORKS is a family of network operating systems and includes PATHWORKS for Digital UNIX and PATHWORKS for Windows NT.

PATHWORKS for Digital UNIX

PATHWORKS for Digital UNIX (Advanced Server) provides the following Windows NT-style enterprise services, allowing Digital UNIX to be a full peer in a Windows NT environment:

- Support for the Advanced Server (LAN Manager) 3.0 SMB protocol.
- Windows NT controller support: UNIX can act as both primary and backup domain controllers.
- Windows NT Trusted Domain support.
- Windows NT wide area domain support (through an LMHOSTS file and WINS client).
- Windows NT management APIs (provide the ability to manage and be managed by Windows NT system management applications).
- Windows NT user and file replication.
- Support for a TruCluster environment for highly available PC services under DIGITAL UNIX and the ability for PCs to browse UNIX NFS shares.

PATHWORKS for Digital UNIX (Advanced Server) provides Windows NT Server networking features for Digital UNIX platforms. In the past, this technology was known as LAN Manager for UNIX. Most recently, additional NT networking features have been added and the technology has evolved to be known as Advanced Server for UNIX.

PATHWORKS for Digital UNIX (Advanced Server) allows full participation of Digital UNIX in a Windows NT domain. The previous version allowed Digital UNIX to act as a backup controller only. PATHWORKS for Digital UNIX (Advanced Server) Version 6.1 ships "TruCluster ready," meaning that your Windows NT files have the high availability and reliability of clustering servers such as Digital UNIX clusters. High availability and reliability are key features for enterprise applications to be deployed on Windows NT.

PATHWORKS for Digital UNIX (NetWare) server software enables your Digital UNIX and native NetWare users — as well as PATHWORKS for DOS and Windows (NetWare) users — to share files, data, mail, applications, disks, printers, and other resources. Multiple NetWare-based or LAN Manager-based clients can concurrently access files stored on the server's disk through the file access modes and byte range locking that Digital UNIX provides.

PATHWORKS for Digital UNIX supports multiple file systems, including:

- UNIX File System (UFS)
- Network File System (NFS)
- Advanced File System (AdVFS)
- CD-ROM File System (CDFS), read-only

File and print services are based on NetWare Core Protocol (NCP) and are available directly from Digital UNIX over the NetWare transport. You can manage file and print services by using standard NetWare utilities such that your investment in NetWare management expertise is preserved.

PATHWORKS integrates the most popular network operating systems, NetWare, and LAN Manager, allowing users within different workgroups to share information and resources.

PATHWORKS supports all of the leading network protocols — TCP/IP, DECnet, IPX/SPX, NetBEUI, AppleTalk, and LAT. For enterprise backbones, Digital also offers a full range of "multilingual" networking solutions, including TCP/IP, DECnet, OSI, X.25, ISDN, and telephone (PSTN) protocols and connectivity to IBM SNA networks.

Through PATHWORKS, NetWare users can share information with UNIX and OpenVMS, as well as LAN Manager-based users, including Windows NT and OS/2 users.

PATHWORKS for Windows NT

PATHWORKS for Windows NT is a member of the PATHWORKS family for Windows NT. PATHWORKS for Windows NT, available for both Windows NT Workstations and Windows NT Server systems, extends the connectivity of Windows NT systems. PATHWORKS for Windows NT gives Windows NT clients additional connectivity to legacy Digital environments by enhancing the clients with LAT, DECnet, and VT terminal emulation access.

NetWare provides file and print server support for a wide range of clients and servers. NetWare is covered in more detail in Chapter 11. Another network operating system that provides heterogeneous file and print connectivity is Vines from Banyan.

Check with your network operating system vendor to ensure that the specific client(s) and the specific server(s) you are planning on using are supported.

NFS

NFS is a standard file-sharing and access protocol invented by Sun Microsystems. It is used widely in the UNIX world. A system running NFS-compliant software can access (open, close, read, and even write to) files on remote systems, and share all or part of its file system with other systems that are NFS compliant. For example, a UNIX network administrator can mount NFS file systems from remote hosts and make the file systems available as though they were local. The directories and files on the UNIX server to be shared with other machines on the network are set up as shared directories using the *exportfs* UNIX command. The *exportfs* command specifies the type of access allowed (read only, write, etc.).

NFS Architecture

Figure 8.7 shows the architecture of NFS and how the different NFS functional layers map to the OSI 7 layer model.

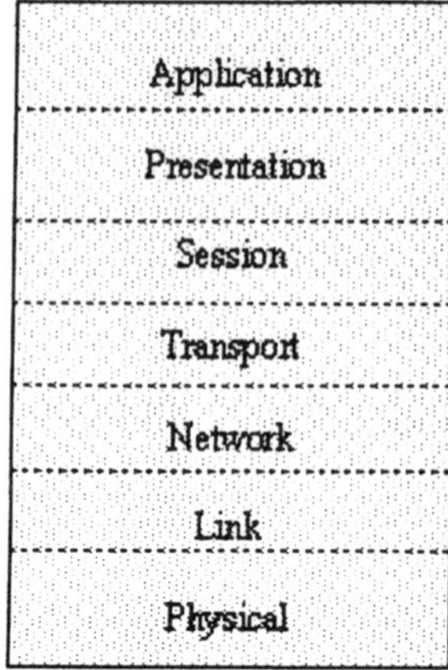

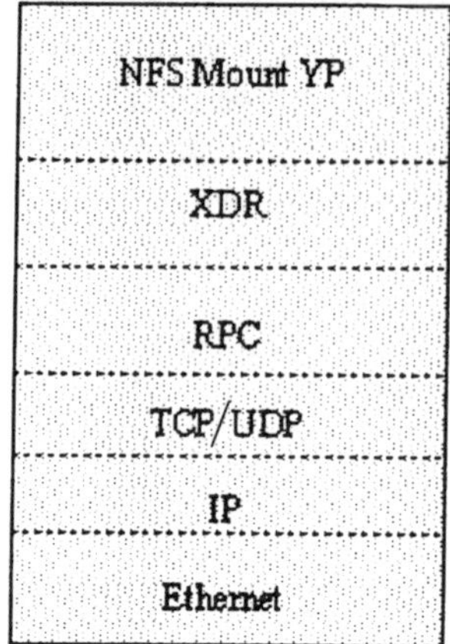

FIGURE 8.7 NFS Architecture mapped to the OSI model.

As shown in Figure 8.7, NFS is an application layer built on top of external data representation (XDR), remote procedure call (RPC), and User Datagram Protocol (UDP).

NFS Components

Typical NFS components include:

- NFS client
- NFS server
- NFS daemons

The NFS client is the code that resides in a client, such as a PC, that handles the client portion of accessing remote drives and directories. To the user, the NFS client interface makes remote drives look the same as local drives. For example, if the client is a Windows machine, the remote drives appear as additional drive letters and the file listings of the remote drives appear in File Manager or Explorer (Windows Explorer not Internet Explorer), in the same way as local drives. Windows does not have a built-in NFS client. If you want to access UNIX NFS volumes from Windows machines, you need to get third-party NFS clients. Some NFS clients support multiple remote drives to be accessed simultaneously and some support peer-to-peer LAN networking as well.

NFS servers respond to NFS client requests. NFS servers provide read and write access to network drives, access network printers, and CD-ROM drives. NFS servers also allow file systems to be exported to other NFS servers on the network. Since NFS servers could be executing on computing environments from different vendors, heterogeneous file sharing is possible.

NFS daemons are meant for the same purpose as any other UNIX or other daemons. They wait and execute in the background, facilitating NFS client/server exchanges. The NFS daemons, their type (core vs. non-core), and the functions they perform are summarized in Table 8.1.

Common NFS Products

There are a number of competing file systems to NFS. They include Remote File System (RFS), Andrew File System (AFS), and Windows NT's NTFS. Although Windows NT has built-in capability of supporting multiple file systems, NTFS is the one most suitable for heterogeneous system file access involving Windows NT. We will discuss NFS because the other file systems are either proprietary and/or do not have as good a market penetration as NFS.

TABLE 8.1
NFS Daemons

Daemon	Type	Function
portmapd	Core	Direct NFS clients to appropriate servers
nfsd	Core	Start file system requests for NFS clients
mountd	Core	Enable NFS clients to mount the file system
pcnfsd	Non-core	Assign NFS client access rights and print request directives
timed	Non-core	Adjusts time between clients and servers
lockd	Non-core	Implements NFS file locking service

Note: pcnfsd and lockd are required when implementing NFS using PCs.

NFS is usually supplied as an extension of the operating system by the UNIX system vendor, and is the standard for distributed file access in UNIX networks. In contrast, Macintosh, DOS, OS/2, Microsoft Windows, Windows NT, and Windows 95 NFS implementations have been developed independently by third-party TCP/IP software developers. Because NFS is built in as a feature of a specific vendor's TCP/IP, most NFS implementations will not run over different TCP/IP stacks, and are not compliant with Windows Sockets. NFS implementations for Windows NT and Windows 95, however, are compliant with Microsoft's TCP/IP kernel.

NFS products for the personal computer are normally offered as separate client and server applications, although there are some vendors that bundle client and server applications together in a single product. There are more than 100 different implementations of NFS for UNIX workstations, mainframes, and personal computers. The majority of NFS products support NFS Version 2 introduced in 1987, and many support the enhancements of NFS Version 3 (1989–1992).

Some of the third-party NFS products include InterDrive NT and InterDrive NT Server from FTP Software, NFS Maestro for Windows NT from Hummingbird Communications, PC NFS, DiskAccess (NFS clients for Windows NT), DiskShare (NFS server) from Intergraph, Chameleon from NetManage, Netpack NFS from Network Computing Devices, and PC NFS for Windows NT from SunSoft. NFS for Windows NT is also available from Beame and Whiteside and Process Software.

Let us take a brief look at the capabilities of some of these products.

NFS Maestro

More information on NFS Maestro is available online from Hummingbird at http://www.hummingbird.com.

NFS Maestro is a family of NFS products that includes:

- NFS Maestro Solo: The NFS client add-on to Hummingbird's eXceed PC X server (eXceed is covered in Chapter 6).
- NFS Maestro for Windows NT or Windows 95.
- NFS Maestro for Microsoft TCP/IP: TCP/IP stack and suite for DOS and Windows 3.x PCs.
- NFS Maestro for DOS and Windows: Client and Server.

Chameleon NFS/X

More details about Chameleon NFS/X are available online at http://www.netmanage.com.

NetManage provides products that enable access to NFS servers, X Window workstations, UNIX/VMS systems, IBM mainframes, and AS/400 systems from any Windows environment — Windows 3.1, 95, or NT. NetManage aims to provide the functions required of an enterprise desktop — host connectivity, e-mail, and messaging, file and printer sharing, Internet access, workgroup collaboration, and desktop management.

Chameleon NFS/X includes an NFS client and server software. Chameleon NFS also has NetManage's X-server, which is X11R6.1 compliant. The product also integrates terminal (TN3270/TN5250/Telnet) emulation. Chameleon NFS/X supports Windows NT 4.0. Cut-and-paste of text and graphics between UNIX and Windows desktop applications is supported.

Access NFS

More information on Access NFS is available online from Intergraph at http://www.intergraph.com.

Access NFS is part of the set of products to aid in the integration of Windows NT and UNIX from Intergraph. Access NFS includes:

- DiskAccess — NFS Client
- DiskShare — NFS Server

DiskAccess features: DiskAccess is an NFS client for Windows 95 and Windows NT based on NFS version 3. You can use your familiar Windows interface (Windows Explorer, Network Neighborhood, or File Manager) to browse and connect to file systems and printers located on UNIX or other NFS systems. DiskAccess replaces the PC-NFS product.

With DiskAccess, you can browse NFS file systems without committing a drive letter, accessing network resources as you need them. You also have the option of establishing a full-time link to your server. You can add frequently accessed NFS folders or files as a short-cut to the desktop. You can also use drag-and-drop or OLE-linked objects to establish connections.

DiskAccess supports UNIX-like symbolic links, and browsed connections are mounted and unmounted automatically, even if the desired file is located on an alternate server. You can manage file permissions using Windows property sheets. DiskAccess supports path-based (UNC) access to NFS files. DiskAccess is implemented as a multithreaded system service on Windows NT. On Windows 95, DiskAccess is implemented as a Virtual Device Driver (VxD). DiskAccess uses Microsoft's native TCP/IP stack.

Some of the other features of DiskAccess are:

- Terminal Emulation support for connecting to IBM mainframes, IBM AS/400, and DEC systems
- Network Time Protocol (NTP) supports NTP client to ensure time synchronization
- File Transfer Protocol (FTP) support
- Security functions through support for PCNFSD and NIS
- Utility to convert text files between DOS and UNIX

DiskShare features: DiskShare is an NFS server that runs on Windows NT and makes files on Windows NT available to UNIX and other non-Windows NFS clients. DiskShare provides NFS sharing directly from Windows' My Computer, File Manager, or Explorer interfaces.

DiskShare is implemented as a kernel-mode service, and runs at the most privileged CPU mode (ring 0). DiskShare uses Microsoft's native TCP/IP stack. DiskShare includes support for port mapper (portmap), extended data representation (xdr), mount protocol (mount), and network lock manager (nlm). DiskShare is available for Intel, PowerPC, MIPS, and Alpha processors. (Keep in mind that recently IBM and Microsoft announced that future Windows NT versions will not be supported on the PowerPC.)

DiskShare is integrated with Windows NT security. A system administrator can create or modify NFS user accounts and then associate them with local or domain-based Windows accounts. Once this is done, Windows takes care of the management and control of NFS access to Windows files. When the Windows NT account is modified or deleted, it is instantly reflected in NFS access to the system.

DiskShare supports PCNFSD version 2 to provide security and printing support for PC-based clients.

Intergraph also sells an NFS Solutions bundle that includes both DiskAccess and DiskShare.

InterDrive

InterDrive NT client (available for Windows NT and Windows 95) and InterDrive NT server are file access products from FTP Software. More details are available online at http://www.ftp.com.

InterDrive NT Client

The features of InterDrive client include:

- Installs on either Intel or DEC Alpha platforms
- Mount, Unmount, and Map File systems
- Displays Long, Uppercase, Lowercase, and NTFS, CDFS, and HPFS File Names
- Support for NT 4.0 Shell Extensions, plus maintains backward compatibility with NT 3.51
- Provides multiprocessor performance enhancements
- Support for UNC filenames
- Support for NFS printing
- Interoperates with other Network Operating Systems, such as LAN Manager, Banyan VINES, or Novell NetWare
- Take advantage of file locking
- Easily view and set file permissions from a command line utility
- Automatic alias support and (optional) server discovery
- Multi-user profile support

InterDrive NT Server

The features of InterDrive server include:

- 32-bit multi-threaded kernel-mode NFS server implementation
- Fully integrated LPD network print server
- Installs as a Windows NT service
- Installs/de-installs through network control panel
- Centralized server control application
- Event logging through Windows NT event logger
- Increased Security through advanced access control
- Case-sensitive file name support
- Long file name support
- Context-sensitive online help

Reflection

Reflection is a family of network products from WRQ. The Reflection family includes an NFS client for Windows 95. More details on the Reflection family of products from WRQ are available online at http://www.wrq.com.

Exceptional NFS (Windows 95 only) runs over the Windows 95 stack or WRQ's TCP/IP stack to facilitate integration with Microsoft desktops.

Features of the NFS support for Windows 95 include:

- Browse for NFS resources on the network
- Support for applications that use OLE file-locking, giving multiple users access to OLE
- Document files on NFS drives
- Full DOS session support
- APIs for developers that allow an application to log on to an NFS authentication server and establish connections to exported file systems and/or NFS printers, disconnect, and log off
- RPC (Remote Procedure Call) functions are also provided
- An NFS Administrator that lets you save time searching for server file systems, print queues, and daemons, and translates files from DOS format to UNIX format, and vice versa

ACCESSING WINDOWS NT SERVER FILES FROM UNIX CLIENTS

You can access Windows NT server files from UNIX clients in one of three ways:

- You can have an NFS server installed on Windows NT machines, and UNIX clients can access the Windows NT files just as they would access any other NFS files. NFS was discussed earlier in this chapter.
- You can use a network operating system such as PATHWORKS from Digital. PATHWORKS file functions were covered earlier in this chapter.
- You can let Windows NT provide ftp server functions and transfer files from UNIX clients using ftp.

File Transfer from Windows NT Server to UNIX Clients

Besides the ftp client function, Windows NT also includes the ftp server function. For simple file transfers, UNIX clients can use their ftp client and access the Windows NT ftp server. UNIX clients can also use third-party NFS products.

Windows NT must be running the ftp server (which is the equivalent of the UNIX ftpd daemon) before the UNIX clients can start transferring files. Windows NT versions prior to Version 4 included the ftp server as part of the TCP/IP service. Starting with Version 4, Windows NT includes the ftp server function with a different service, the Peer Web service.

ISSUES IN FILE TRANSFERS

There are issues involving file system differences that you may face when transferring files between UNIX and Windows.

- UNIX supports long file names and you may have to come up with a name in the 8-dot-3 format for DOS or Windows systems using the FAT file system.
- UNIX names are case sensitive and you have to be careful not to overlay files. For example, the files "SampFile" and "Sampfile" are two different files in UNIX, but cannot be two different files in the FAT file system used by DOS and Windows 3.x. Even Windows NT (with NTFS) is case-aware, but not fully case sensitive. Windows NT using NTFS preserves the case of file names when the name was generated and displays the

case in file displays such as Windows NT explorer, but does not use the case information in other file functions such as file searches.

- UNIX files use a linefeed (LF) character for line separation, while Windows NT files use carriage return and linefeed (CRLF). Whether this is a problem depends on the type of file you are transferring and how you use the file after the transfer. If you transfer a text file from UNIX to Windows NT and attempt to print it, this difference could cause a problem. On the other hand, if the file is a program source file and you compile it, then it may not be a problem. Many porting tools, including N*u*TCRACKER, automatically take care of inserting a carriage return (CR) character when required.

PUBLIC DOMAIN PROGRAMS FOR HETEROGENEOUS FILE ACCESS

There are freeware and shareware tools that permit heterogeneous files access. The most popular one is probably Samba. Samba is a program suite that allows clients such as Windows to access files and printers on a server using the SMB (Server Message Block) protocol. Samba started with UNIX. Versions of Samba are now available for NetWare, OS/2, and VMS. A frequently asked question (FAQ) list on Samba is available online at http://samba.canberra.edu.au/pub/samba/docs/faq/sambafaq.html.

NETWORK DIRECTORIES

When you want to access directories in a Windows environment, you can do this in one of two ways. You can map network directories to drive letters. Alternately, you can have directory replication.

MAPPING NETWORK DRIVES

You can map a network directory to a drive letter. After this mapping, you can access directories and files using the drive letter, just as you would any local drive. Typically, the drive letters a: and b: are used for local floppy drives, and the drive letter c: for the local primary hard drive or partition. Additional partitions and CD-ROM drives are assigned drive letters starting with D:. When you assign drive letters for network drives, you are free to choose any unassigned letter. You can map a network directory using Windows NT explorer.

DIRECTORY REPLICATION

Directory replication, as the name implies, is the mechanism by which copies of directories on a server are replicated on client workstations. If you or your users are frequently accessing files across the network, then directory replication will be of interest to you. Both Windows NT Server and Windows NT Workstation support directory replication.

How Does Replication Work?

You create a set of exported directories on a file server. The exported directories are imported by the client workstations on the network. Changes to the contents of the exported directories on the server are automatically reflected on the imported directories at the workstations. This capability is useful in creating a standard directory setup for all the machines on a network.

COMPARING REPLICATION AND DRIVE MAPPING

The primary difference between replication and drive mapping is that the directories imported through replication reside on the local disk and behave the same way as other local mappings. This means that the performance of accessing the replicated directory is faster than accessing the

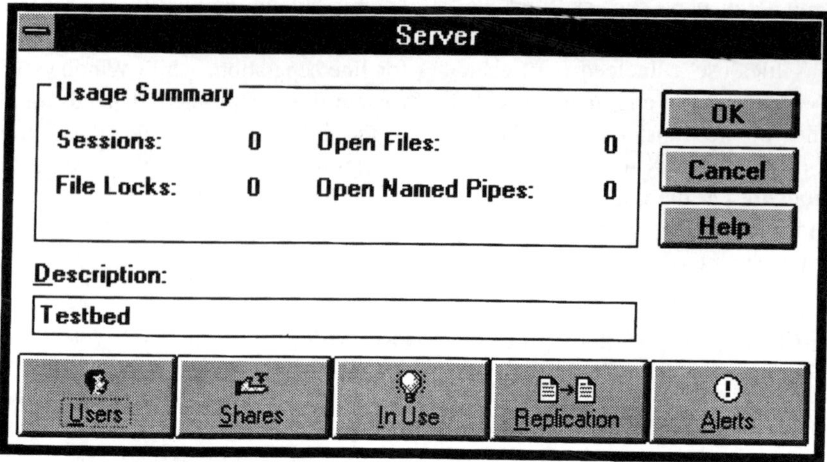

FIGURE 8.8 Selecting directory replication in the Server dialog.

same directory across a network. Probably, a more significant benefit of replication is that changes in server and network configurations may cause consequent changes to your drive mappings. This may cause setup and application problems where the mapped drive letters are used. Use of a local drive for replication shields many of these changes from your client workstation setup and applications.

Setting up and Monitoring Directory Replication

You can set up directory replication at a Windows NT workstation by following these steps:

- Set up a logon account at the server for the workstation replication service. Since this is a not a "real user" account, typical user account features such as expiring passwords should not apply to this account. In addition, ensure that the account has backup rights.
- Choose the **Replication** button from the Server Dialog box (Figure 8.8).
- In the Directory Replication dialog box, select the **Import Directories** option (Figure 8.9).
- Change the path name where the replicated directories will be created, if you do not want the default that Windows NT provides.
- Click the **Add** button to get a Select Domain dialog box as shown in Figure 8.10.
- Select a domain from the list provided, and click **OK**.

You can monitor replication activity in your Windows NT server or Windows NT workstation using the Server applet in the Control Panel.

PRINTING FROM WINDOWS CLIENTS TO UNIX NETWORK PRINTERS

In a UNIX network, UNIX clients use software called Line Print Requester (LPR) to issue print requests to UNIX servers that control the printers. The UNIX servers run a daemon — the Line Printer Daemon, which receives requests with the print output from the LPRs and transfers the print output to the print queue. The printers can be attached directly to the UNIX machine or directly to the network.

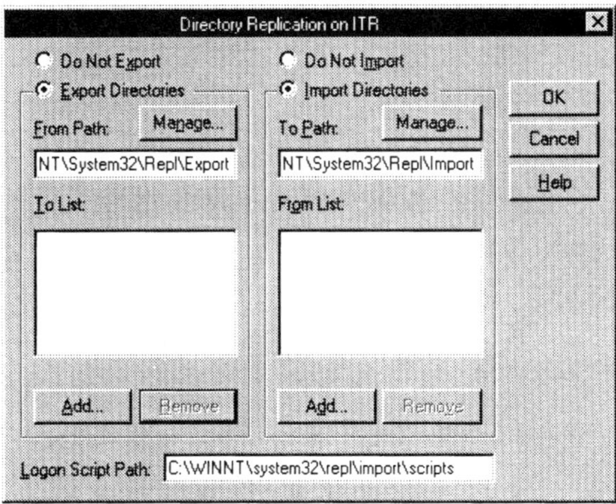

FIGURE 8.9 Main menu of server applet in control panel.

To access a UNIX network printer from a Windows client, you need to set up TCP/IP with the following set up information:

- The IP address (or the remote system alias)
- The name of the remote print queue
- TCP/IP printing option installation and configuration information

Once you collect the information, you can install TCP/IP printing service in Windows NT using the following steps.

1. Double-click the network icon from the **Control Panel,** under **Settings**, under **Start**.
2. Click the **Services** tab, and then click the **Add** button.
3. Click the Microsoft TCP/IP Printing Service from the list and click OK. This installs the TCP/IP printing service and the service is available to use when you restart your computer.

Once you have set up Microsoft TCP/IP printing services, you need to set up a printer port for the UNIX printer you want to print to. The following steps add a printer port.

1. Select **Printers**, under **Settings**, under **Start** (you can also use the control panel and double-click the printer icon). Note that the number and names of existing printers in your dialog will be different.
2. Double-click the **Add Printer** icon. Don't be concerned by the title "Add Printer." Add Printer not only adds printers, but it is also used to add printer ports.
3. Click the **My Computer** button (even though you want to print to a network printer).
4. Click **Add Port** and get to the Add LPR-compatible dialog.
5. Enter the IP address (or DNS name alias) and the printer (or printer queue) name.

Windows NT will try communicating with the printer and will give you an error message if it is not able to communicate with the printer. (If this happens, then it is most likely because your setup information is incorrect.)

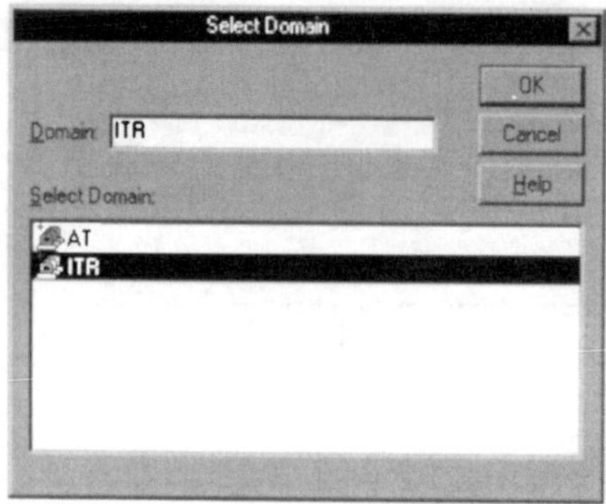

FIGURE 8.10 Directory replication status.

Once you have added a port, you assign the UNIX network printer to the port by following these steps.

1. Click the box next to the port entry you just created for the network UNIX printer.
2. Select the manufacturer and model of your printer. Depending on your setup, Windows may prompt you to insert the Windows NT CD-ROM to copy the printer drivers for your printer from the CD-ROM.
3. Once the drivers are successfully copied, enter a name for the printer that makes it easy to identify the printer. This name will show up when you select Printer setup (or similarly named) function that lets you select the printer.
4. Optionally, you can share the printer with other computers. If you opt to share, you need to enter a share name and the computers that will be sharing the printer.

You may want to test your setup and access to the printer by printing a page.

Once you complete the setup, using the printer is just the same as using any shared printer attached to a Windows NT network.

PRINTING FROM UNIX CLIENTS TO WINDOWS NETWORK PRINTERS

In the prior section we looked at printing from a Windows client to a UNIX printer. You can go the other way too. You can print from a UNIX client to Windows NT-accessible network printers. The printer can be directly attached to a Windows NT server, or can be directly attached to the network, or can even be a NetWare printer that Windows NT can access.

Printing to a Windows network printer is transparent to a UNIX client. The UNIX client uses *lpr* just as it would for printing to a UNIX network printer. Windows NT server should be running the *lpdsvc* for the *lpr* to communicate to. You can start the *lpdsvc* if it is not already running, either by using the command line (key in *net start lpdsvc* at the command prompt) or using the GUI (Click Start, Settings, Control Panel, double-click Services, click TCP/IP Print Services, click Start). If you print regularly from UNIX clients to Windows network printers in your environment, then it may be more convenient to automatically start the TCP/IP Print Services whenever the system is booted. To designate that TCP/IP Print Services should be started automatically, select TCP/IP services as mentioned earlier, click the Startup button, and set the start-up type to Automatic and click OK.

You can check on the status of your print requests using the UNIX *lpq* command (just as you would for any UNIX network print request).

Accessing MS-DOS Files from UNIX

You can use Mtools to access diskettes and other media using the MS-DOS file system. Mtools is a public domain collection of programs that allow UNIX systems to read, write, and manipulate files in an MS-DOS file system, such as a diskette. Due to the differences in the environments, it is not possible to reproduce the command exactly as in MS-DOS. Each program attempts to emulate the MS-DOS equivalent command as closely as practical. There is a lot of information available on the Internet about Mtools, and the following is a brief extract. Information on Mtools is available at http://wauug.erols.com/pub/knaff/mtools.

Table 8.2 summarizes the commands available as part of Mtools.

TABLE 8.2
Mtools Commands and Descriptions

Mtool Command	Description
mattrib	Change MS-DOS file attribute flags
mcopy	Copy MS-DOS files to/from UNIX
mcd	Change MS-DOS directory
mdel	Delete an MS-DOS file
mdir	Display an MS-DOS directory
mformat	Add an MS-DOS file system to a low-level formatted diskette
mlabel	Make an MS-DOS volume label
mmd	Make an MS-DOS subdirectory
mrd	Remove an MS-DOS subdirectory
mread	Low-level read (copy) an MS-DOS file to Unix
mren	Rename an existing MS-DOS file
mtype	Display contents of an MS-DOS file
mwrite	Low-level write (copy) a Unix file to MS-DOS

MS-DOS filenames are optionally composed of a drive letter followed by a colon, a subdirectory, and a filename. Subdirectory names can use either the '/' or '\' separator. The use of the '\' separator or wildcards will require the names to be enclosed in quotes to protect them from the shell.

The regular expression "pattern matching" routines follow the Unix-style rules. For example, '*' matches all MS-DOS files in lieu of '*.*'. The archive, hidden, read-only, and system attribute bits are ignored during pattern matching.

Not all UNIX filenames are appropriate in the MS-DOS world. The Mtools commands may have to alter Unix names to fit the MS-DOS filename restrictions. Most commands have a -v (verbose) option that will display the new names if they have been changed. The following table (Table 8.3) shows some examples of filename conversions.

Unlike UNIX, MS-DOS filesystem is not case sensitive.

All options use the '–' (minus) flag, not '/' as you'd expect in MS-DOS.

The *mcd* command is used to establish the device and the current working directory (relative to the MS-DOS filesystem); otherwise, the default is assumed to be A:/.

All the Mtools commands return 0 on success, 1 on total failure, or 2 on partial failure.

Conclusion

In this chapter, we looked at how you can access a UNIX server from Windows clients for print and file services. We also looked at the reverse of accessing a Windows NT server from a UNIX client.

TABLE 8.3
UNIX and Windows File Name Conversion

UNIX Name	MS-DOS Name	Reason for Change
Thisisatest	THISISAT	Filename too long
Emmet.gray	EMMET.GRA	Extension too long
prn.txt	XRN.TXT	PRN is a device name, not allowed in filename
.abc	X.ABC	Null filename
Hot+cold	HOTXCOLD	Illegal character

This concludes the coexistence part. In Part Three, we will take a look at system administration and other considerations such as e-mail and Internet access in heterogeneous environments.

Part Three

Systems Administration and Other Considerations

Thus far, we have focused on applications. In Part One, we looked at porting current applications and developing new applications. In Part Two, we looked at application coexistence in heterogeneous environments.

Now let us focus on systems administration aspects in heterogeneous environments. We will start by taking a look at the different administration functions in managing heterogeneous environments. Then we will look at what UNIX administrators use every day — UNIX shell and utilities — and look at some tools that let the UNIX shell and utilities be available in Windows NT. Subsequently, we will look at some typical systems administration functions and see how equivalent functions are implemented in Windows and UNIX. Finally, we will look at Windows and NetWare. Microsoft has included a number of built-in functions in Windows NT to coexist in NetWare networks. Microsoft also provides tools to let NetWare users migrate to Windows NT without having to recreate valuable systems administration data.

9 Managing Heterogeneous Environments

INTRODUCTION

In a heterogeneous network that includes Windows NT and UNIX, there are products available that let you perform systems administration functions for the complete heterogeneous network from either a Windows NT workstation or a UNIX workstation. Full coverage of these topics is beyond the scope of this book. The book will focus on just the migration and coexistence aspects. The systems administration functions in a heterogeneous environment include:

- Enterprise systems management
- Disk and file backup and restore
- System performance management
- Security management
- Helpdesk software
- Background job scheduling
- Software distribution and asset management
- Output management
- Network management
- Application management

Enterprise systems management provides cohesive, integrated administration of the entire IT infrastructure of an organization, which could include systems, networks, applications, and databases, Internet access, desktops, processors, and PDAs. *Disk and file backup* provides these functions across heterogeneous environments. *System performance management* collects and displays performance data from heterogeneous systems in a consistent manner. *Security management* functions are typically provided by the operating system, and the level of security provided is indicated in a scale. The scale ranges include D (least secure level) to A (most secure level), with intermediate classifications. The level that most operating system vendors aim for and that is required in many federal computer procurements is C2. Windows NT meets the requirements for the C2 security level and so does Digital UNIX. With an optional product, DEC MLS+, Digital UNIX can meet some security requirements at the B1 level. Digital UNIX, starting with version 4.0, also includes support for Access Control Lists (ACLs). ACLs are standard in Windows NT. UNIX includes some basic *background job scheduling* functions such as *cron* and *at*. Windows NT includes *at*. But many organizations need much more sophisticated job scheduling functions and typically use third-party software. Output management deals with printing, spooling, paging, and other output operations in a heterogeneous environment.

Table 9.1 lists the different system administration functions to be performed and the various vendor products that are available.

TABLE 9.1
Systems Administration in a Heterogeneous Environment

	Enterprise Systems Management	Disk and File Backup and Restore	System Performance Management	Security Management	Help Desk Software	Background Job Scheduling	Software Distribution and Asset Management	Output Management	Network Management	Application Management
Computer Associates	CA-Unicenter TNG		POLYCENTER Performance Manager				POLYCENTER Asset Works		POLYCENTER PathDoctor, Unicenter TNG	
Open Systems Management	COSMOS					COS/Batch	COS/Relay	COS/Report COS/Print		
OpenVision Technology	AXXiON family	AXXiON NetBackup		AXXiON						
PLATINUM Technology	System Management Suite	PLATINUM Tsreorg	ServerVision		PLATINUM Apriori	AutoSys	AutoXfer	AutoDeliver	WireTap, Trans Tracker	DBVision
Tivoli Systems	TME 10						TME 10		TME 10 NetView	TME 10/Plus
Cheyenne Software		ARCserve 6								
Digital Equipment		POLYCENTER Networker	Resource Broker						PATHWORKS, ServerWorks	
Spectra Logic		Alexandria Backup Librarian								
BGS Systems			BEST/1							

BMC Software	Knowledge Modules							PATROL
Candle	Candle Command Center, OMEGAMON							
Compuware	EcoTOOLS, EcoSCOPE							EcoTools
Datametrics System	ViewPoint							
Axent Technologies		OmniGuard						
Applix			Applix Enterprise					
Silvon Software			Helpline		Insite			
Unison Software				Maestro				
Novadigm					Enterprise Desktop Manager			
DAZEL						DAZEL Output Management System		

UNIX SHELL AND UTILITIES ON WINDOWS NT

Developers and system administrators in the UNIX environment make extensive use of the UNIX shell — the command prompt environment of UNIX. GUI environments such as the Common Desktop Environment (CDE) have been added to many UNIX systems. But the shell is still very popular. The situation is analogous in the Windows world. DOS is a pure command prompt environment. Initial versions of Windows overlaid a GUI environment on top of DOS. In subsequent versions of Windows, with Windows GUI user acceptance, the user interface has become primarily graphical, although it is still possible to use the command prompt.

Users starting to use Windows NT after using UNIX have the same reaction as the first DOS users who started using Windows. They want to "drop down" into the command prompt environment. You can delete a file, for example, in one of two ways. You can use the DOS *delete* command and key in the file name to be deleted. You can also use the File Manager or Windows Explorer, select the file, and delete the file using a few clicks of the mouse.

UNIX Shell and Windows Command Prompt

The advantage that the command prompt offered then and what the shell offers now is the same — familiarity. UNIX users starting to use Windows NT can use Windows right away if the familiar shell is still available on Windows. This is the main idea behind offering the UNIX shell on Windows NT. There are other advantages of being able to use a UNIX shell on Windows, and these are covered later in this chapter.

Keep in mind, however, that the UNIX shell is much more powerful compared to the functions of the DOS or even Windows NT command prompt. Windows NT has *cmd.exe,* which is a souped-up version of the *command.com* of DOS with added commands and additional options to existing commands. UNIX shell functions include:

- The primary difference in power comes from the fact that the shell is more like a programming language than a scripting language, with support for variables, arrays, expressions, procedures, test and branch options, and looping.
- Multi-command buffering to permit you to retrieve prior commands and avoid retyping (DOS permits recall of the last command with the **F3** key, and Windows NT command prompt supports the last few commands with the up arrow) as well as the ability to search prior commands.
- Synchronize the date and time of files on a group of files that need to synchronized — such as the files that make up one version of a product.
- Search all source code files in a directory for specific characters.
- Support for command aliases.
- Sophisticated support for completing partial file names compared to the * and ? options.
- Perform batch processing of commands. This is conceptually the same as the *bat* files in DOS. However, since the commands themselves are more powerful, you can accomplish much more with batch processing compared to *bat* files.
- Schedule tasks on your computer for later processing.

If you are a manager and you are trying to decide if you should invest in a third-party product that provides the UNIX shell on Windows NT, then you have to decide if the cost of the third-party product is worth the advantages listed below:

- Allows your developers and systems administrators to be productive without having to undergo an extensive learning curve

- Existing investment in scripts for application development and systems administration can be protected and reused with very little change

So far, we have been talking about the UNIX shell as if there was just one shell. Actually, there are three primary shells — Bourne, Korn, and C shells. The Korn shell, for the most part, is compatible with the older Bourne shell. The C shell, on the other hand, is not compatible with either Korn or Bourne shells. When you are looking at products that support the UNIX shell on Windows, ensure that the product you select supports the shell(s) you use. The MKS toolkit, for example, supports the Korn shell, while the Hamilton C Shell supports the C shell, and Portage supports both the Korn shell and the C shell.

UNIX shell support in Windows can come from three sources:

- Shareware and freeware sources
- Microsoft, which has developed some UNIX tools
- Third-party sources

As mentioned earlier in the book, the main problem you face with public domain software is one of support. That said, UNIX shell is one area where you get better public domain software compared to other software areas.

Shell Support from Microsoft

Microsoft has some built-in commands that are also used in UNIX. These include TCP/IP commands such as *ping, ftp,* and *rcp.*

Microsoft also includes additional shell commands. These are not built into Windows NT, but they are available in the Windows NT Resource kit. Besides the popular ones such as the *vi* editor, the applications-building utility *make*, the kit also includes *ar, cat, cc, chmod, chown, cp, find, grep, ld, ln, ls, mkdir, mv, rm, rmdir, sh, tape, touch,* and *wc*. The kit doesn't include *diff*, but does include an equivalent utility called *windiff.*

While the list included with the Windows NT Resource kit may be sufficient for some users, it is normally not enough for power UNIX users. UNIX shells are available from third-party sources to provide a more complete UNIX shell environment on top of Windows NT. The third-party shells include:

- MKS Toolkit from Mortice Kern Systems (MKS)
- Hamilton C shell from Hamilton Laboratories
- Portage Base System
- OpenNT from Softway

MKS Toolkit from Mortice Kern Systems (MKS)

More details on the MKS Toolkit are available online from MKS at http://www.mks.com.

The MKS Toolkit is more than a shell. It includes the Korn shell, the *vi* text editor, *make* for building applications, the data reporting *awk* language, a *visual diff* utility (a graphical equivalent for the text-based source comparison utility *diff*), and a graphical scheduler to run backup and other unattended jobs.

The MKS Korn shell supports three modes of command line editing:

- Native mode, which emulates the DOS box in Windows
- vi mode to emulate the *vi* editor
- EMACS to emulate the popular EMACS editor

The MKS Toolkit includes online help and an electronic manual. The *tar* format is commonly used on UNIX systems to read and write tapes. Using the MKS Toolkit, you can create a *tar* formatted tape on Windows for use with UNIX systems. The MKS Toolkit is available on Windows 95 and all of Windows NT's supported hardware platforms.

The N*u*TCRACKER product to port applications from UNIX to Windows, from Datafocus, includes the MKS toolkit. N*u*TCRACKER is discussed in Chapter 3.

Hamilton C Shell from Hamilton Laboratories

More details on the Hamilton C Shell are available by e-mail (hamilton@bix.com).

Hamilton C Shell recreates the UNIX shell environment on PCs running Windows 95 or on workstations running OS/2 or Windows NT on all platforms supported by Windows NT (Intel, Alpha, PowerPC [up to Windows NT 3.51], MIPS). The Hamilton C Shell supports the UNIX development shell environment with support for *cat, cp, diff, du, head, mv, rm, tail, touch, tr, wc,* among others. Like the MKS Toolkit, the Hamilton C Shell also supports the *tar* format for generating UNIX-compatible tapes in Windows NT. The Hamilton C Shell supports the Windows NT command line editing keys as in Windows NT and adds functionality by using additional keystroke combinations.

Portage Base

The following is a brief summary of Portage from Consensys Web pages. More details on the Portage Base are available online from Consensys at http://www.consensys.com. (Be careful when you type in Consensys, as there is another company with the name Consensus and the address http://www.consensus.com). Consensys also provides products to port from UNIX to Windows, and these are discussed in Chapter 3.

Let us look at the UNIX shell and utilities function provided by the Portage Base.

The UNIX Shell in Portage

Portage provides both the Korn Shell (*ksh*) and the C Shell (*csh*). Both of these shells run in the console. This means that you can set a very large buffer size, say 200 lines or more, and keep that much interactive history available for browsing. You can launch a *ksh* or *csh* from icons in the Portage program group. You can also simply type *ksh* or *csh* at an NT command prompt. If you want to run multiple shells (maximum of 20 can be active at any one time), the preferred method is probably to use the Portage Windows Interface to start them.

Once you are running *ksh* or *csh*, you are in a UNIX environment. The shell window provides an emulation of a VT100 terminal (a VT100 subset), and your *term* environment variable will be set to vt100. The window also provides a limited *tty* line discipline, and you can use *stty*(1) to view the options in effect or to change a subset of them.

In general, you should be unable to tell the difference between the behavior under one of the Portage UNIX shells and a native SVR4 implementation. A list of the few known differences is provided in the Portage documentation.

If you prefer graphical user interfaces, Portage includes the Portage Windows Interface, which serves a number of important functions:

- It allows you to easily start up and manage multiple UNIX shells.
- It allows you to customize the default settings of your shell windows (e.g., size, colors, etc.).
- It provides a dialog box interface to all Portage UNIX commands.
- It provides easy access to online manual pages for every command.

You can start up the Portage Windows Interface by clicking on its icon in the Portage program group. The program's main feature is a set of 140 buttons providing dialog-box access to UNIX utilities. The Portage SDK has an even larger set of buttons (170) than the Base System. Screen shots are available at http://www.consensys.com.

UNIX Utilities in Portage

All Portage utilities can be run from the NT Command Prompt or console. Since the Command Prompt passes command line arguments to programs unchanged (unlike UNIX shells, which perform wild-card expansion and much more), Portage programs are able to provide an overlapping set of UNIX-like and DOS-like syntax. In particular, from the Windows NT Command Prompt, path names can use either UNIX style / or Windows style \\ notation. Supported functions include:

- Pattern matching is UNIX style, including '*', '?', single quotes, and double quotes
- The Portage environment variables (UNIXROOT, UNIXTMP, SYMLINKS \& CASE-NAMES) are in effect

Of course, shell-specific features like \$X for environment variables and backquotes for sub-shells are not available from the Command Prompt.

An example of a valid Command Prompt command line is *ls -lrt /bin/b**.

There are several name conflicts between NT commands and Portage UNIX utilities. The echo command is built into the Command Prompt (as it is in UNIX shells), so it will always use the NT syntax. Other commands like *more* and *mkdir* are not built in, so you will get whichever one is found first by following your PATH environment variable.

When Portage is installed, the *bin* directory is added to the end of your PATH, so by default you will get the NT version of these utilities. You can change the PATH environment variable but that may break existing batch and other Windows NT functions using the Path. The simplest solution is to use one of the UNIX shells, where \$PORTAGE/bin is added to the front of the PATH environment variable by default.

N*u*TCRACKER

More details on N*u*TCRACKER are available from http://www.datafocus.com. As mentioned earlier under MKS Toolkit, N*u*TCRACKER includes the MKS Toolkit under an agreement between Datafocus and Mortice Kern Systems. N*u*TCRACKER also has some additional utilities such as *chmod, whoami, process, sdiff*, etc. The N*u*TCRACKER *Installation and Porting Guide* included in the CD accompanying this book has a complete list of the utilities.

If you are used to using GNU tools, Congruent Corporation provides Toolbuster which provides GNU utilities, compilers, debuggers, editors, etc. for Windows NT.

HETEROGENEOUS NETWORK MANAGEMENT USING SNMP

SNMP stands for Simple Network Management Protocol. It is a standard protocol that is used in many system management software products, including system management software for UNIX systems and heterogeneous systems. Some of the products that use the SNMP protocol include Openview from HP, and TME 10 Netview from Tivoli Systems (part of IBM).

System management software provides centralized and formatted status information about all SNMP supporting devices on the network. The devices that support SNMP could range from simple hardware devices to complete computer systems. The software in these devices that inform the system management software running on servers are called SNMP agents. SNMP agents convey status information to SNMP-based system management servers in one of two ways:

- Send alerts
- Respond to queries

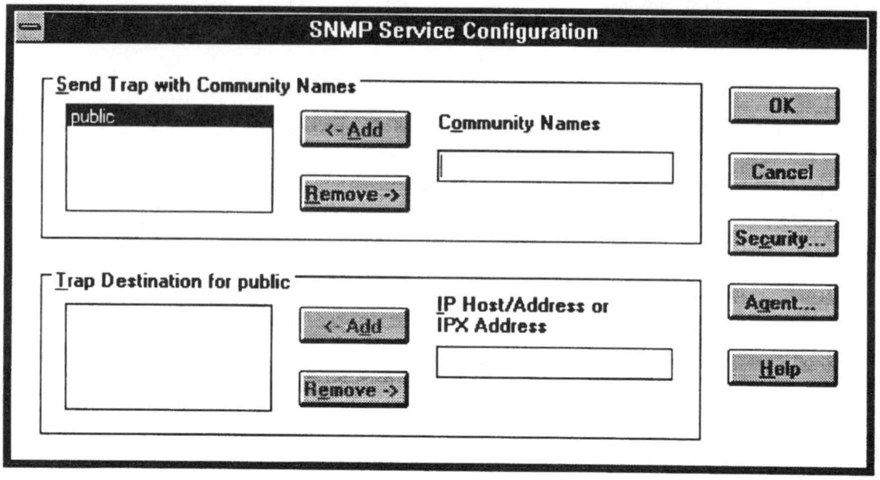

FIGURE 9.1 SNMP service configuration.

Alerts are for serious errors and are broadcast by the device over the network to get attention. Queries are specific communications between the system management software and the SNMP devices and are typically used to communicate regular status messages.

Most UNIX systems and Windows NT support SNMP.

Installing and Configuring SNMP in Windows NT

SNMP support is implemented as a service (a *service* in Windows NT is the equivalent of a *daemon* in UNIX) in Windows NT, and you install this service the same way as you would any other Windows NT service. (From **Start**, select **Settings**, then choose **Control Panel** and double-click the network icon in the Control Panel. Select the **Services** tab and, from the list of services shown, click SNMP service and click OK.) The SNMP is installed and will be available the next time you restart the machine.

Configuring SNMP involves specifying community names for sending traps and specifying IP addresses. The menu in Windows NT to specify SNMP service configuration information is shown in Figure 9.1.

DIRECTORY SERVICES MANAGER FOR NETWARE

NetWare 2.x/3.x and 4.x servers (those that are managed via the NetWare bindery) have to be managed individually. This includes managing the users in each server as well. Windows NT Server includes global directory services and can help users manage multiple environments. Windows NT server offers users the possibility of single network logon to all services, including applications, and provides administrators with a central point of administration.

With Windows NT Server and DSMN, NetWare customers can centrally manage their mixed Windows NT and NetWare environments with the Windows NT Directory Services. DSMN copies the NetWare user accounts to the Windows NT Directory Service and then propagates any changes back to the NetWare server. This is done without the need to install any software on the NetWare servers.

DSMN simplifies network administration tasks. Administrators can centrally manage their Windows NT Server and NetWare account information while having to maintain only one user account and associated password for each end-user on the network. DSMN includes:

- A point-and-click interface for propagating user and group accounts from NetWare 2.x/3.x (and 4.x in bindery emulation mode) to Windows NT Directory Services.
- Multiple options for setting up initial passwords, selecting which user accounts to propagate each way, handling account deletions, and even doing a "trial run" to test a propagation strategy.
- Windows NT Directory Service manages Windows NT Server from the server console, or from anywhere else on the network (including remotely via dialup) from a Windows NT workstation or, new with version 4.0, Windows 95-based desktop.
- Account database backup and replication to any location on the network.

DSMN simplifies end-user network access. DSMN also simplifies network access for end-users in the following ways:

- New users are up and running quickly because the administrator does the setup in Windows NT Server directory services, and the user account is automatically propagated back to all authorized NetWare servers.
- Each user's account name and password are identical on all NetWare and Windows NT servers, so they use the same name and password regardless of where they log on.
- Using Windows NT server remote access services (RAS), users can log on via dialup with the same account name and password.
- Windows NT Directory Service can authenticate users to applications running on Windows NT server. Thus, with a single logon, users can get access to business applications in addition to Windows NT server file and print services.

DYNAMIC HOST CONFIGURATION PROTOCOL

If you have played around with TCP/IP configuration information such as IP addresses and subnet masks when you set up your Internet service, you have a pretty good idea of the complexity involved in setting up TCP/IP. In a business setting, the administrators used to spend a fair amount of time setting this configuration, primarily because it was necessary to set this up at each client and making changes meant making them at the client level.

Windows NT supports the Dynamic Host Configuration Protocol (DHCP) to reduce the work associated with network configurations, in particular setting IP addresses. DHCP dynamically assigns addresses and ensures that there are no duplicates and thus relieves the major problems with manual configurations. Since it is the DHCP (and not an administrator) that keeps track of addresses, it is easy to reuse addresses and manage the IP address allocation and management centrally.

DHCP lets the administrator specify some parameters for the IP addresses such as "lease durations." When DHCP assigns an IP address to a client, the address is actually assigned temporarily for a finite time called "lease." Lease durations specify how long a computer can use an assigned IP address before having to renew the lease with the DHCP server.

The typical scenario that happens in many businesses that administrators used to dread is when a computer is moved from one subnet to another. Administrators are used to manually assigning a new address and deleting the old one. With DHCP, the IP address is released automatically when the DHCP client is removed from a subnet, and a new address is automatically assigned when the (moved) DHCP client is reconnected on another subnet. There is no manual intervention (from either the user or the administrator) to accomplish the address change. Contrast this with the earlier manual scenario. The dynamic address assignment feature is particularly useful for portable computer users.

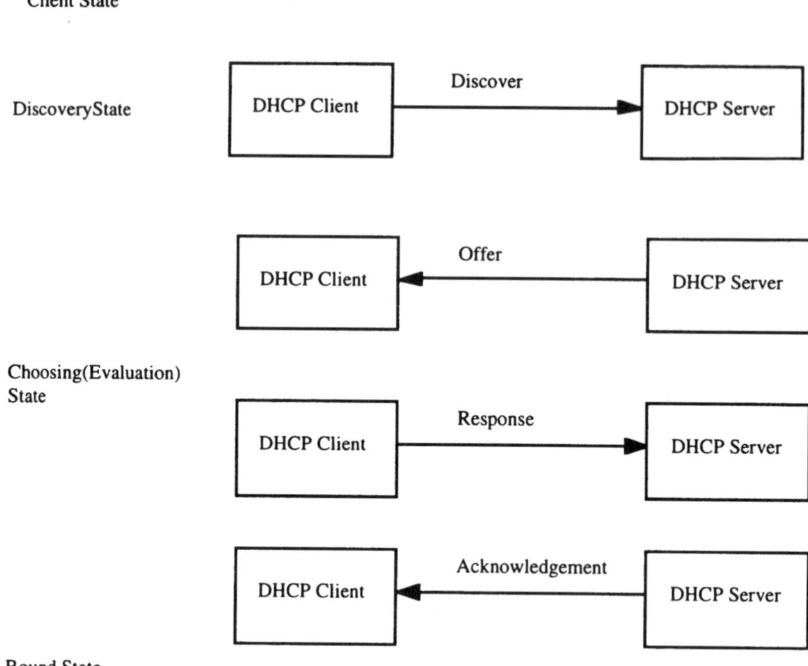

FIGURE 9.2 DHCP IP address assignment process.

How Does DHCP Work?

DHCP is implemented at the client and the server. The DHCP server assigns the addresses while the DHCP client asks for an address. When a DHCP client boots up, the DHCP client broadcasts a discover message. This message is sent to all DHCP servers in the local network as well as other DHCP servers set up to receive the broadcasts. Every DHCP server that receives a *discover* message responds with an *offer* message. The *offer* is sent to the requesting DHCP client (not broadcast). The *offer* contains an IP address and valid configuration information for the client that sent the request. The DHCP client may thus receive multiple responses to its broadcast. The DHCP client must then choose one of the offers. It does this and is said to be in a *choosing state* when it is evaluating the *offers*. Once the DHCP client decides on the offer, it then responds to the offer to complete the address setup.

The selected DHCP server receives the response from the DHCP client to its offer. The DHCP server then sends a DHCP acknowledgment message to the DHCP client. The acknowledgment message contains the address it sent with the offer (in response to the discover message). The acknowledgment message also contains a valid lease for the address and the TCP/IP network configuration parameters for the client. The client receives the acknowledgment and enters a bound state.

The DHCP client can now participate on the TCP/IP network. Since this process occurred some time during the bootup, the client completes the rest of the booting process. If a network connection could not be established (for example, if the computer is not connected to a network or the network card is not installed), the address assignment will not occur and the bootup indicates errors. The address that has been assigned is valid for the lease duration. As mentioned earlier, system administrators decide valid lease durations for the installation. The DHCP client attempts to renew the lease when it is about to expire, if an IP address is still required. Typically, it would renew the existing lease. If for any reason, it is unable to renew the lease (the server that assigned the lease is not available, for example), then the DHCP client restarts the discovery process. Figure 9.2 illustrates the DHCP IP address assignment process.

Windows NT Server includes a DHCP Manager. Windows NT system/network administrators use the DHCP manager to define policies for address allocation, leases, etc.

WINDOWS INTERNET NAMING SERVICE (WINS)

WINS solves the problem of locating network resources in a TCP/IP-based Microsoft network. WINS performs this function by configuring and maintaining the computer name and IP-address mapping tables, which can be looked up whenever a name-address mapping is required. WINS performs the mapping updates automatically. Because it maintains the mapping table, WINS can detect, alert, and correct error situations such as duplicate names and addresses. WINS is a complementary service to DHCP and is not a prerequisite. WINS also includes the user interfaces required for administration and configuration of the WINS servers, static name tables, and replication information.

WINS CONFIGURATION

We saw earlier how the message exchanges between DHCP clients and servers. Once the DHCP client gets an address with a valid lease, and is in the bound state, the client registers its name with the designated WINS server. The client issues a direct request to the WINS server and sends the *NameRegistrationRequest* with the DHCP client's computer name and leased IP address.

The WINS server uses its mapping table to validate that the requesting computer name is unique on the network. It responds to the client with either a positive or a negative WINS name registration response message. A positive response indicates a successful WINS registration. As part of the registration response, the WINS server includes the Time To Live (TTL) for the name registration. This is roughly equivalent to the lease duration issued by the DHCP server. If the WINS server is unable to complete registration (e.g., if the validation for name uniqueness fails), it sends a negative registration response message. The user is notified of the error.

WINS TTL renewal

Renewal of TTL for a WINS client is, for the most part, simple and automatic. The NetBIOS over TCP/IP (NBT) client process automatically registers the computer name with the WINS-based server whenever the NBT client process is started. The WINS server automatically renews (issues a new TTL whenever NBT registration occurs). There is also a timer service to request an NBT registration in the event that no automatic NBT registration happened in the interim.

10 Comparing NT and UNIX System Administration

INTRODUCTION

Continuing our focus on *system administration* aspects, this chapter will go into various system administration functions and point out how equivalent functions are performed in UNIX and Windows NT.

The primary difference between system administration in UNIX compared to Windows NT is in the end-user interface. Windows NT uses the graphical user interface, while the command line (character-based interface) is used heavily in UNIX. UNIX shells and Windows command prompts are discussed in Chapter 9. There are some system administration functions in some UNIX systems using the X-Windows-based graphical interface. However, the X-Windows is an add-on that may or may not be used, unlike Windows NT where the primary means of user interface is the Windows GUI.

The second important difference stems from the fact that Windows NT is based on the client/server model. This changes the concept of users, user administration, and other system administration functions as well.

EQUIVALENT WINDOWS NT, UNIX ADMINISTRATION FUNCTIONS

The primary menu for system administration functions in Windows NT is shown in Figure 10.1. You get to this menu by double-clicking **Windows NT Administration**, under **Programs**, under **Start**, in Windows NT 4.0.

In UNIX, you log on as the "root" to perform system administration functions.

LOGON/LOGOFF

Administrator logon

UNIX: The administrator logs on as the "root." This automatically sets all the privileges required by the administrator to perform administration functions, as shown in Figure 10.2.
Windows NT: The administrator logs on as the "administrator" (Windows is not case sensitive, in general). You can get to the logon screen by pressing CTRL+ALT+DEL when no one is logged onto the system. This brings up a screen to enter userid and password. If some user is already logged onto the system, remember to log the user off because the user may not have the administrator privileges you need to perform system administration functions.

Changing Administrator Privileges

UNIX: You can change your ID and privileges using *su*. When you logon from a terminal other than the system console, your system may not allow you to logon as "root" as shown in Figure 10.3.

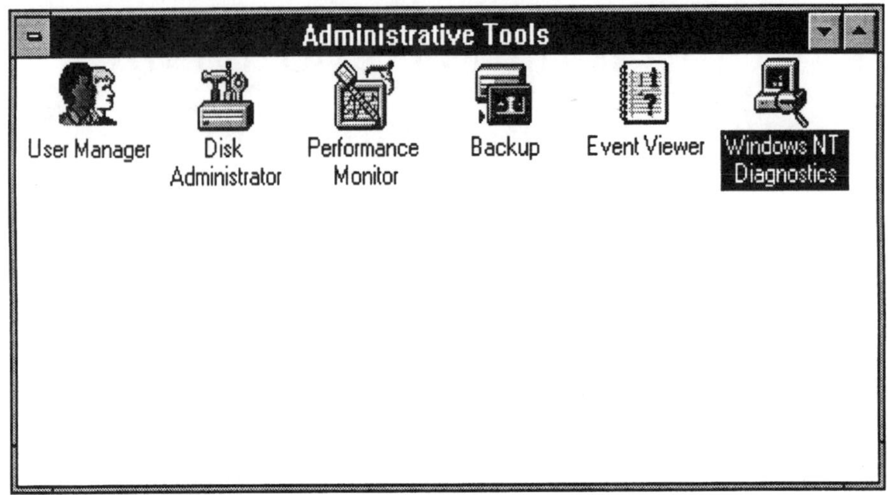

FIGURE 10.1 Main system administration menu in Windows NT.

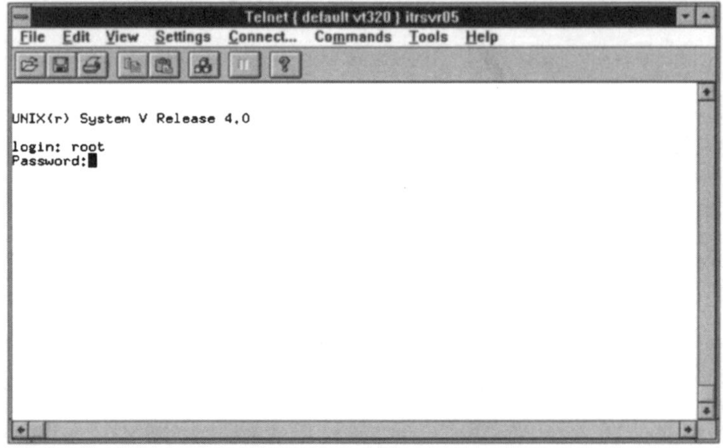

FIGURE 10.2 UNIX system administrator logs in as root.

If this is the case, logon as another user (this is one example where you should have your personal id, besides "root"). Then you can get the privileges of "root" by using the *su* command as shown in Figure 10.4.

Windows NT: An alternate way of performing administrative functions in Windows NT (other than logging in as administrator) is to grant administrator privileges to your personal (non-administrator) account via the User Manager. Of course, this privilege can be granted the first time only when you log on as the administrator. However, it is a good idea to keep the administrator privileges only with the administrator ID. From time to time, if you want to check if some functions are not available to non-administrator IDs, the simplest way is to use your personal ID (without special privileges). This is another reason for keeping your personal ID separate from your administrator ID.

There is no direct equivalent of *su* in Windows NT. If you want to change your ID, you need to log off and log on as another user.

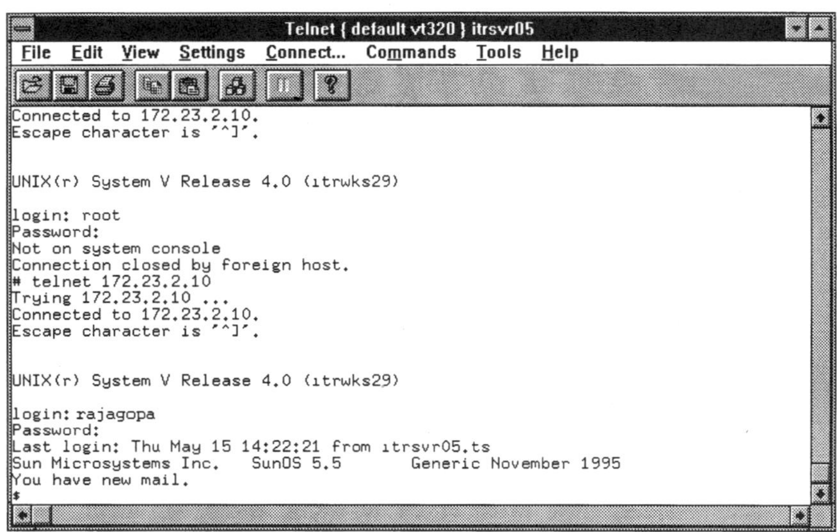

FIGURE 10.3 Prevent system administration login from non-system console.

Changing Administrator Password

UNIX: You can change passwords using the *passwd* command.
Windows NT: You can change your password in two ways:

- Use the User Manager
- Press Ctrl-Alt-Delete (Don't worry — unlike DOS, your machine is not going to reboot automatically). Click the **Change Password** button.

This is another thing you need to get used to in Windows. There are multiple ways to accomplish the same function. As another example, if you are looking for files, you can use **Find** in the **Start** menu, Use the My Computer icon, or use Windows **Explorer**. If users are asking for your help, you need to figure how they got there in the first place. Also, if you are writing instructions for users on how to access system resources, keep in mind that there may be more than one way of doing it.

Shutting Down the System

UNIX: You typically perform a UNIX shutdown using a script that you wrote or one supplied by the UNIX vendor. The script ensures that file system updates are complete by using a *sync* command. After all users have logged off and backup processes are done, *init* is soft killed.
Windows NT: You can shut down a Windows NT system in one of the following ways:

- Click on **Start** and choose **Shutdown** (Windows NT 4.0).
- Click on **File** in the **Program Manager** Menu and choose **Shutdown** from the pull-down menu (Windows NT 3.5x).
- Press Ctrl-Alt-Delete and choose **Shutdown.**

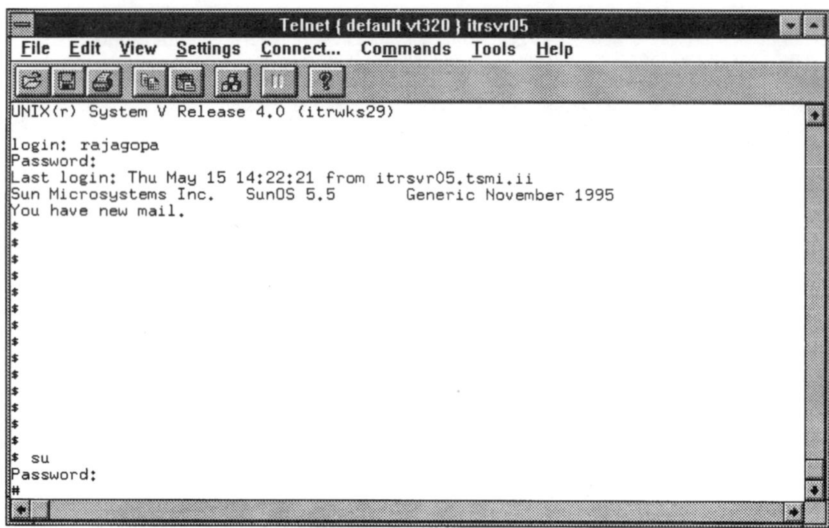

FIGURE 10.4 Using *su* to change privileges.

Disk Administration

Partition Disk

UNIX: Partitioning is many times already done by the UNIX system vendor or the disk manufacturer (when operating systems are preloaded). Some UNIX systems include *fdisk* for managing partitions.
Windows NT: Use the Disk Manager.

Creating Stripe/Volume Sets

UNIX: No direct equivalence, functions vary by UNIX implementation.
Windows NT: Use the Disk Manager.

Remote Disks

UNIX: Each machine has a single directory tree that includes all local and remote drives.
Windows NT: Each local and remote drive gets assigned a "drive letter." The drive letters are the alphabet letters A through Z. A file on drive A called **Myfile** shows up in Windows menus as **A:\Myfile**. Typically, the letters A and B are used for local floppy drives, and the letter C for the main (or only) local hard drive. Additional local hard drives are denoted starting with D. You are not constrained to assign the letters in alphabetical order, although you cannot assign a letter already assigned. You can access remote drives on the network using **Connect** in the **File Manager** or use the **Explorer**.

File Services

File Security

UNIX: File security is determined by permissions (rwxrwxrwx), as shown in Figure 10.5.

The left-most character is not permissions related. It is *d* for directories, *c* for special character files, - for regular files, etc. The remaining letters are composed of three user segments, each with three letters. The three user segments are owner, a group of users, and any other. For each segment, *r* indicates read permission, *w* indicates write permission, and *x* indicates execute. In Figure 10.5,

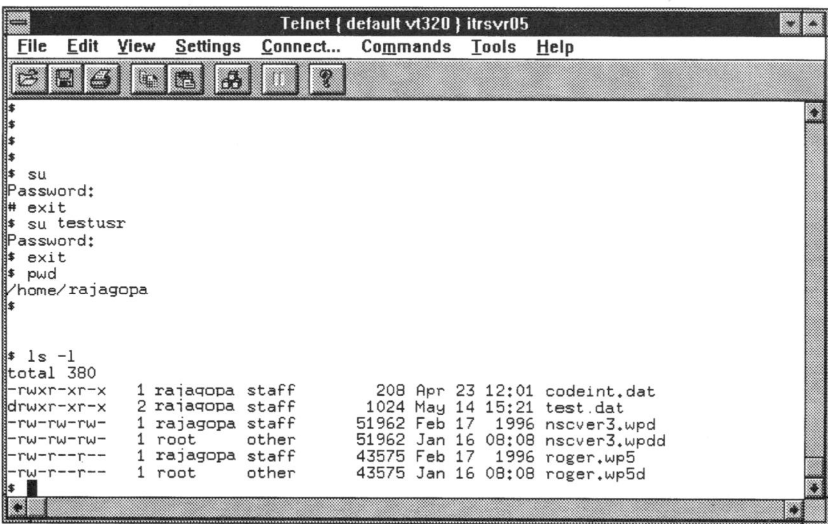

FIGURE 10.5 UNIX File Permissions.

for the file codeint.dat, the owner has read, write, and execute permissions while other users do not have write permissions.

Windows NT: File security is controlled through Access Control Lists (ACLs). Use the Security tab in the Properties menu to administer file directory security. You can use the menu shown in Figure 10.6 to set security-related attributes.

You can also set up Directory permissions using the menu shown in Figure 10.7, which you get by clicking the Permission button in the dialog shown in Figure 10.6.

File Names

UNIX: File names are not restricted to the 8-dot-3 format and can contain almost any character.

Windows NT: Windows NT supports multiple file systems (FAT, NTFS, etc.) and the file name restrictions depend on the file system. FAT file names must follow the 8-dot-3 format. If a file with a long file name is copied into 8-dot-3 restricted file system, Windows NT changes the name and truncates it to fit in 8-dot-3 format.

Sharing Files

UNIX: The most common method to share disks, directories, and files in UNIX is to use NFS. NFS is covered in Chapter 8.

Windows NT: To share disks across Windows NT machines, use the **Share** option in **File Manager**. See Figure 10.8. To share disks, directories, and files in a heterogeneous environment with UNIX and Windows NT machines, use either the Network Operating System functions or a third-party NFS package. NFS is discussed in Chapter 8.

Print Services

Printer Sharing

UNIX: Once set up, use *lpd* to spool print requests from all users (with *lpr*) to print.

Windows NT: Use the **Share** option in **Print Manager.**

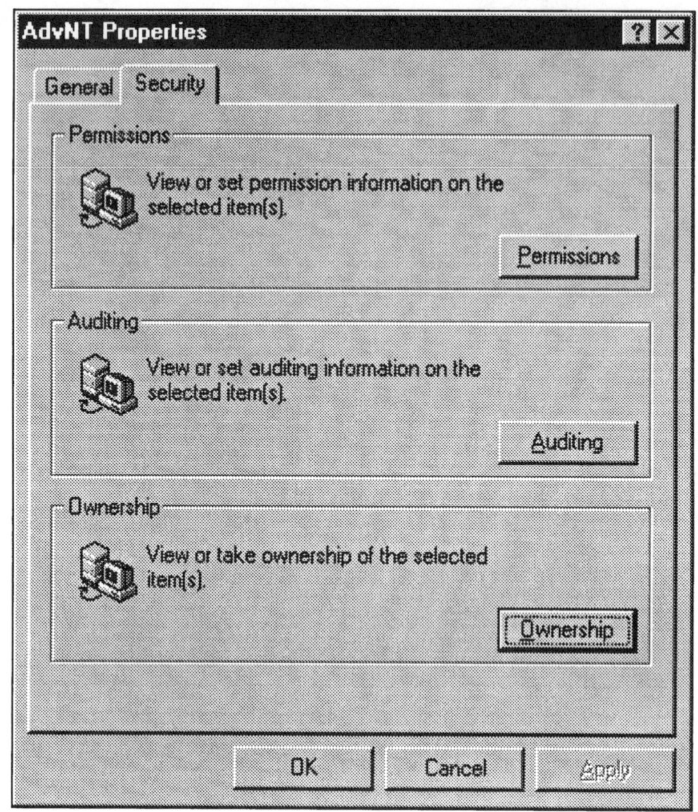

FIGURE 10.6 Setting security-related attributes.

Remote Printers

UNIX: Most NFS packages also provide remote printer support besides file access.
Windows NT: Use the **Connect** option in **Print Manager.** See Figure 10.9.

Adding/Changing Printers, Printer Drivers

UNIX: Printer drivers are in */etc/printcap.*
Windows NT: You add or change printer divers (when adding a new printer or updating an old copy of the printer driver) by using **Create Printer** in the **Print Manager**.

Communication Services

TCP/IP Setup/Change

UNIX: You can add and edit IP addresses in */etc/hosts.* You can *ping* to verify connection.
Windows NT: You can browse and update a machine's TCP/IP address using TCP/IP software module in the **Network** icon in the **Control Panel.** The TCP/IP Configuration menu is shown in Figure 10.10.

Advanced TCP/IP Configurations are set using the menu shown in Figure 10.11. You get the menu shown in Figure 10.11 by clicking on the **Advanced** button in the menu shown in Figure 10.10.

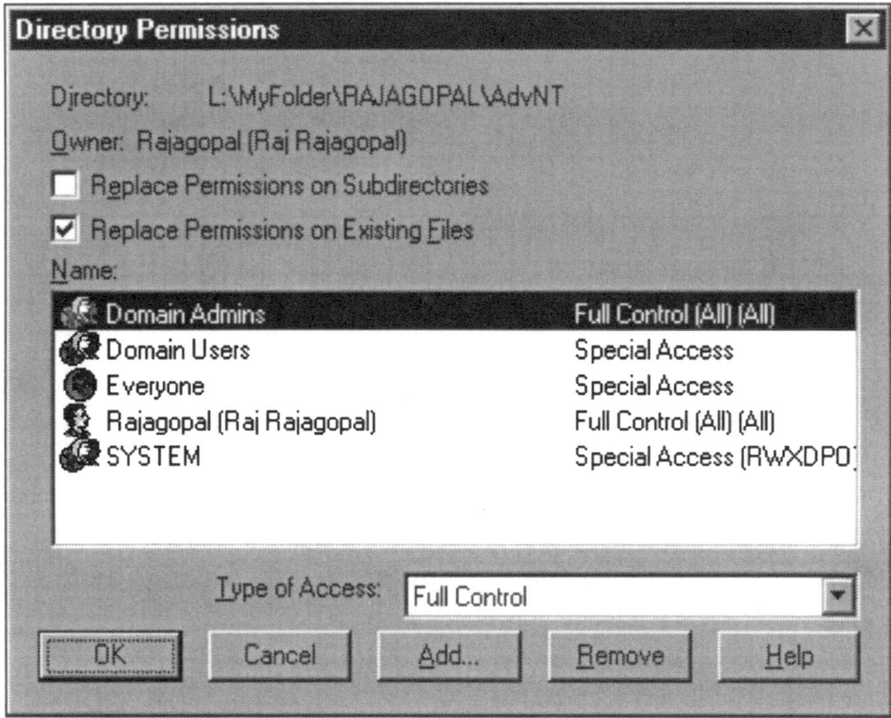

FIGURE 10.7 Directory Permissions.

Shared Resources

Sharename	Uses	Path
ADMIN$	0	C:\WINNT35
C$	0	C:\
DRIVE1	0	c:\
IPC$	0	
USERS	0	c:\users

Connected Users Time In Use

Connected Users: 0

Close Disconnect Disconnect All Help

FIGURE 10.8 Shared Resources in Windows NT.

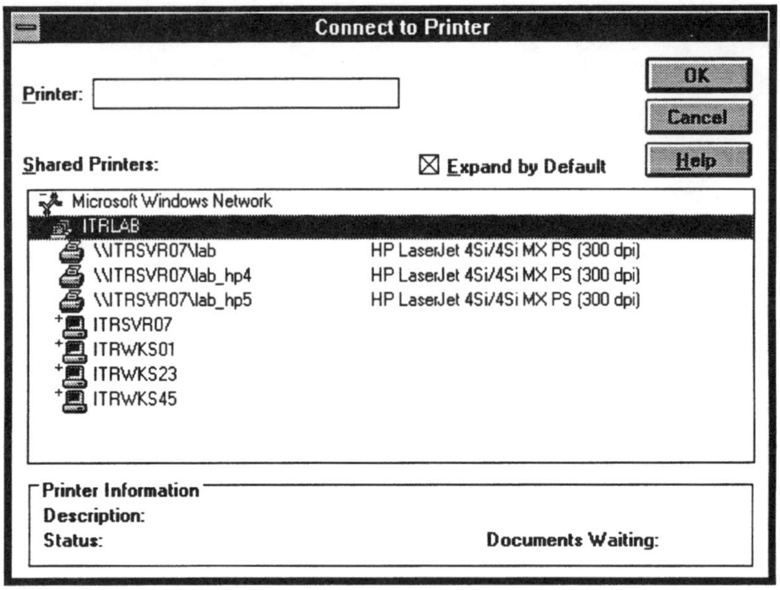

Connect to Printer

Printer:

OK

Cancel

Help

Shared Printers:

Expand by Default

Microsoft Windows Network

ITRLAB

\\ITRSVR07\lab	HP LaserJet 4Si/4Si MX PS (300 dpi)
\\ITRSVR07\lab_hp4	HP LaserJet 4Si/4Si MX PS (300 dpi)
\\ITRSVR07\lab_hp5	HP LaserJet 4Si/4Si MX PS (300 dpi)

ITRSVR07

ITRWKS01

ITRWKS23

ITRWKS45

Printer Information

Description:

Status:

Documents Waiting:

FIGURE 10.9 Connecting to a printer.

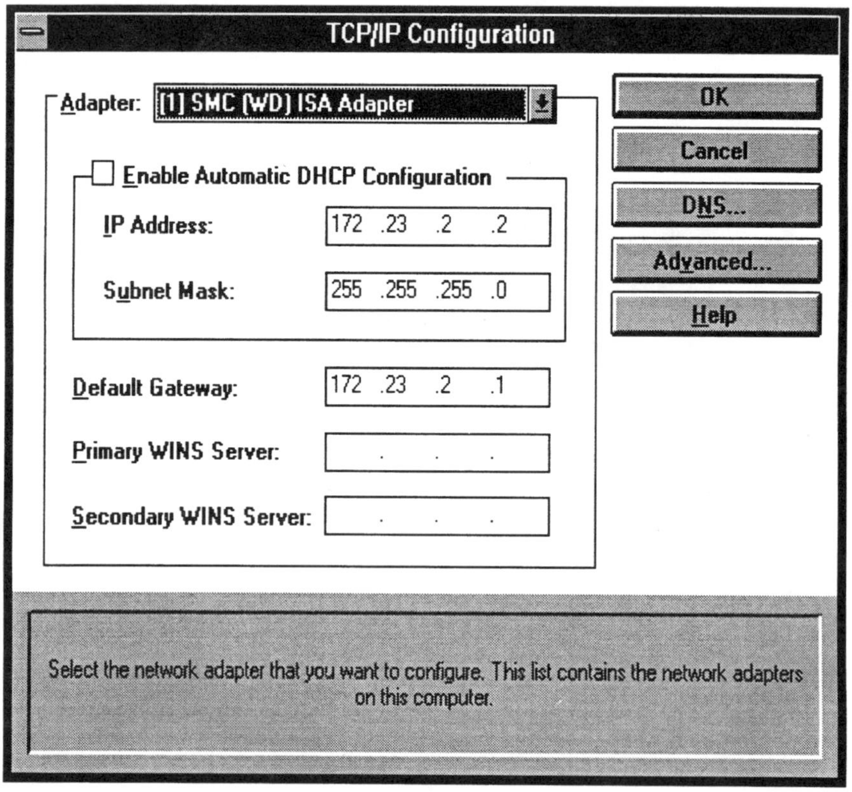

TCP/IP Configuration

Adapter: [1] SMC (WD) ISA Adapter

OK

Cancel

DNS...

Advanced...

Help

Enable Automatic DHCP Configuration

IP Address: 172 .23 .2 .2

Subnet Mask: 255 .255 .255 .0

Default Gateway: 172 .23 .2 .1

Primary WINS Server:

Secondary WINS Server:

Select the network adapter that you want to configure. This list contains the network adapters on this computer.

FIGURE 10.10 TCP/IP Configuration in Windows NT.

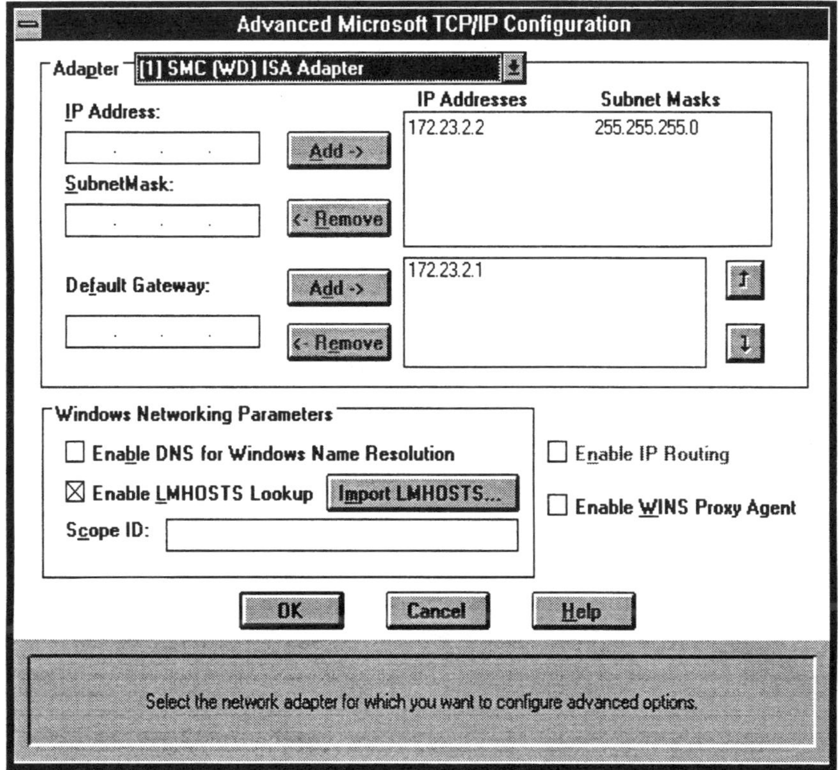

FIGURE 10.11 Advanced TCP/IP Configuration.

FTP, TFTP, RCP, and Telnet

UNIX: FTP, TFTP, RCP, and Telnet are commands executed from the command line.
Windows NT: Windows NT includes command line versions of FTP, TFTP, RCP, and Telnet. Windows NT also includes a graphical version of FTP. A sample FTP session showing how to download a file using the graphical FTP is included in Chapter 8. A sample Telnet session showing how to log on to a remote host is included in Chapter 6.

e-mail

UNIX: e-mail is automatically enabled as a part of creating a user account.
Windows NT: e-mail has to be separately enabled. You create a post office and an associated administrative account. You then allow shared access to the post office. After this, either you can set up users to access the post office or the users can set up themselves.

Talk/Chat

UNIX: Talk is a standard command in UNIX, executed from the command line.
Windows NT: In Windows, the equivalent function to UNIX Talk is called Chat. Chat is built-in in Windows NT. You can access Chat by double-clicking on the Chat icon in the Accessories Group (or search for "chat" in Help, under **Start**). The Chat menu is shown in Figure 10.12. Clicking on conversation shows a list of computers you can chat with.

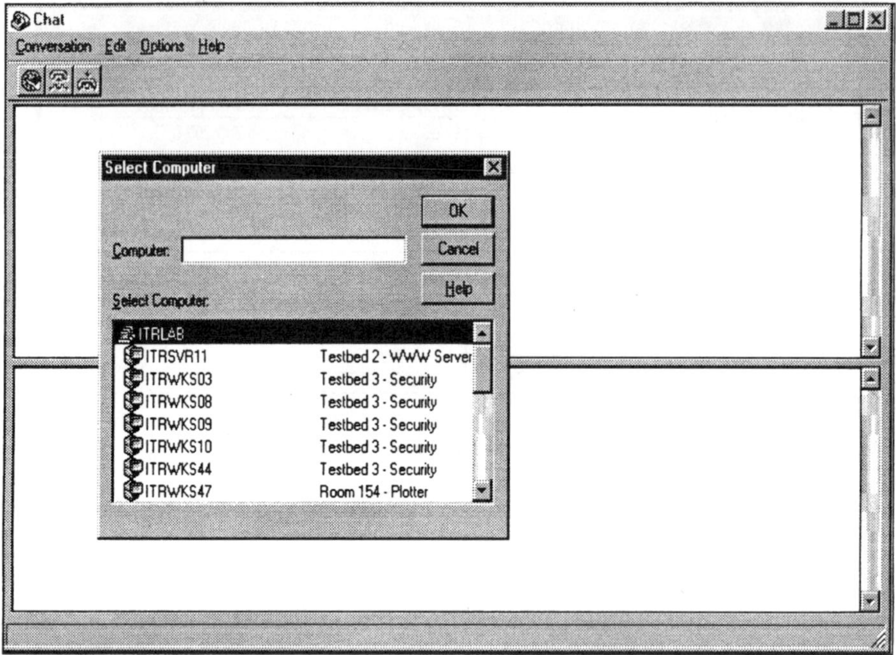

FIGURE 10.12 Chat menu in Windows NT.

User Messages

UNIX: You **write** a message to a user or **wall** a message to all users.
Windows NT: You can either use the **net send** command (See Figure 10.13), or when using a domain controller, use the **Send Message** option.

BACKUP/RECOVERY

Tape Backup — tar/dump

UNIX: You use **tar** or **dump** to make tape backups.
Windows NT: Use **Tape backup** in the Administrative Tools group or (more likely) use third-party backup software.

pkzip/tar

UNIX: You can also use **tar** to save subdirectory trees into a single file.
Windows NT: You can use a shareware utility like *pkzip* or *Winzip* to compress and save all files within a subdirectory tree.

COMPRESS/UNCOMPRESS/EXPAND

UNIX: You use **compress** and **uncompress** to reduce file sizes and later restore the file sizes.
Windows NT: The equivalent of **compress** is **compress.** The equivalent of **uncompress** is **expand.** The zip utilities mentioned earlier also compress while saving multiple files to a single zip file.

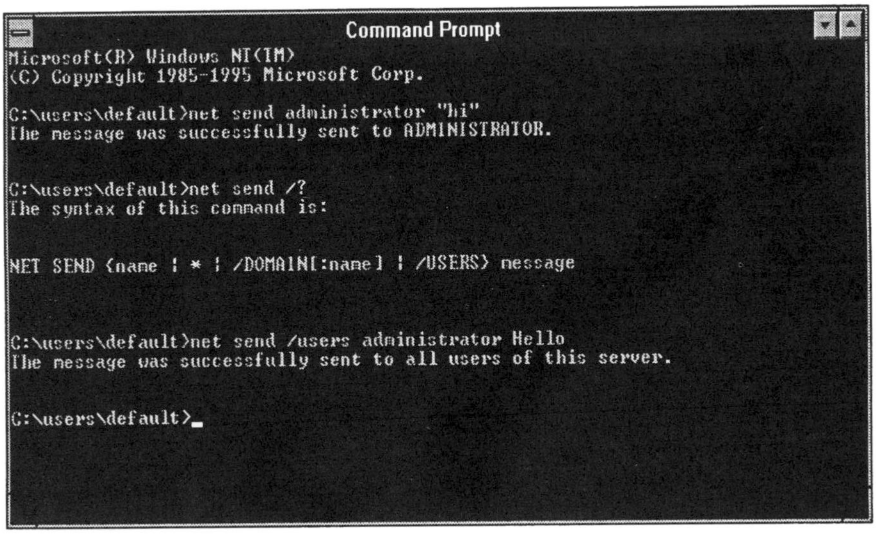

```
Command Prompt
Microsoft(R) Windows NT(TM)
(C) Copyright 1985-1995 Microsoft Corp.

C:\users\default>net send administrator "hi"
The message was successfully sent to ADMINISTRATOR.

C:\users\default>net send /?
The syntax of this command is:

NET SEND {name | * | /DOMAIN[:name] | /USERS} message


C:\users\default>net send /users administrator Hello
The message was successfully sent to all users of this server.

C:\users\default>_
```

FIGURE 10.13 Sending a message to users in Windows NT.

System Log Files

UNIX: The main log file is the syslog file. Most log files in UNIX contain plain text that can be read with a text editor.
Windows NT: Look for all log files under **Event Viewer** (see Figure 10.21) which is part of the **Administrative main menu** shown in Figure 10.1. The log files use an internal format and cannot be viewed with text editors.

Process/Task Management

Task Priority

UNIX: You can use the *jobs* command to view a list of executing and suspended shell's job. In many UNIX systems, particularly those based on BSD, you can use the *renice* command to alter the priority.
Windows NT: Use the **System** icon in the **Control Panel**.

Automatic Job Scheduling

UNIX: Use the **CRON** and **at** facilities to schedule job executions.
Windows NT: Use the **at** command in conjunction with the **Schedule** service. Windows NT Resource kit also includes **Command Scheduler**, a graphical utility.

If you are using third-party data center operations software such as POLYCENTER from DEC or CA-Unicenter from Computer Associates, check with the vendor to see if they have versions for your environment.

System Load Balancing

UNIX: Use the *w* or *uptime* commands to monitor system load.
Windows NT: Use the **Performance Monitor** in the **Administrative Tools** group.

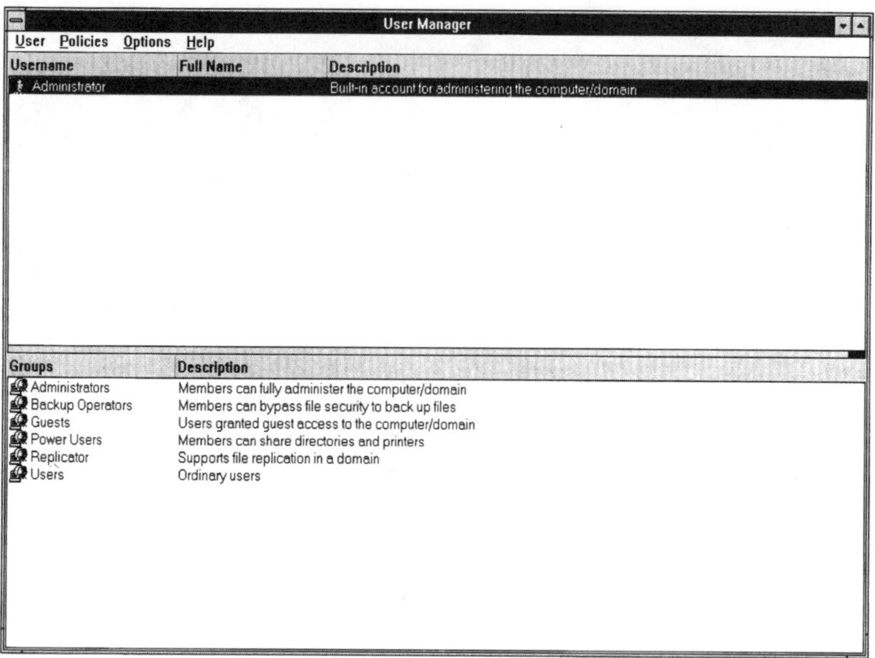

FIGURE 10.14 User Manager in Windows NT.

Terminate Process/Task

UNIX: Use the *ps* to get a list of processes and *kill* to kill a process.
Windows NT: Use the *pview* application (it is available in the SDK). You can get a task list and select individual tasks and kill them.

Daemons

UNIX: Daemons are constantly running background processes which typically wait for and process messages.
Windows NT: The functionality of Daemons is implemented using *Services*. Use **Service Manager** in the **Control Panel**.

User Management

User Accounts, Groups, and Profiles

UNIX: Information about all users is stored in **/etc/passwd,** (user) group information is stored in **/etc/groups,** and user profile information in **/etc/profile files.** Updates are performed to the user data by editing these files using an editor like *vi*. Information about a specific user is contained in the *$home* environment variable and **.profile** and **.kshrc files**
Windows NT: The User Manager and User Profile editor are used to maintain user information. You can specify the path where user profile information should be stored and you can also change the path. The User Manager icon is normally found in the Windows NT Administrator main menu, as shown in Figure 10.1. Double-clicking on the User Manager icon brings up the menu shown in Figure 10.14. The menu is divided into two halves. The bottom half shows the list of valid user groups, and the top half shows the list of valid users within the group selected in the bottom half.

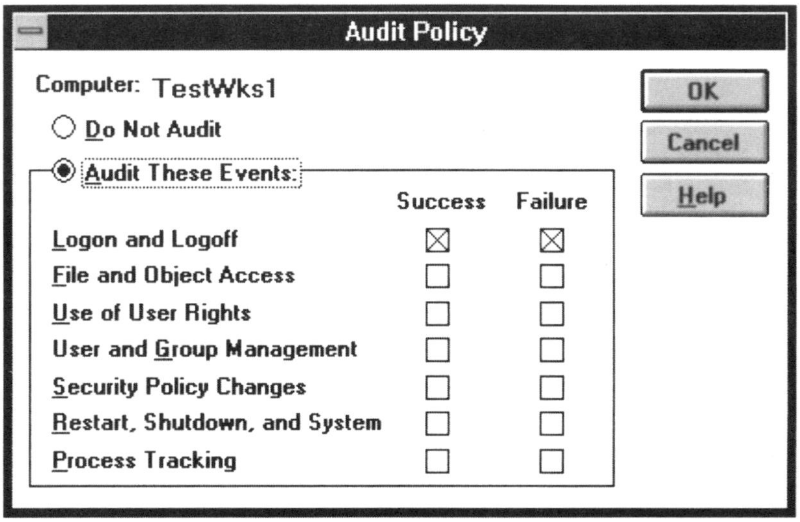

Audit Policy

Computer: TestWks1

Do Not Audit

Audit These Events:

	Success	Failure
Logon and Logoff	☒	☒
File and Object Access	☐	☐
Use of User Rights	☐	☐
User and Group Management	☐	☐
Security Policy Changes	☐	☐
Restart, Shutdown, and System	☐	☐
Process Tracking	☐	☐

OK Cancel Help

FIGURE 10.15 Setting Audit Policy for a user in Windows NT.

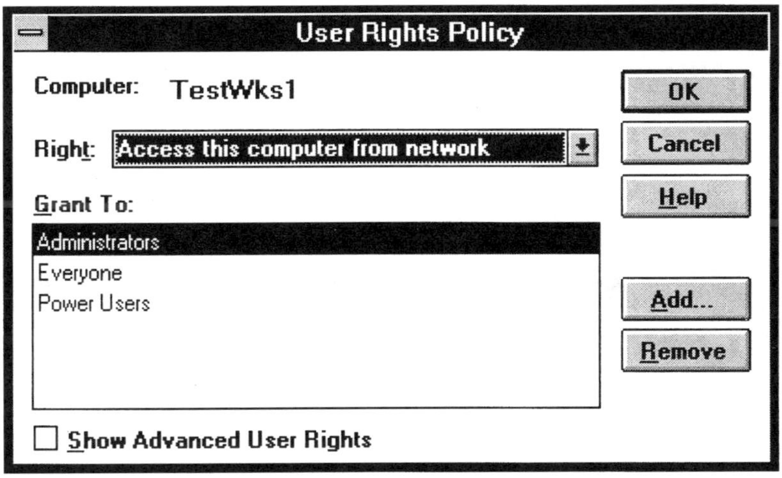

User Rights Policy

Computer: TestWks1

Right: Access this computer from network

Grant To:

Administrators
Everyone
Power Users

Show Advanced User Rights

OK Cancel Help Add... Remove

FIGURE 10.16 Setting User Rights Policy.

One of the administration functions you can perform for each user is to the audit policy for that user. You can set the audit policy using the menu shown in Figure 10.15 You can get this menu by clicking an individual user (click on one user entry in Figure 10.14) and selecting **Policies**, **Audit**, from the pull-down menu. You can audit user events such as logon and logoff, file and object access, etc.

Another user administration function is to set the User Rights Policy. Figure 10.16 shows the User Rights Policy menu that you can use to set user rights policy.

You can set the user account policy using the menu shown in Figure 10.17.

You can set the user properties using the menu shown in Figure 10.18.

You can set up the user environment, such as whether the user will have a login script and the name of the script, using the menu shown in Figure 10.19.

You can specify user group information using the menu shown in Figure 10.20.

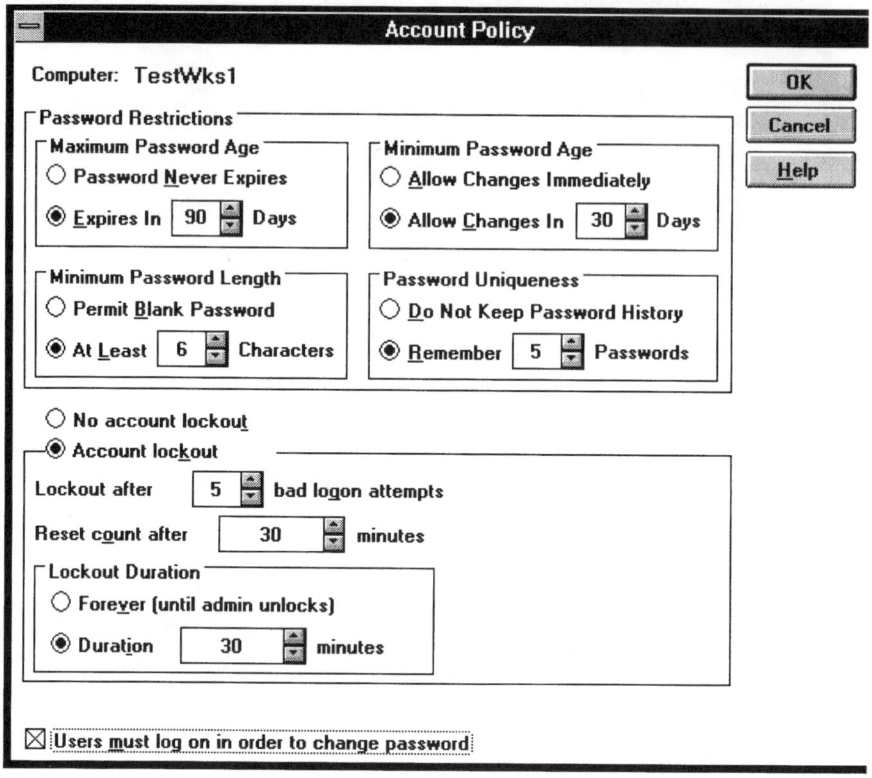

Account Policy
Computer: TestWks1
OK
Cancel
Help
Password Restrictions
Maximum Password Age
Password Never Expires
Expires In 90 Days
Minimum Password Age
Allow Changes Immediately
Allow Changes In 30 Days
Minimum Password Length
Permit Blank Password
At Least 6 Characters
Password Uniqueness
Do Not Keep Password History
Remember 5 Passwords
No account lockout
Account lockout
Lockout after 5 bad logon attempts
Reset count after 30 minutes
Lockout Duration
Forever (until admin unlocks)
Duration 30 minutes
Users must log on in order to change password

FIGURE 10.17 Setting user Account Policy.

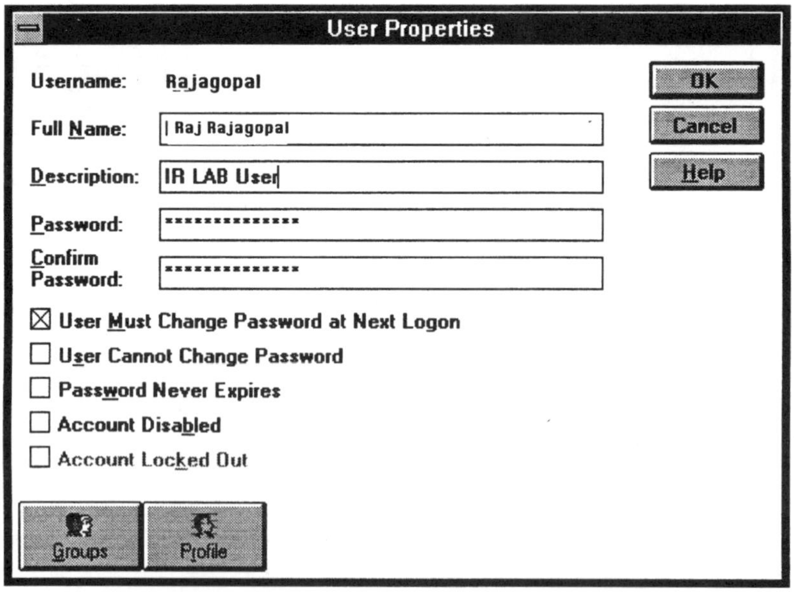

User Properties
Username: Rajagopal
Full Name: Raj Rajagopal
Description: IR LAB User
Password: **************
Confirm Password: **************
OK
Cancel
Help
User Must Change Password at Next Logon
User Cannot Change Password
Password Never Expires
Account Disabled
Account Locked Out
Groups
Profile

FIGURE 10.18 Setting User Properties.

Migration Solution for Migrating NetWare Users

Windows NT includes a migration tool that lets system administration information such as user data be copied from one or more NetWare servers to a Windows NT server. The migration tool is discussed in Chapter 11 — *Windows NT and NetWare.*

LOGGING IN WINDOWS NT AND UNIX

Both Windows NT and UNIX support a number of logs that provide an audit trail of events about users, files, networks, etc. There are two primary differences between UNIX and Windows NT for logging:

- The logging administration and browsing utilities in UNIX for the most part are non-graphical, whereas Windows NT uses the GUI for logging administration and browsing.
- Many logs in UNIX store the log data in ASCII (plain text), whereas the log information in Windows NT is stored in a special format.

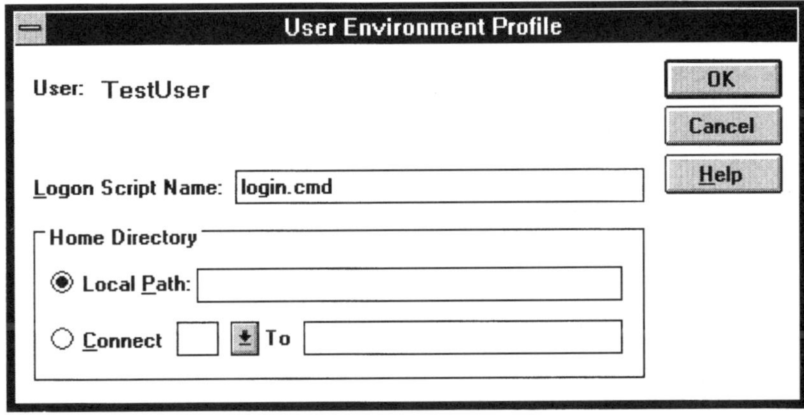

FIGURE 10.19 Setting the User Environment Profile.

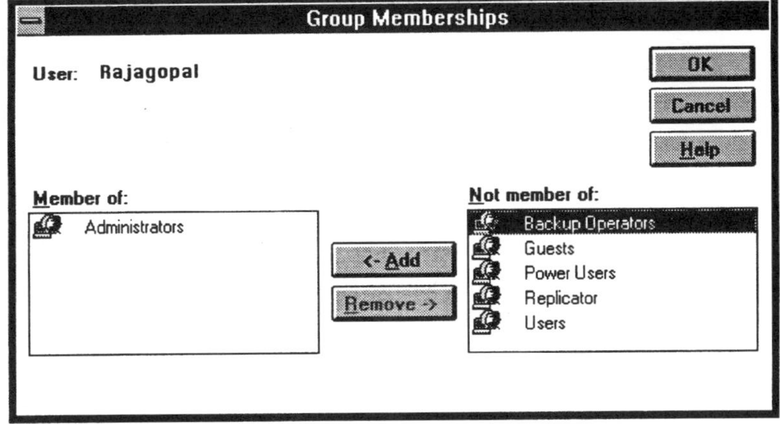

FIGURE 10.20 Setting User Group Memberships.

UNIX: The most important log is syslog, the system log, which logs various system-related information. Some logs that store user information are lastlog, UTMP, WTMP, sulog, etc. Logs that store file access information include LOGFILE (normally records UUCP activities). You use built-in UNIX functions or public domain tools to browse the logs.

Windows NT: Windows NT uses three logs — the system log, the security log, and the application log. The security log has information about system accesses, illegal file accesses, invalid password entries, privileged objects accesses, user name and password changes, etc. The system log contains information about the system generated by system components. Application logs contain information generated by Windows NT applications. For example, an application that encounters a file access error logs the error in the application log. You use the Event Viewer shown in Figure 10.21 to view the Windows NT logs.

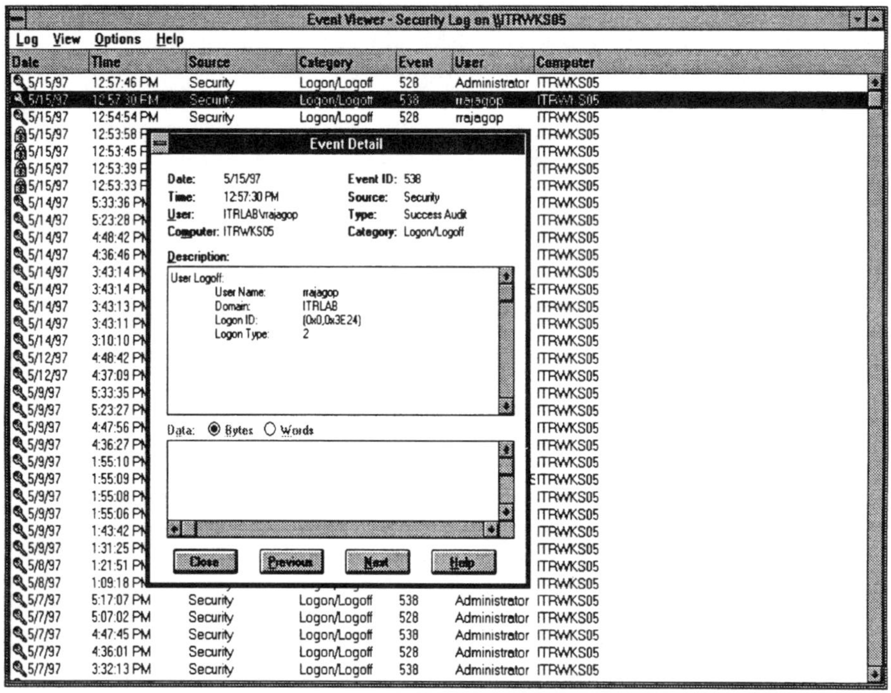

FIGURE 10.21 Using Event Viewer to view Windows NT logs.

LOGGING ERROR LEVELS

UNIX: UNIX uses an eight level system to classify logging error levels. These levels and the associated descriptions are summarized in Table 10.1.

Windows NT: Windows NT uses a five-level system to classify logging error levels. In addition, Windows NT uses colored graphical symbols to indicate the error. The error symbols and the associated descriptions are summarized in Table 10.2.

NETWORK COMMANDS

Windows NT also includes network commands that help you in your management of files and computers on your network. Table 10.3 summarizes the network commands. Keep in mind that there are more network commands and you can get a list of them with their descriptions by using

TABLE 10.1
UNIX Logging Message Levels and Descriptions

Error Level	Description
emerg	Emergencies
alert	Alert conditions that require prompt administrator action
crit	Critical condition
err	Non-critical errors
warning	Warnings
Notice	Messages that need action, but are not errors
info	Informational messages
debug	Debugging messages

TABLE 10.2
Windows Logging Message Symbols and Descriptions

Error Symbol	Description
Red stop sign	Serious error (that needs attention) message
Yellow circle with an exclamation point	Warning message
Blue circle with the letter "I"	Informational message
Gray padlock	Invalid authorization message
Gold key	Authorization successful message

TABLE 10.3
Windows NT Network Commands and Descriptions

Network Command	Description
net computer	Add/Delete computers to Windows NT server domains
net file	Displays all open shared file names on a server
net help	Displays network command names and descriptions. Optionally, you can include a command name for more description about the command
net helpmsg	Displays help information about a network error message
net print	Monitor and administer printers and printer queues
net start	Net start is actually a family of commands to start services and utilities such as the spooler, event log, etc. You specify the specific service or utility name after net start
net use	Displays current drive mapping information

the command *net help*. In addition, you can perform the functions performed by these commands by selecting from the graphical user interface instead of the command line.

The *net help* command is illustrated in Figure 10.22, and the *net use* command is illustrated in Figure 10.23.

```
Command Prompt

C:\users\default>net help
The syntax of this command is:


NET HELP command
     -or-
NET command /HELP

   Commands available are:

   NET ACCOUNTS             NET HELP            NET SHARE
   NET COMPUTER             NET HELPMSG         NET START
   NET CONFIG               NET LOCALGROUP      NET STATISTICS
   NET CONFIG SERVER        NET NAME            NET STOP
   NET CONFIG WORKSTATION   NET PAUSE           NET TIME
   NET CONTINUE             NET PRINT           NET USE
   NET FILE                 NET SEND            NET USER
   NET GROUP                NET SESSION         NET VIEW

   NET HELP SERVICES lists the network services you can start.
   NET HELP SYNTAX explains how to read NET HELP syntax lines.
   NET HELP command | MORE displays Help one screen at a time.

C:\users\default>
```

FIGURE 10.22 Net Help command.

Conclusion

We looked at some common system administration functions and reviewed the equivalent ways of executing the functions between UNIX and Windows NT. In the next chapter, we will look at some migration and coexistence topics between Windows NT and NetWare.

```
Command Prompt

C:\users\default>net use
New connections will be remembered.


Status       Local     Remote                    Network

-------------------------------------------------------------------------------
             D:        \\TSMI\TSMIDSK2           NetWare or Compatible Network
             E:        \\TSMI\TSMIDSK2\myfolde0\rajagopa
                                                 NetWare or Compatible Network
             T:        \\tsmi\sys                NetWare or Compatible Network
OK                     \\TSMSVR05\IPC$           Microsoft Windows Network
The command completed successfully.


C:\users\default>
```

FIGURE 10.23 Net Use command.

11 NetWare Considerations

INTRODUCTION

In this chapter we will look at migration and coexistence options between Windows NT and NetWare. Novell NetWare was, and still is, the predominant Network Operating System. However, recently Windows NT is gaining market share from NetWare. Windows NT had one advantage in its competition with NetWare compared to UNIX. Unlike UNIX with its many variants, NetWare is a well-defined target. NetWare was relatively easy to develop migration and coexistence solutions for. Just as it introduced WordPerfect compatibility features (such as document translation filters for WordPerfect documents and user guides that provide comparable Word functions for WordPerfect functions) to appeal to the WordPerfect install base, Microsoft included NetWare compatibility features in Windows NT. Besides Windows NT, Windows 95 and Windows for Workgroups integrate with NetWare as well. These include:

- File and Print Services for NetWare (FPNW)
- Client Services for NetWare (CSNW)
- Gateway Services for NetWare (GSNW)
- Migration tool to migrate NetWare information to Windows NT

These compatibility features have been used by many customers, and you should find these very helpful if you are exploring migration and coexistence options between Windows NT and NetWare. We will cover these features in this chapter. We will also look at Novell server and client products that work in the Windows environment. Also in this chapter, we will look at system administration features that let you monitor and update the NetWare server using Windows NT functions.

WINDOWS NT AND NETWARE MIGRATION AND COEXISTENCE OPTIONS

You have a good set of migration and coexistence options when you want Windows NT and NetWare to coexist. For example, you can:

- Access NetWare Servers using Microsoft Clients, access files on disks attached to the NetWare Server, and print to printers attached to the NetWare Server
- Access Windows NT Server using NetWare Clients, access files on disks attached to the Windows NT Server, and print to printers attached to the Windows NT Server
- Administer a NetWare server using built-in functions of Windows NT
- Migrate from NetWare to Windows NT; there are tools that permit you to copy the administration data (such as user data) from the NetWare server to the Windows NT server

Let us look at these options in detail.

Accessing Novell NetWare Servers Using Windows Clients

If you are using Microsoft Windows-based desktops and you want to access files and printers attached to Novell NetWare, you can do one of the following:

1. Get a Windows operating system with built-in NetWare client support. Windows operating systems that provide this support include Windows NT Workstation and Windows 95. The built-in client to access NetWare is also called Client Services for NetWare (CSNW). Using CSNW, you have full access to NetWare 3.1x (and below) servers. These clients also allow you to access NetWare 4.x servers in bindery emulation mode. Depending on the version of Windows 95 you have, you may not have built-in NDS support. Windows 95 started including full NDS support with Service Pack 1. Service Packs are available for download from **http://www.microsoft.com/windows/software/servpak1/enduser.htm**. You can also find Service Pack 1 in Microsoft's Software Library forum on CompuServe (GO CIS:MSL-30; Search for SNumber S15768). CSNW is covered in more detail later in this chapter.
2. Get a NetWare client from Novell. Novell provides NetWare clients that work in Windows 3.1, Windows 95, and DOS. Novell NetWare clients provide all the functionality for NetWare 3.1x and NetWare 4.x, including NDS access on NetWare 4.x. Novell NetWare client can coexist with the Microsoft client on the same machine (older versions of the NetWare client did not support this). You can download the 32-bit client for Windows 95 from **ftp.novell.com/pub/updates/nwos/ nc32w952**, and for DOS/Windows 3.1x from **ftp.novell.com/pub/updates/ nwos/cl32dw21**. Novell also provides support through its NetWire forum on CompuServe. You can also access NetWare information through the World Wide Web at http://www.novell.com.
3. Install Gateway Service for NetWare (GSNW) to let clients running only Microsoft Networking client software access NetWare server resources via gateway services provided by Windows NT Server.

These options are shown in Figure 11.1.

***Tip**: Both Microsoft and Novell provide products that have basically the same functions. If you are in an environment where both products coexist, try looking at the features in detail of both products, even though you may be very familiar with one. You may find that for some of your most commonly used functions, one of these products provides a simpler or faster way of accomplishing your functions.*

Your choice depends on the level of NetWare support you need, the types of client your users prefer, costs involved, and the administrative skill set you have. Let us look at each of the options in detail.

Using Windows Operating System with Built-in NetWare Client Support

Windows includes Client Services for NetWare (CSNW) in Windows 95 and Windows NT. CSNW supports NetWare access by using the Multiple Provider Router (MPR) API. Support for the MPR API is available in Windows 95 and Windows NT 4.0's Workstation and Server versions. MPR is not an acronym for the similar-sounding Multi-Protocol Routing Service. The multiple provider router ensures proper routing. For example, remote requests to Windows servers are sent to the proper server by the Windows redirector, while requests to NetWare servers are routed appropriately.

MPR exports Win32 networking APIs and interacts with Network Providers and network DLLs. Figure 11.2 shows layers 5, 6, and 7 of International Standards Organization's Open System Interconnect (OSI) model and the components of the Windows NT operating system that implement these layers.

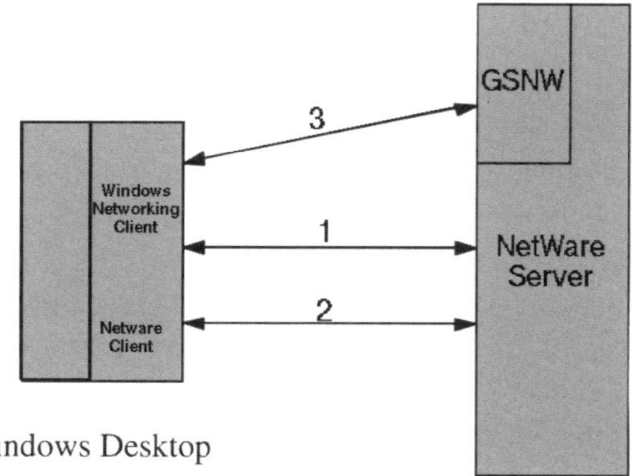

FIGURE 11.1 Accessing NetWare Server from Windows Desktop. (1) Windows built-in Networking Client accessing NetWare Server. (2) Novell's NetWare Client accessing NetWare Server. (3) Windows Networking Client accessing NetWare Server through Gateway.

OSI Layer	Windows NT Operating System Components
	RPC | Providers | Named Pipes
7. Application	User Mode
6. Presentation	Kernel Mode
5. Session	NetBIOS Driver | Redirectors | Servers | WinSock Driver

FIGURE 11.2 Upper layers of OSI model and Windows NT components.

In Figure 11.2, for each redirector at the session level, there exists a provider at the application level. When there are multiple providers available, MPR handles the routing of a network service request to the appropriate provider. MPR facilitates user interfaces such as Windows Explorer to access the underlying networks. All network providers request network services such as connecting to servers, browsing servers, and disconnecting from servers through MPR. Besides NetWare Server access, the MPR API is also used as an application programming interface to the local file system and remote Windows network servers. In this scenario, there is no need for a NetWare-specific protocol stack.

Bindery: Access to file directories and printers on NetWare networks is on a per-user basis. When a NetWare server gets a request, it needs access to the list of authorized users to validate the request. In NetWare 3.x and earlier, access control information such as users, groups, passwords, and rights are stored in a database on the server called the *Bindery*. One of the problems with the bindery is that each server had its own bindery. If you wanted to let a user access multiple NetWare, then that user's information should be updated in the bindery of all the servers, one bindery at a time. NetWare fixed the bindery problems with the introduction of NetWare Directory Services (NDS). NDS uses an object-oriented approach to network management. For compatibility purposes, NDS emulates the presence of a bindery, by default. Windows 95 can use the bindery of one NetWare server.

Windows 95, NetWare, and Security

In NetWare environments, it is common for multiple departments to have a NetWare server of their own and provide access to selected users from other departments as required. NetWare does this through the concept of NetWare domains and NetWare Name Service (NNS), an add-on service, that obtains user lists. Windows 95 can specify only one bindery and does not support the use of NetWare domains or NNS. This means that Windows 95 users can access the resources on one NetWare server, but cannot obtain pass-through validation on other NetWare servers. One suggestion to solve this problem, according to Microsoft documentation, is to list all NetWare users on one NetWare server. This server acts as the security clearing house for all Windows 95 users using File and Print Services for NetWare.

Using CSNW

You can access a NetWare server using the built-in client services of Windows; the following lists the sequence of activities that you need to follow:

- Install the necessary software and set up accounts
- Set up the NetWare connection configuration
- Set logon, printing, and other options

Let's look at these activities in detail:

Installing Software and Setting up Accounts

The following are the steps involved in installing the necessary software and setting up the required accounts. The steps presume that your client Windows operating system and the NetWare server operating system software have already been installed.

1. Install Networking support in your client workstation. This may have already been installed when the client operating system was installed. If it is not installed, then you (or your Network Administrator) need to install this first.
2. Set up a user account on the NetWare server, if one doesn't already exist. For NetWare 3.x and earlier, use the SYSCON, NETADMIN NetWare administration utility. For NetWare 4.x, use the NWADMIN utility that is part of NDS.
3. Install NWLink transport and related protocol support.

In following these steps, remember to check for the latest drivers from Microsoft and/or Novell. Successful installation of NetWare client support adds the CSNW applet to your control panel, as shown in Figure 11.3.

Configuring the NetWare connection

You use the CSNW applet that was added to your control panel to configure the NetWare connection. Double-clicking on the CSNW applet brings up the screen shown in Figure 11.4.

The three main parts of your configuration are the server specification (or tree/context specification if you are using NDS), your print options, and whether you want to use login scripts. If the NetWare server you specify runs NetWare 3.x or earlier, then bindery emulation is automatically used. For NetWare 4.x, then there is a choice between bindery emulation and NDS. If you choose to use NDS, then you should specify the name of a tree and context. Note that although NetWare natively includes support for both a preferred server and a default tree/context, Windows NT restricts you to choose one or the other.

Regardless of the version of the server, you must have an account in the NetWare server you want to access. You can specify *None* as a server name, in which case Windows NT will attempt to log you to the nearest available NetWare server, but this is not a good idea for two reasons. First,

FIGURE 11.3 CSNW applet in the Control Panel.

NetWare requires that a user account must be created before the user logs on. This means that an account must be set up for you in potentially all the NetWare servers that are near you. Second, this negates attempts by system administrators to distribute load on servers by assigning users to servers.

Follow these steps to configure NWLink:

1. In **Control Panel**, double-click **Network**
2. Click the **Protocols** tab
3. Click **NWLink IPX/SPX Compatible Transport** (See Figure 11.5)
4. Click **Properties**
5. Select either **Auto Frame Type Detection** or **Manual Frame Type Detection**
6. If you select Manual, click **Add**, and enter a Frame Type and Network Number for each type you want to add, and then click **Add**
7. Click **OK** to save your changes

Note*: Although NetBIOS is not very common in the NetWare world, NetWare supports its own version of NetBIOS that some users use. Besides NWLink IPX/SPX protocol support, Microsoft also includes an NWLink NetBIOS protocol for compatibility.*

Setting Your Options

Your logon options depend on the NetWare server version, as mentioned earlier. Your print options available with CSNW include form feeds, completion notification, and printing a banner page, as shown in Figure 11.4.

Form feeds are required for compatibility with older applications that did not automatically include a form feed. If an older application just printed text for example and if this option is not

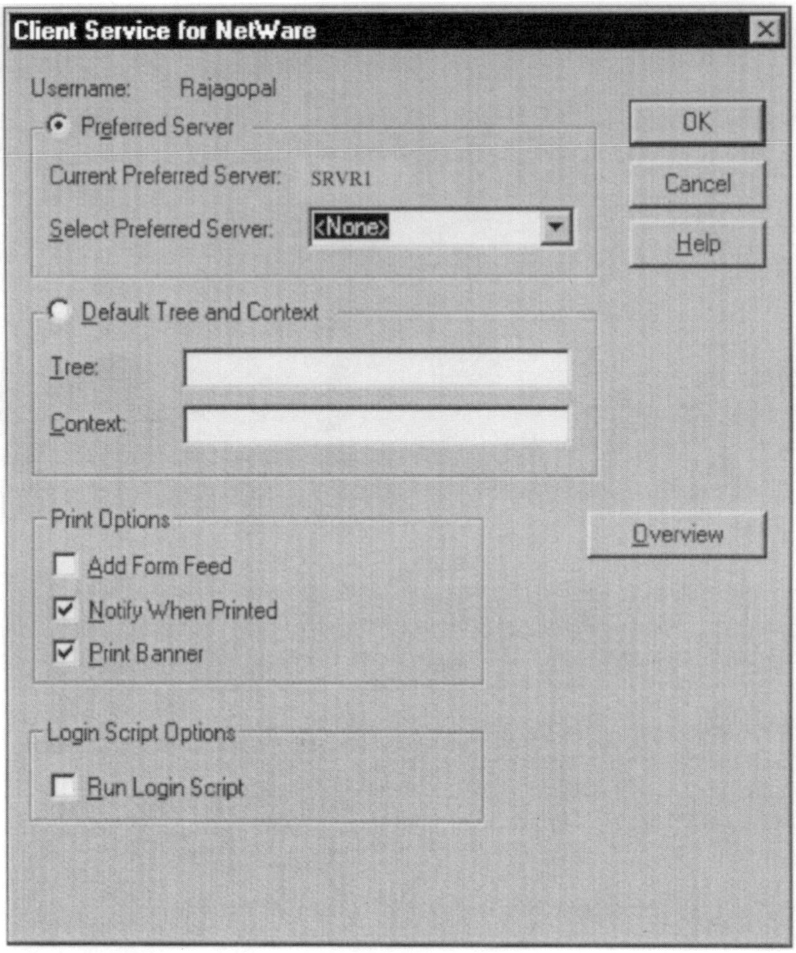

FIGURE 11.4 Configuring the NetWare connection using CSNW.

selected, then the output of another application sent to the same printer will start after the output of the older application without any separation.

However, most new programs automatically include the form feed at the end of the print output, and selecting this box will add an additional form feed, resulting in waste of paper. Select this option only when you know you have older applications that do not include form feeds.

The print completion notification option informs you when the background printing is complete. If you have a printer attached to your computer and use it for printing or you do not want to be disturbed by the completion notification, then you can turn this option off.

Selecting the banner page option inserts a banner page with your user information along with your printed output to help separate print output of different users. Again, you don't need this if you have your own printer.

The other option you can specify when configuring CSNW is whether you want to use Login Scripts. This option is useful if you have login scripts that have already been created and are residing on the NetWare server. For example, you may have login scripts to handle security functions or for creating automatic search mapping. The system login script of a NetWare server (using bindery emulation) is in \PUBLIC\NET$LOG.DAT and individual user scripts are in the user's \MAIL directory. You can specify the location of your login script using the User Environmental Profile

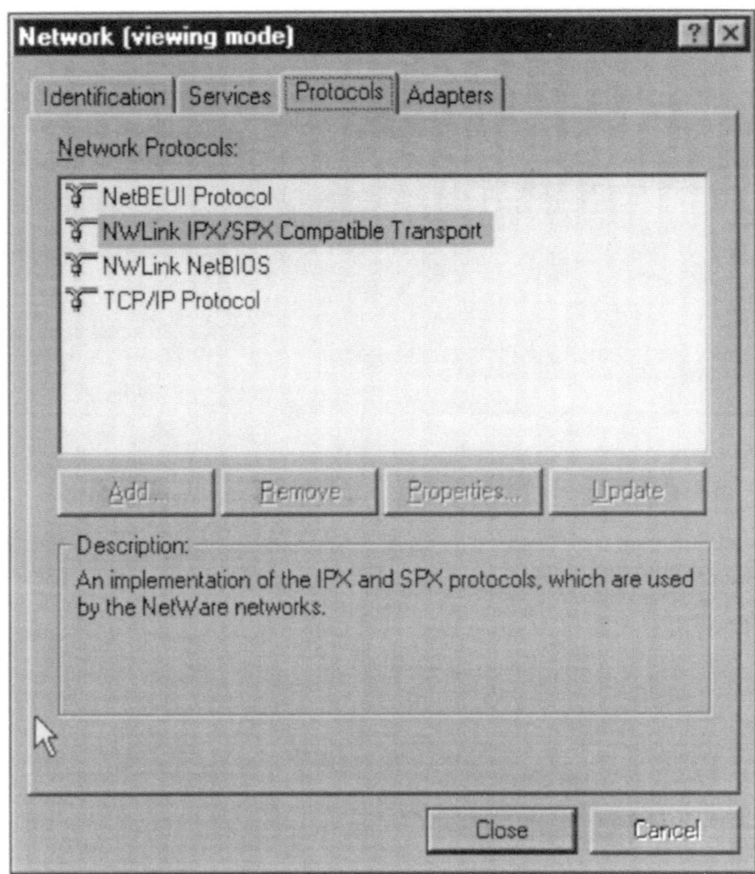

FIGURE 11.5 Selecting IPX/SPX compatible protocol for NWLink.

Dialog Box under User Manager. NDS login scripts can be edited using a GUI interface, while the older scripts are typically edited using simple DOS editors.

Tip: *You may be able to reduce the time taken to process your login script (and hence your logon time) by eliminating commands no longer needed or applicable in a Windows NT environment. One such command is the Greeting command.*

Locating and Logging to a NetWare Server

If you need to find the NetWare servers in your network, you can use the **Explorer** under **Start**, **Programs**. You can also use the Network Neighborhood or the **Computer** under **Start**, **Find**.

Figure 11.6 shows accessing a NetWare server using **Find** while Figure 11.7 shows how to access the same server using Network Neighborhood.

Once you have located the server icon or entry, double-clicking the icon or entry brings up the logon screen.

To logoff, select the server from the Network Neighborhood as you did for logon. Then choose **File**, **Log Out**. Confirm that you want to logoff from the confirmation dialog box, as shown in Figures 11.8.

You can logon to another server, if you choose. At any time, you can check the server you are logged on to and connection type by selecting **File**, **WhoAmI** when the server is selected in the Network Neighborhood window, as shown in Figure 11.9.

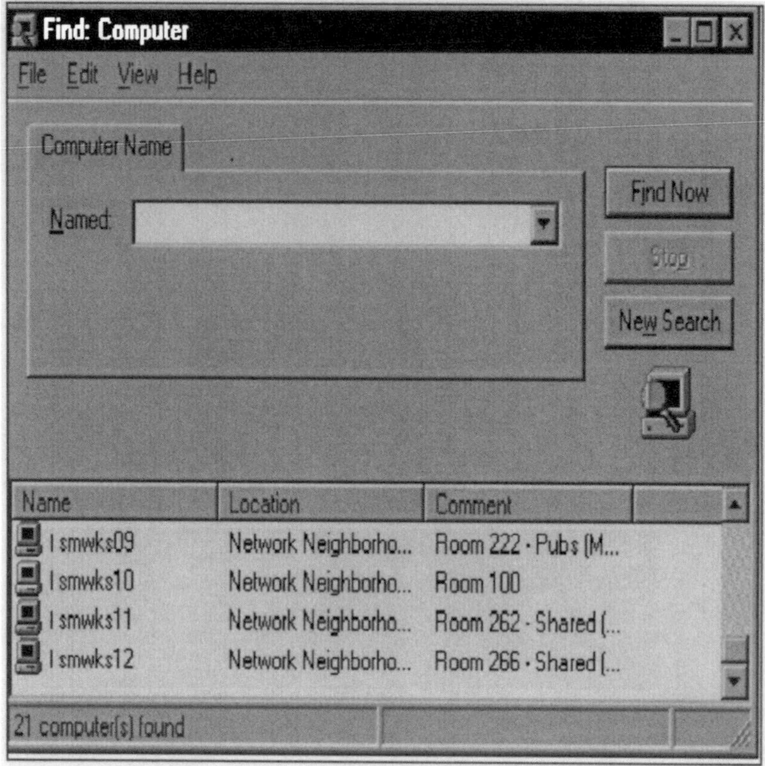

FIGURE 11.6 Locating a NetWare server using Find.

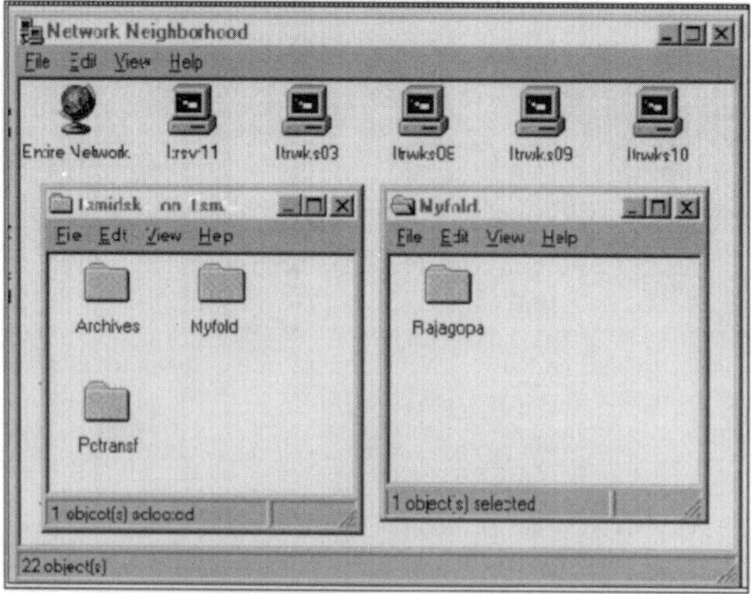

FIGURE 11.7 Locating a NetWare server using Network Neighborhood.

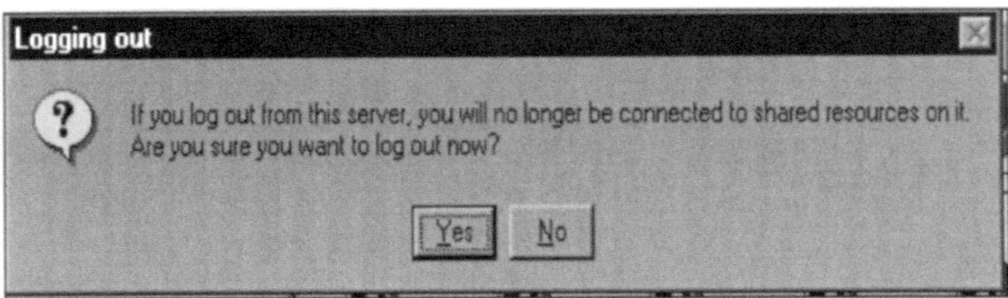

FIGURE 11.8 Logging out of a NetWare server.

Accessing NetWare File Services

Once you have located your NetWare server and logged on to the server, you can access the directories and files on the NetWare server using the standard Windows functions.

You can access disks, directories, and files using Windows Explorer, Network neighborhood, and the File Manager. The File Manager is the standard interface for files in Windows NT 3.5x and Windows 3.x. Although the Explorer replaced the File Manager, you can still use the File Manager, if you prefer, by selecting **Start**, then **Run**, and keying in *WinFile*. An example of accessing a NetWare server using the Explorer is shown in Figure 11.10.

The use of the same interfaces for a NetWare server as a Windows NT server means that you do not have to learn anything new to use the directories and files on the NetWare server. Some functions that are available with a Windows NT server, such as sharing workstation directories, are not available when you access the NetWare server.

If you anticipate repeated access to specific directories and drives, you can set up drive mapping in Windows NT to make it easier and faster to access NetWare server and directories.

You can map a drive by selecting the Network Neighborhood and selecting the drive or server or folder you want to map to, as shown in Figure 11.11.

Alternatively, you can also use NetWare's MAP command to access drives, directories, and files.

Accessing NetWare Print Services

It is very common to share expensive laser printers in a NetWare network. Once a Windows client establishes connection, it can use the NetWare network printers. NetWare supports three ways to attach a printer to a NetWare network as follows:

- Attach the printer to a server machine running Novell NetWare. The NetWare server manages the print queues and other administration functions of the printer.

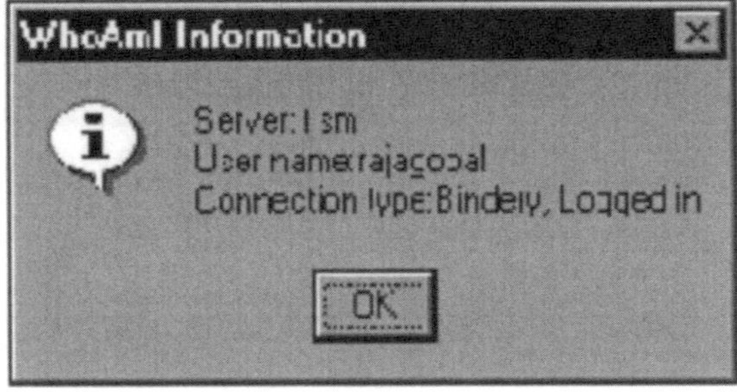

FIGURE 11.9 Determining the NetWare server logged on and the connection type.

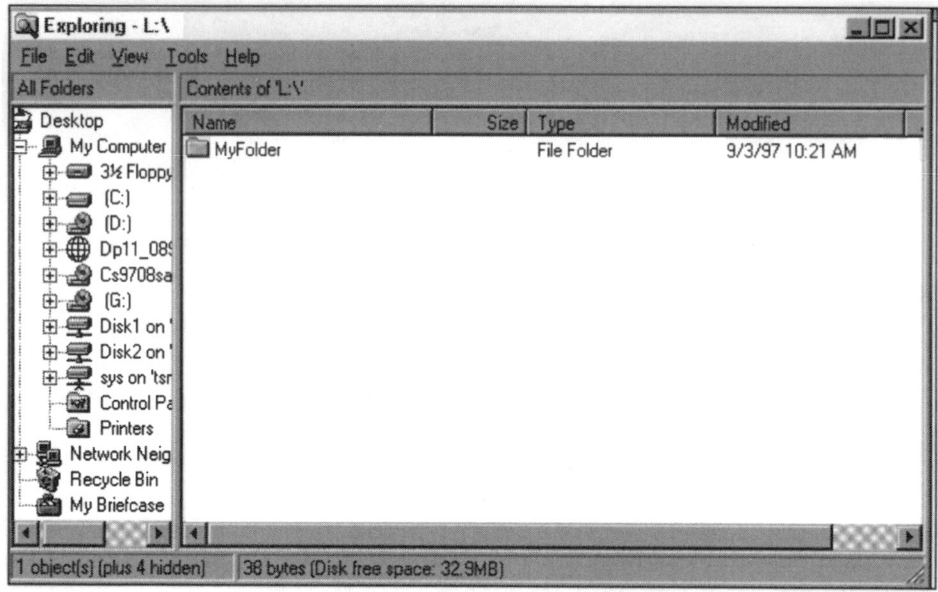

FIGURE 11.10 Accessing a NetWare server using Explorer.

- Attach the printer directly to the network (with a network card in the printer), and manage the queues and administration of the printer from a NetWare server elsewhere on the network.
- Attach the printer to a PC as a simple print server using a spooler.

Regardless of how the printer is attached to the network, you can set up the printer for printing as follows.

Setting up a Novell NetWare Printer in Windows

You typically select printers the first time you log on or want to print. You can choose the printer in one of two ways. Before you select one of the ways and proceed with the steps that follow, make sure that you have a userid and password on the NetWare server and you are logged on to the Novell network.

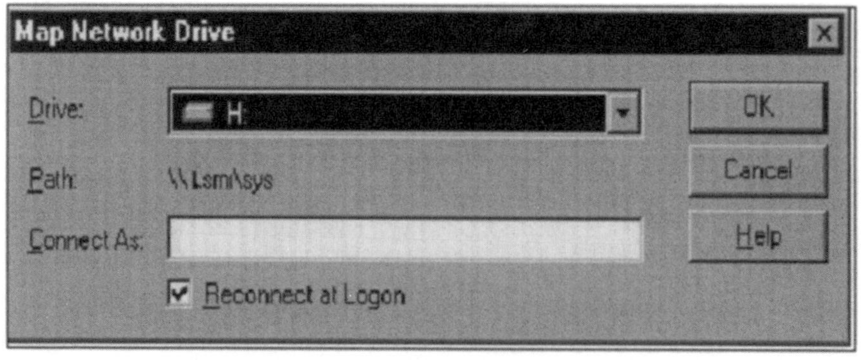

FIGURE 11.11 Mapping a Network Drive.

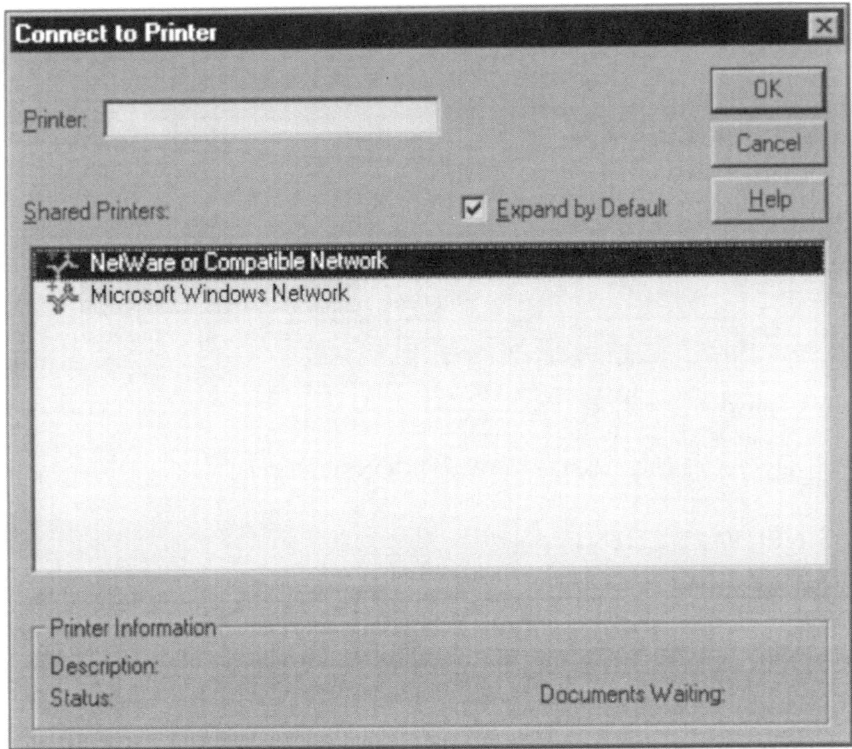

FIGURE 11.12 Locating NetWare printers.

From **Start**, select **Settings**, and then select **Printers**. Choose the option to **Add** printer and select Network printers. This will bring up the menu shown in Figure 11.12. Double-clicking on the NetWare Compatible Network entry will expand and eventually show all the NetWare printers you can use to print.

You can also use the following steps to set up a Novell NetWare printer.

- From the **Start** menu, choose the **Control Panel**.
- In **Control Panel**, choose **Printers** option.
- Select the option to add a printer. In the setup wizard, select a network printer instead of a local printer.
- Browse the network to find your printer; you will see the NetWare attached printers.

Select the one that you want (depending on the printer, you may need to use a driver diskette from the printer manufacturer) to complete the printer installation. When installation is complete, you can start using the printer. Repeat the above steps to add other network printers.

Managing Printers

Once you have set up a NetWare printer, you print from your application the same way as you would to any other printer. You can query and set any network printer as your default and you can change your default. You can also query about print jobs waiting at a printer and cancel outstanding print requests on a NetWare printer just as you would query or cancel any other print request as shown in Figure 11.13. To cancel a print request, select the entry from the print queue shown in Figure 11.13 and click on **Document** in the menu bar. From the pull-down menu, select **Cancel**.

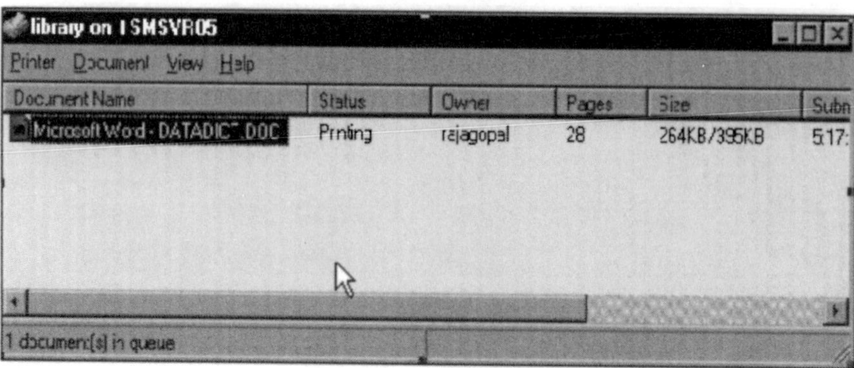

FIGURE 11.13 Print queue for a NetWare printer.

Alternatively, you can also use the NetWare PCONSOLE command to manage print queues.

NOVELL'S NETWARE CLIENT

You can avoid some of the limitations, such as accessing only one bindery or having to define a NetWare server with all users for security, by using NetWare clients from Novell. Novell NetWare clients are available for DOS, Windows 3.x, Windows 95, Windows NT, OS/2, UNIX, and Macintosh. The advantages and disadvantages of this approach compared to using CSNW are summarized in Table 11.1.

With NetWare 4.0, Novell included some significant enhancements to the client software. These include:

- The NETx shell used in prior NetWare versions clients was replaced by a Virtual Loadable Module (VLM) requester.
- The IPX driver (IPX.COM), which has some serious limitations, such as hardcoded network addresses and support for only one IPX protocol stack, has been replaced by Novell Open Datalink Interface (ODI).
- Drivers to facilitate interoperability between ODI and NDIS.

Regardless of whether you use NETx or VLM requester, you are better off using the newer ODI driver because it lets you run other protocols besides IPX, which is very important from a heterogeneous coexistence viewpoint.

TABLE 11.1
Comparing Novell Windows Client and Microsoft Built-In NetWare Client

Advantages	Disadvantages
• Provides NetWare server access even when the native operating system doesn't provide built-in support • The NetWare client typically is a full function NetWare client without limitations • Has more features, particularly for the System Administrator. Some of these features include: • Support for 3270 emulators requiring DOS TSR capability • NetWare Internet Protocol support • NCP Packet Signature support • Custom component support	• Another piece of software that has to be installed and maintained • Additional resources such as memory (for a NetWare stack) and disk space required for the installation and operation of the NetWare client • The additional features seem to make the NetWare client a little slower for some functions compared to the Microsoft product

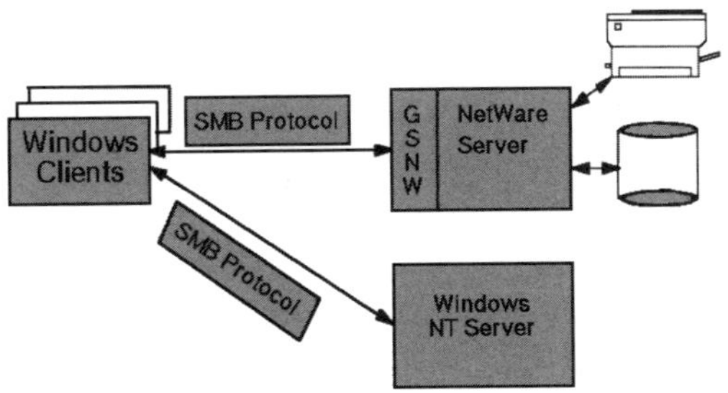

FIGURE 11.14 Gateway Services for NetWare (GSNW).

GATEWAY SERVICE FOR NETWARE (GSNW)

GSNW allows clients running Microsoft client software to access shared files resident on a NetWare server. GSNW also allows Microsoft clients to print to NetWare printers.

Microsoft uses the Server Message Block (SMB) protocol for communication between an NT server and its clients running various Windows software. Novell uses the NetWare Core Protocol (NCP) for communication between NetWare server and NetWare clients. If Windows clients are to access a NetWare server transparently (thinking that they are still talking to Windows NT), translation is required between the SMB and NCP protocols. GSNW is the translator. GSNW translates the upper layer SMB calls to and from NetWare NCP calls. GSNW is part of the Windows NT Server 4.0 Directory Services Manager for NetWare (DSMN). The role of GSNW is shown in Figure 11.14.

GSNW is included with Windows NT Server 4.0. GSNW is implemented as a Windows NT service.

To use GSNW, you need to install GSNW on your Windows NT server. This step is covered below. You also need to configure your NetWare server; this step is covered later in this chapter.

You install GSNW on a Windows NT server using the following steps:

1. From **Start**, click **Settings**, and click **Control Panel**, which brings up the Control Panel. Double-click the Network icon and select the Services tab in the Network Property sheet.
2. Click **Add** button, which displays the Select Network Service dialog. Choose Gateway client service for NetWare from the list of services and then click OK to bring up the Windows NT setup dialog.
3. Specify the complete path information where GSNW files are stored and click Continue.
4. When all files are copied, the Network Property sheet is displayed. The list of services now includes GSNW. Click **Close** and you will be prompted to restart the computer to activate the GSNW service.
5. The first time you use GSNW after installation, it will prompt you to enter a default NetWare server to which GSNW will connect (if more than one NetWare server exists on your network).

GSNW can be used along with Remote Access Service (RAS) built into Windows NT to allow remote Microsoft Networking clients to access NetWare file and print services transparently.

Some considerations in using GSNW:

1. If you use GSNW and want to print to a postscript printer, be sure to turn off the default option of including a banner page. Even though you are printing a postscript file, the banner page is non-postscript and the printer cannot handle the banner page.
2. NDS support — GSNW works fine in NetWare 2.x/3.x environments. GSNW doesn't support Novell NDS, and a GSNW client can access a NetWare 4.x server only in bindery

TABLE 11.2
Comparing Direct and Gateway Connections

Connecting through GSNW	Connecting Directly
Only one logon ID is required for the gateway at the NetWare server; clients accessing the gateway do not need their own NetWare logons	Each client workstation logging into the NetWare server needs a logon ID in the NetWare server
Easy to isolate the NT network and NetWare network and separate the traffic (e.g., by using different network cards for each network)	Difficult to separate the networks and traffic when multiple clients access both Windows NT server and NetWare server independently
Setup is more involved; setup is required at the NetWare server, gateway, and the clients	Setup is simpler; only the NetWare server and the clients need to be set up
The gateway becomes a central routing point for traffic, which could mean delays, downtime (a single point of failure)	Traffic is not centrally routed

emulation mode. If you do not want these limitations, then you can use the Novell NetWare client.

3. GSNW uses a single connection and a group account to the NetWare server that is used by all GSNW clients, including remote clients. This has many implications:
   a. All GSNW clients have identical trustee rights and permissions (those of the one group account).
   b. The number of clients as seen by NetWare is reduced; this has license and system administration implications.
   c. All requests from GSNW clients to the NetWare server are routed through GSNW. This has performance implications. This central routing also implies that if GSNW or the machine goes down, then all the GSNW clients are affected even though the NetWare server they are trying to access may be up and running.
   d. The GSNW clients cannot have individual login scripts since NetWare doesn't recognize them as individual clients.
   e. NetWare's built-in backup cannot be used to back up GSNW clients.

We have discussed different ways for a Windows desktop to access a NetWare server. Table 11.2 compares the advantages and disadvantages of accessing a NetWare server directly vs. through a gateway.

There are multiple ways to attach a Windows client to access NetWare servers. Your choice depends on your environment, the types of NetWare services you need, and the skills you have for network administration.

ACCESSING WINDOWS NT SERVER USING NETWARE CLIENTS

Just as you can transparently access a NetWare server from a Windows client, you can transparently access a Windows NT server from a NetWare client using File and Print Services for NetWare.

File and Print Services for NetWare (FPNW)

FPNW allows the Windows NT Server to emulate a NetWare server. NetWare clients can access shared files and printers in the same way that they would access shared resources on any NetWare server. The Windows NT printers appear as print queues on a NetWare network. FPNW does not

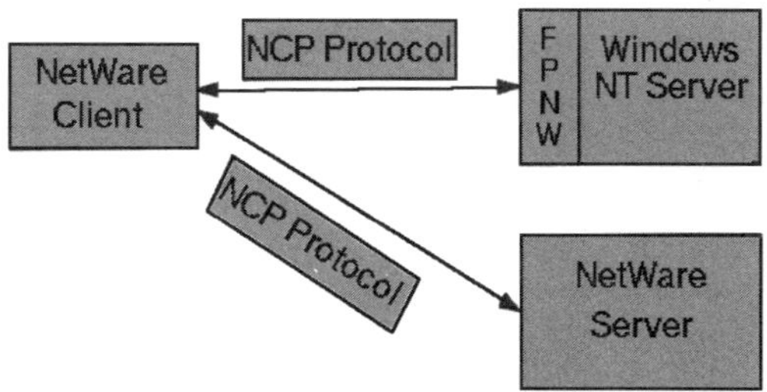

FIGURE 11.15 File and Print Services for NetWare (FPNW).

translate between SMB and NCP. It supports the NCP Protocol so that NetWare clients continue to use that protocol. The role of FPNW is shown in Figure 11.15.

NETWARE ADMINISTRATION FUNCTIONS FROM MICROSOFT

When you are administering NetWare servers and clients in a Windows environment, you have two choices. Microsoft includes network management functions as part of Windows NT. These functions are available in the Control Panel, Network Neighborhood, etc. We will look at some of these functions in this section.

Your other choice is to administer NetWare servers and clients in a Windows environment using software from Novell. We will cover this approach in the next section.

Sometimes it is convenient to monitor and control a NetWare server using Windows NT functions rather than using NetWare administration functions. This may be the case, for example, if you are managing several servers using Windows NT facilities and a NetWare server happens to be one of them.

One of the Windows NT facilities to manage networks is the Server applet in the Control Panel. See Figure 11.16.

Double-clicking the server applet shows the Usage Summary area, which provides the following useful information:

- Sessions: shows the current number of open logons (the same user who logged in twice is counted as two logons)
- Open Files: shows the current number of open data and executable files
- File Locks: shows the current number of file locks (including locks on system, data, and executable files) active
- Open Named Pipes: shows the number of named pipes and mailslots that are open

USER ADMINISTRATION USING THE SERVER APPLET

Besides the information about the server listed, you can perform user administration functions such as viewing and disconnecting one or more users logged onto a NetWare server. To do this, you click on the Users box from the server main menu.

In the user menu that comes up, each user with an active logon has an entry here. You can disconnect a single user by clicking on the user entry and clicking **Disconnect**, or sometimes you may want to disconnect all active users (for example when you want to perform maintenance on the server). Before disconnecting one or more users, ensure that the users are aware that they are going to be disconnected, because they might lose data otherwise. If you have the privileges, you can log the users out as well.

FIGURE 11.16 Server applet in Control Panel.

Shared Resources

You can see what server resources are being shared and by whom in one of two ways. The first way is by using the Shared Resources dialog box, which is accessed by clicking the **Shares** button in the server dialog box.

The top half of the Shared Resources dialog box shows the complete list of resources and a count of the number of users using each resource. If you are interested to see the actual list of users for a specific resource, select the resource by clicking it. The bottom half of the dialog box shows the list of users using that resource. You can disconnect a user or all users from this dialog box as well.

The second way you can see what server resources are being shared and by whom is by using the Open Resources dialog box. You invoke the Open Resources dialog box by clicking the In Use button in the server dialog box. The Open Resources dialog box gives a snapshot of the list of resources that any user has currently open and you can disconnect any resource a user has open. In contrast, if you disconnect a user using a shared resources dialog box, then all the resources that the user has open are disconnected. You can disconnect all resources (this comes in handy if you want to bring down the server, for example). You can also see the number of open file locks for a resource. You can update the snapshot at any time by clicking the **Refresh** button.

Alerts for a Windows NT Administrator about a NetWare Server

You can alert a Windows NT administrator about an event in a NetWare server, besides creating a log entry for the event. Windows NT provides this capability. You can set up alerts by clicking the **Alerts** button on the server applet that displays an Alerts dialog box.

You can send the alert to a computer or the administrator. In the Alerts dialog box, type the name of the administrator or a computer that the alert is to be sent to.

TABLE 11.3
NWADMIN Menu Options

NWADMIN Menu Option	Description
Details	Displays user location and contact information. You can use this option to set up login scripts and security for a user
Rights	Displays the rights of the currently selected object for using/modifying other objects
Object Trustees	Displays the users/groups that have the rights to access and manipulate an object; selecting a trustee entry displays the rights for that trustee
Browse	Displays the contents of a container object; container objects hold (or contain) other objects; an example of a container object is the organizational unit
Create	Displays a dialog box that has a list of the object types that can be contained by the container object
Delete	Removes the current object and all other objects contained within it

NETWARE ADMINISTRATION FUNCTIONS FROM NOVELL

The network management utility from Novell that runs in the Windows NT environment is called NWADMIN. NWADMIN provides a list of network objects, including users, servers, groups, printers, etc. You can add your own objects as well.

Older versions of NetWare used a number of DOS command-type utilities. The nature of these utilities was very similar to the DOS *.bat* files, except that these NetWare utilities had an *.ncf* extension. NWADMIN replaces all the old DOS utilities with a centralized management environment.

The major menu options provided by NWADMIN and their descriptions are summarized in Table 11.3.

Older versions used a number of DOS utilities, and Table 11.4 is a summary of these. Most of these utilities will run in the Windows NT command prompt.

PROTOCOL SUPPORT AND ADMINISTRATION

Another system administration function that you will be dealing with in heterogeneous environments is choosing the communications protocol. The vast majority of Novell NetWare networks use the IPX/SPX protocol for communication between NetWare clients and servers.

Windows NT supports multiple protocols, including IPX/SPX and NetBEUI (which are commonly used in Windows networks), and TCP/IP (which is commonly used in UNIX networks and the Internet). Novell has recently started including support for TCP/IP. Each of the protocols has strengths and weaknesses.

IPX/SPX is proven and is a routable protocol, but it is not an open protocol as TCP/IP is. NetBEUI is a simple protocol, but is not routable and does not handle well such complex tasks as database access. TCP/IP is open and is proven, but has complex setup and configuration. If you have played around with TCP/IP, Winsock, etc. to get connected to an Internet service provider, then you know the configuration work involved with TCP/IP.

You can have both Windows NT and NetWare servers and Windows clients accessing the servers in different ways, as discussed earlier. This may cause different protocols such as IPX/SPX and NetBEUI to coexist on the same network. For example, you can have workstations running Windows NT, and Windows 95, Windows for Workgroups on the same network with a NetWare server.

While the Windows NT workstation is communicating with the NetWare server, the other Windows workstations may be communicating with a Windows NT server using the NetBEUI

TABLE 11.4
NetWare Utilities

NetWare Utility	Description
Fconsole	Console operations such as handling broadcast messages, console messages, file server status, etc.
Filer	Provides data about files such as Size, Owner, etc.
Rconsole	Provides file server console functions from a workstation
Salvage	Recovers deleted files
Session	Provides menu functions for network drives
Slist	Displays a list of NetWare servers
Syscon	Controls users, groups, servers, etc.

protocol. In addition, the same workstation may be using TCP/IP to access the Internet in one window, for example, while browsing NetWare resources using IPX/SPX in another. Although Windows NT supports coexisting protocols, occasionally you may run into network problems due to protocol conflicts.

***Tip**: When you have different types of networks coexisting, try to get consistency in the way the networks are administered. For example, try to have a common response center and helpdesk, and try to get a single userid and password for different networks. If the same userid and password are not feasible, maintain consistency between different networks by using the same password lengths and duration for which passwords are valid, etc.*

Configuring Gateway Services for NetWare

If you plan to use GSNW, then you need to configure your NetWare server to use GSNW by following these steps (you will need supervisor access because you need to use the SYSCON utility):

- Run the SYSCON utility (SYSCON.EXE) and create a NetWare group calling it NTGATEWAY (this name must be used exactly as specified).
- Grant appropriate file, directory, and printer rights to this group. Remember that this is the group of all current and potential GSNW users.
- Create a NetWare user with supervisory rights in addition to file, directory, and printer rights. You can logon to a Windows NT server as the user you just created and perform maintenance functions and also run the migration tool provided by Microsoft (see Migration tool later in this chapter).
- Create other GSNW user accounts within the NTGATEWAY group.

Besides the setup at NetWare, you should also install GSNW on your Windows NT server before GSNW clients can access NetWare files and printers. This was addressed earlier in the chapter.

MIGRATION TOOL TO MIGRATE FROM NETWARE TO WINDOWS NT

Windows NT includes a migration tool to help customers migrate from NetWare to Windows NT. Besides migration, the tool can also assist in network reconfiguration.

The *migration tool* is useful to Network administrators. It automatically migrates NetWare user and group accounts, files and directories, and security and permissions from NetWare server(s) to a Windows NT server. The tool can also help network consolidation since administrators can use the tool to migrate different configurations such as a single NetWare server to a single Windows NT server, multiple NetWare servers to a single Windows NT server, etc. System administrators can use the migration tool to perform a trial migration. The migration tool generates detailed log files that provide an audit trail of changes that may occur during the migration process.

The migration tool just extracts the information from one or more NetWare servers and does not affect the data in the NetWare server. Once copied, the user information is available to other Windows NT server-based BackOffice applications such as SQL Server, SNA Server, and Exchange Server since these applications share the same user account database as the Windows NT server.

NetWare and UNIX

Novell sold UnixWare to SCO. Prior to the sale, Novell had started enhanced compatibility between NetWare and UnixWare. UnixWare NetWare Services allows NetWare access for SCO UNIX clients. Additional information on UnixWare NetWare Services is available at http://www.sco.com/unixware.

SCO UnixWare NetWare Services (NWS)

Starting with version 2.1, UnixWare provides standard NetWare 4.1 networking services in addition to the standard UNIX networking and application services. These services, called NetWare Services (NWS), provide NetWare 4.1 server capabilities that integrate seamlessly into existing Novell and UNIX environments.

With NWS, UnixWare can also act as the primary network server for businesses that need NetWare 4.1 file, print, and directory services, LAN security, and multiple client support.

NWS allows administrators to use native MS Windows-based NetWare tools like NWADMIN and PSERVER to administer the LAN environment.

NWS features include:

- Full NetWare File, Print, and Directory Services on a native SCO UnixWare environment
  - File services include:
    - Enables users to share files and information across the entire network
    - Supports DOS, Windows, Windows 95, UNIX, Mac NCP, and OS/2 clients
    - Works with standard SCO UnixWare 2.1 file systems (vxfs, ufs, sfs, s5) including NFS
    - Mounted file systems
    - Synchronized with host file system
    - Graphical volume manager
    - Combined security of NetWare and UNIX
  - Print services include:
    - Allows users to access any printer on the network by simply knowing the printer's name
    - Graphical printer setup utility
    - NDS based
    - Print Server v4.1
    - Remote printer print monitor for job status
- Full support for Novell Directory Services, NDS APIs, and Novell Cross Platform Services. NDS functions include:
  - Provides detailed map of available network users, resources, and services
  - Common source code with native NetWare, co-developers with Novell

  - Includes functionality for RSA authentication, schema, objects, partitions, replicas, and access
  - Controls, service controls, bindery emulation, and time synchronization
  - Multithreaded for scalable SMP performance
  - Administration using standard NetWare tools
- Supports up to 150 concurrent connections and can achieve performance close to native NetWare performance
- Graphical administration tools for installing and configuring all aspects of NWS operations:
  - NDS administration and repair
  - Administration of NetWare and UNIX System printers from a single tool
  - NWS volume administration
  - NWS networking configuration and tuning
- Supports DOS, Windows, Windows 95, UNIX, Mac, NCP, and OS/2 clients
- Works with standard SCO UnixWare file systems, including NFS-mounted file systems
- Transparent to clients, administrators, and network management system (like Novell ManageWise, etc.)
- Supports a range of protocols common in NetWare environment, including:
  - IPX, SPX2, IPX/SPX diagnostics protocols
  - SAP, RIP routing protocols
  - NCP and NCP Extensions (NCPx)
  - Novell Virtual Terminal (NVT2) terminal emulation over IPX/SPX
  - SNMP network management

Banyan VINES and Windows NT

Although NetWare is the predominant network operating system, there are other network operating systems that are being used as well. One of them is VINES from Banyan. If you have VINES and are interested in integrating with Windows NT or if you are interested in adding directory services to your Windows NT environment, then you may want to consider StreetTalk from Banyan. Banyan has a version of StreetTalk that runs natively on a Windows NT server. This product ties together the StreetTalk Access capabilities with a local copy of StreetTalk, STDA (StreetTalk Directory Assistance service), and Banyan's security and authentication service. Information on Banyan's products is available at http://www.banyan.com.

Basic features of StreetTalk include:

- StreetTalk, STDA, and Banyan's Security Service running as native Windows NT services, at the same level as VINES
- Full interoperability with StreetTalk in VINES
- Runs on Windows NT Server 3.51 and 4.0
- Integrated with Windows NT's Event Monitor and Performance Monitor, which can be SNMP-enabled
- Enhanced VINES protocol stack, enabling multiple sessions per server
- Support for Banyan's Sequenced Routing Transport Protocol
- Support for DOS, Windows 3.x, Windows 95, Windows NT, and OS/2 clients
- Support for both Windows NTFS and FAT file systems
- File and print services support (includes all of the capabilities of StreetTalk Access)
- Long file name support for Windows 95 and Windows NT clients
- Support for international file names, including double byte Kanji characters
- Support for OS/2 Extended Attributes

- TCP/IP support for Windows 95 and Windows NT clients
- A new 32-bit management tool ("StreetTalk Explorer" for Windows 95 or Windows NT) to manage all services

Banyan has issued two additional releases, adding such functionality as:

- Banyan's Intelligent Messaging Service
- Server-to-Server TCP/IP
- Enhanced StreetTalk Explorer functionality including modules for Users, Groups, Organizations, Lists, Nicknames, Security, StreetTalk, STDA, and Intelligent Messaging
- Optimize and Audit function to keep list, nickname, and user names current
- Remote restart and time synchronization services
- Enhanced backup and restore utilizing Legato's Networker for Windows NT
- Guaranteed login for DOS, Windows 3.1, Windows 95, and Windows NT clients
- Developers toolkit for integration of third-party services
- Support for Windows 95 System Policies

Conclusion

We looked at accessing Windows NT server from NetWare clients and vice versa for file and print services. Both Microsoft and Novell offer products for accomplishing these functions. We also looked at network administration functions from Microsoft and Novell, and briefly looked at the tool Microsoft provides to migrate from NetWare to Windows NT.

12 e-mail and Internet in Heterogeneous Environments

INTRODUCTION

In earlier chapters we looked at porting applications from one environment to another, developing applications that could run in multiple environments, connecting clients to heterogeneous servers for file and print access, etc. Another function that has become almost as commonplace as the telephone is the e-mail function. e-mail is used for both intra-organization communications and for communications with others who are not part of the organization.

As you would expect, this explosive growth in e-mail has resulted in the availability of e-mail products from a number of vendors. Some of the products are host or mainframe based, while others are LAN based. In either case, you also have a number of dialup remote users who need access to e-mail. As you may also expect, these products are not completely compatible and you may have problems sending and receiving mail between the different products. Continuing our network focus, let us look at migration and coexistence issues that pertain to e-mail and the Internet.

If you are considering migrating from one environment to another (say UNIX to Windows NT), pay special attention to e-mail since the number of users of e-mail is typically more than any production application you may have, most users are not likely to tolerate even a short outage of the e-mail application, and there is no way to shut down inputs to the e-mail system if your e-mail users can receive external e-mail.

HETEROGENEOUS e-MAIL SYSTEMS

There are a number of different e-mail systems. Some of them use proprietary protocols. While most systems easily handle simple inline text, e-mail becomes a problem when you attempt more complicated functions such as multiple attachments where some of the attachments contain graphics and other multimedia messages. Some of the e-mail systems commonly used include:

- All-in-One from DEC
- PROFS/OfficeVision from IBM
- Notes and cc:Mail from Lotus/IBM
- Microsoft Mail for PC and AppleTalk networks
- Microsoft Exchange Server
- MCI Mail
- AT&T Mail, etc.

Before we look at migration and coexistence issues involving e-mail systems, let us take a look at the components of an e-mail system and how these components are implemented in UNIX mail systems and Windows NT exchange server.

MAIL SYSTEM COMPONENTS*

The components of any mail system include:

- Computer servers acting as "post offices," collecting mail, and providing it to users (storing and forwarding it). Mail servers include support for the following:
  - Message transport protocol specific to mail messaging systems.
  - Server support for user access. In centralized mail systems, this is an engineered integration between mail user agents and the server. In distributed, client/server mail implementations, this is a message access protocol, shared by clients and servers. A protocol is chosen based on desired clients, or client behavior.
  - A method of properly presenting message formats to users (e.g., sending a Microsoft Word document to a UNIX workstation user in a manner the recipient can use as a document).
  - Directory services, which have two basic functions: to store and provide proper mail addresses to all mail users, and to synchronize directories across mail servers for updated, correct addresses.
- The network between servers, including:
  - Physical and logical network (e.g., cable or satellite connections, Internet and/or intranet).
  - Network protocol (e.g., TCP/IP).
- A mail client running on a desktop PC or workstation, or a character-based terminal. The user agent varies based on the user's desktop device and preferences.
- Management utilities, ranging from ad hoc to dedicated management stations.

Figure 12.1 shows the components of a mail system.

Let us look at how these components are implemented in UNIX and Windows NT environments.

E-MAIL SYSTEM COMPONENTS IN UNIX

This section discusses the components of a mail system in a typical UNIX installation.

Mail Server Functions

UNIX mail systems, until recently, have been centralized mail systems, as opposed to logically distributed client/server implementations, even when including UNIX workstations in the environment. For example, when UNIX workstation users write and send mail from their workstations, their mail agent software is working on the central server, providing access to the server's mail application. This centralized characteristic of traditional UNIX mail systems represents the greatest challenge when considering integration with Windows NT, which is a client/server implementation.

The mail server functions in a UNIX system include:

- Message Transport protocol: SMTP (Simple Mail Transport Protocol) is implemented in most vendors' UNIX systems as the Sendmail utility. The Sendmail utility handles more than just the store and forward function between mail servers.
- Server support for user access: In centralized UNIX mail environments (the typical case for both System V and BSD UNIX systems), the mail user's agent software connects to the Sendmail program on the UNIX server, which allows the user to send, receive, and manipulate mail.
- Recent customer demand for client/server implementations of mail systems result in support for an additional access method for UNIX users, a message access protocol

* Reproduced with permission from Digital Equipment Corporation.

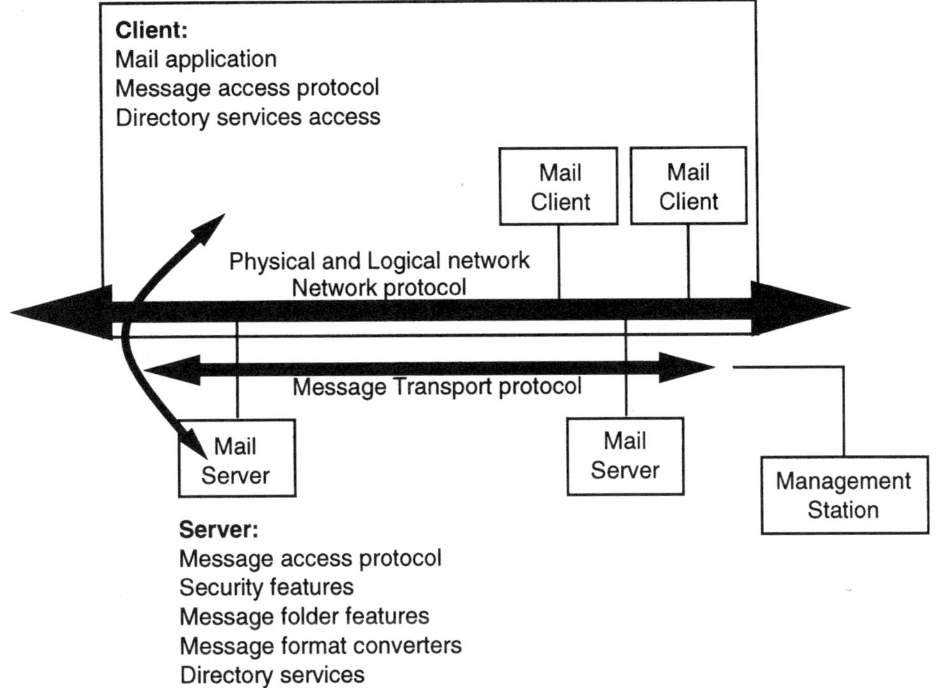

FIGURE 12.1 Components of an e-mail system.

called POP3 (Post Office Protocol Version 3). POP3, when supported by both the mail server and client, enables downloading of messages to the client desktop.

- Directory services: Lists of mail users and their proper addresses, as handled by UNIX mail systems, are kept in one of two places:
  - System-wide database of user names, available to Sendmail.
  - User-specific files that define aliases.
- Definitions of nicknames or user names and their mail addresses are available to the user who owns the file.

Network Between Servers

The network between servers includes:

- Physical and logical networks: The UNIX message transport protocol SMTP is now the standard protocol for Internet mail. This development may affect how you choose to implement UNIX and Windows NT integration. For example, if you use Internet mail heavily, your investment in UNIX SMTP-style mail systems transfers directly to this new environment
- Network messaging protocol: These include TCP/IP, and in some Digital installations, DECnet.

Mail Client

The mail client varies, based on the user's desktop device and preferences. UNIX users have several choices of mail user agents. UNIX users with character-based terminals rely on the following command line user agents.

- *binmail*: A command line user agent that ships with most System V and Berkeley-based UNIX systems.
- *mh*: The Rand mail handler (public domain software bundled by some UNIX vendors, including Digital), a command line interface to centralized SMTP mail systems, and using a Sendmail interface.
- *mailx*: A command line user agent that ships with most System V and Berkeley UNIX systems.

UNIX users with graphical workstations or X-terminals have additional options, including:

- *xmh*: This is the Motif-compliant X Windows-based, public domain graphical user agent built on *mh*.
- *dxmail*: This is the X Windows-based graphical user agent, built on mh, that is POP3 aware, meaning it can perform client/server mail functions in cooperation with a POP3 SMTP mail server *dtmail*.
- *dtmail*: This is the graphical user agent that ships with CDE (the Common Desktop Environment). The *dtmail* agent, as shipped by Digital, is POP3 aware, meaning it can perform client/server mail functions in cooperation with a POP3 SMTP mail server.

Additionally, some versions of *dtmail* are MIME capable, meaning those users enjoy automatic format conversion for files sent through the mail system. Digital and Sun Microsystems both ship MIME-aware versions of dtmail.

Traditional UNIX mail systems, centralized with users logging into the server, manage communication from the user to the server via application-to-application communication. Clients use *Sendmail* to log onto the host mail server, communicating directly with the *Sendmail* application on the server, allowing users to read, forward, delete, create, and send messages.

More recent client/server implementations of UNIX mail systems support POP3 in client user agents. Both *dtmail* and *dxmail* are POP3 enabled. Directory services access is provided to mail clients through the mail server and is limited to the use of personal alias files or system-wide Sendmail user databases.

Mail Management Utilities

Management utilities in UNIX mail installations are typically part of the operating system. While some vendors have provided mail management tools, UNIX mail management generally is handled with ad hoc utilities, as opposed to a dedicated mail management station. Useful utilities for system administrators include:

- *sendmail.cf* configuration file: Defines how messages travel throughout an SMTP-based mail system of servers.
- *mailqueue* command: Lists the queue of mail messages being sent, where they are in the network, and why they are where they are.
- *aliases* command: Defines users and their mail addresses at a personal or system-wide level.
- *newaliases* command: Converts alias files from text to binary format for performance improvement in large installations.
- *mailconfig* graphical application: Ships with Digital UNIX to configure mail servers and clients in an SMTP environment. This application supports multiple network protocols (uucp, DECnet, TCP/IP) and other variances in mail systems.

e-Mail System Components in Windows NT Exchange Server

Mail Server Functions

A mail server consists of a Windows NT system, either Intel- or Alpha-based, running Microsoft Exchange Server software. It includes a message transport protocol. Messages between Exchange Servers travel via Microsoft's RPC (Remote Procedure Call) protocol. RPC is particularly desirable over local area networks, which are typically reliable and fast.

Exchange offers the option of SMTP as a transport protocol, sufficient for participating in a UNIX SMTP mail environment. The Exchange Internet Mail Connector product provides SMTP capability to an Exchange server.

Microsoft implements Mail Application Programming Interface (MAPI) as the message access protocol for Exchange Server, shared by Exchange clients. MAPI is a multifunctional interface for applications that involve mail and messaging, such as Electronic Data Interchange (EDI) applications between different companies.

File Format Conversion

Between Exchange Server and Client, Exchange uses an internal format for converting different file formats between users. When using the X.400 transport, Exchange Server employs a format standard called the File Transfer Body Part to identify different document formats — a Microsoft Word document, for example, contained within a single mail message.

Directory Services and Synchronization

The X.500 International Directory Service Standards were designed to provide a global directory capability for heterogeneous environments. Microsoft based the design and the internal structures of the Exchange Directory on many of the recommendations outlined in the X.500 standards, and has committed to be fully compliant in a future release of Exchange Server. In addition, most of the older mail systems vendors have committed to implement the X.500 directory standard at some time in the future. However, at present, few mail systems are X.500 compliant, so for practical purposes gateways are required among the different mail directories.

The Microsoft Exchange Directory Synchronization Agent (DXA) allows system managers to perform directory synchronization with other mail systems based on Microsoft's MSMail Directory Format. The DXA also uses Microsoft Mail synchronization, rather than directory-to-directory automatic replication and synchronization, which would allow other X.500 directories to communicate directly with the Exchange Directory.

Digital X.500 Directory Synchronizer acts as a partner to the Exchange directory by allowing synchronization among Exchange's directories and other directories that may be used within the enterprise. In effect, the Digital X.500 Directory Synchronizer can filter all directories within an enterprise to ensure that everyone can share directory information, no matter what mail system they use.

Mail Client

For Windows NT users, the mail client varies, based on the user's desktop device and preferences. The mail user agent of choice in an Exchange environment is Exchange Client. Exchange Server also supports clients with MAPI Service Provider Interfaces (SPIs). The message access protocol shared between Exchange Client and Exchange Server is MAPI or POP3. Clients access available directory services via either MAPI or LDAP (Lightweight Directory Access Protocol).

Mail Management

Microsoft Exchange features a dedicated management station for Exchange installations.

HETEROGENEOUS e-MAIL SYSTEM OPTIONS

When a new environment is introduced for one reason, there is a possibility that the environment would be used for other functions available in the environment. For example, an organization may decide to introduce Windows NT to replace an existing application in UNIX, or use Windows NT as a Web server. Subsequently, the organization may look at using Microsoft Exchange for its e-mail needs.

When you have more than one e-mail system in your organization and you are considering the e-mail functions in a new e-mail system, you have the following options:

- Coexist with multiple e-mail systems for the foreseeable future and provide for passing e-mail back and forth between the different systems as needed.
- Migrate from one e-mail system (or multiple e-mail systems) to one e-mail system in a phased manner, coexisting with different systems in the meanwhile.
- Migrate from one e-mail system to another in one step without any coexistence period (also called "hot cutover").

Let us look at the characteristics of each of the options. Let us also look at some tools that will assist you in your e-mail migration and coexistence.

e-MAIL COEXISTENCE

In Chapter 1 we compared the advantages and disadvantages of homogeneous and heterogeneous environments. That discussion also applies to e-mail systems. In cases where you have two (or more) large installed bases of users using different e-mail systems, the appropriate option might be to leave the systems as is and not attempt to migrate. This could happen for example when two companies merge or when two or more divisions of a company merge.

While there may be some advantages in reduced maintenance and better compatibility with one e-mail system instead two, the costs and risks involved in migrating the e-mail systems and retraining a large user base are likely to outweigh the potential advantages. But since you are likely to require that the users of the different e-mail systems communicate with each other, you need tools that will facilitate e-mail systems to coexist.

You need tools to pass messages from one e-mail system to another and to permit sharing the user directories between the e-mail systems. If sharing a physical directory is not possible and you are maintaining two or more directories, you should ensure that the directories are consistent between the different systems at all times. If there is no automatic way to ensure consistency, then you may need to come up with manual ways to accomplish this.

You may also have to come up with utilities and procedures when one of the e-mail systems can handle a certain type of attachment that another e-mail system cannot. When you are performing system configuration updates to one or more of the e-mail systems, you have to try to ensure that these changes are not transparent to external users of the e-mail systems.

PHASED e-MAIL MIGRATION

If the number of users is not large and/or if one or more of the e-mail systems is old and is being considered for replacement, then it may be worthwhile to consolidate e-mail systems and migrate from one e-mail system to another. The longer-term reduced costs of a consolidated e-mail system may outweigh the initial upfront costs of migrating from one e-mail system to another. You have a better return on your IT investment when you have multiple business applications using the same hardware and software environment.

You should ensure that the mail received in one system for a user in another system is transferred seamlessly and without delay. If a user's e-mail ID has to change, you should provide enough lag time to allow for receipt and forward of e-mail at the old address. Migration tools are available to move user and other system setup information from one e-mail system to another.

One of the choices that must be made in migrating to a new e-mail system is whether existing e-mail messages, attachments, etc., should be moved. If existing messages are not moved, then the users must be asked to manually clean up their mail. Migration tools sometimes also migrate individual user's custom setup data besides system setup data.

When you have a large number of e-mail users, you typically will have a number of interconnected post offices. Interconnection ensures that the mail is forwarded to the right post office. Each interconnected post office serves a portion of the user community. One strategy for a phased migration is to migrate one post office at a time. Since the post offices are interconnected, you must update the interconnection information after the migration.

Before you start migrating, ensure that you are not migrating unnecessary data to the new system. For example, there may be outdated data about users no longer on the e-mail system. Check the administrative tools in your current e-mail system that let you identify unnecessary data. One example of such a utility is the PODIAG utility for Microsoft Mail.

One-Step e-Mail Migration

This is an option that is available only in limited circumstances when the number of users using the e-mail system is small and all the users can be migrated at one time, the data to be migrated are small, and the total migration can be done in a short time. When you are planning for any change to your e-mail system, a one-step migration in particular, extensive planning with administrators and users is required.

The plan should also include fall-back procedures in the event that the migration or other changes to the e-mail system runs into problems. As in phased migration, migration tools are available to move user system setup, and user's custom setup information from one e-mail system to another. For example, Microsoft includes a number of migration tools to migrate information from popular e-mail systems to Microsoft Exchange.

One-step migration involves installing and testing the new e-mail system well ahead of the migration date. For example, you can set up the e-mail clients at user workstations. The new e-mail server should be operational and setup data that is not likely to change should be preloaded as much as possible. One-step migrations are also easier to accomplish when the migration is between different versions of the e-mail systems from the same vendor (for example, if you are migrating from Microsoft Mail server to Microsoft Exchange server).

You should arrange for limited testing after the migration from selected user workstations to ensure that the migration was successful. You should also include a list of steps users need to perform (such as setting up the profiles or any custom setups that could not be migrated) before the new e-mail system can be used. One benefit of the one-step method is that, if successful, you are finished, compared to what may be a long, drawn-out process for a phased migration.

e-MAIL CHARACTERISTICS

Before we look at some tools that will help in your migration and/or coexistence of e-mail systems, let us look at some characteristics of e-mail systems. Open Standards are playing an increasing role in e-mail systems. The common standards include X.400, X.500, and the Simple Mail Transfer Protocol (SMTP).

Unlike other business production applications, e-mail systems cannot normally have scheduled downtime when there will be no e-mail activity. e-mail is also a way of spreading viruses (particularly through attachments). e-mail application, more than most other business applications, is required to be accessed remotely by people in the organization who are traveling or working from home.

Besides the mail messages themselves, there are other important functions in an e-mail system, including:

- Public and private address lists
- Handling mail attachments that can have different data types
- Securing e-mail becomes more important as more business transactions are conducted through e-mail
- Privacy issues associated with e-mail, unlike most other business applications

E-MAIL MIGRATION AND COEXISTENCE TOOLS

The following tool functions will assist in your e-mail migration and coexistence:

- Ability to interface with external e-mail systems
- Ability to pass e-mail between the different e-mail systems within an organization
- Ability to keep the different user and other directories in synchronization or migrate directories from one e-mail system to another
- Ensure the security of e-mail messages
- Ability to have a universal mail client

Let us look at some of the tool functions in greater detail.

INTERFACING WITH EXTERNAL E-MAIL SYSTEMS

Gateways or connectors are used to exchange e-mail between different e-mail systems in an organization as well as exchanging e-mail with users external to the organization. The external users are very likely to use a number of different e-mail systems (the common ones were listed in the beginning of the chapter). Interfacing with external e-mail systems is typically performed using gateways or connectors. Check with your e-mail system provider to see the built-in connectors provided. You can typically develop your own connector if you need to interface with an e-mail system that does not have a built-in connector.

The Microsoft Exchange Server, for example, includes three built-in connectors:

- MSMail connector to interface with the older MS Mail PC or AppleTalk systems
- Internet Mail Connector (IMC) to interface with the Internet for e-mail
- X.400 Connector to interface with systems using the X.400 standard

There are also a number of connectors available from third parties for fax, wireless connections, etc.

PASSING E-MAIL BETWEEN E-MAIL SYSTEMS

You need to pass e-mail between the different e-mail systems being used in your organization if you decide to have coexisting e-mail systems or if you go for a phased migration. You can pass e-mail messages in one of the following ways:

- Use the Internet
- Use a public X.400 network
- Acquire or develop a custom gateway between the e-mail systems you want to pass e-mail messages between

Use of a custom gateway may be more expensive and may take time to develop. But custom gateways can typically do a better job of seamless passing of messages. Custom gateways also tend to be more secure and reliable.

Check with your e-mail vendor to see if they provide tools to pass e-mail between e-mail systems.

If you are trying to coexist with MSMail and Microsoft Exchange, then the MSMail Connector Interchange (part of the MSMail Connector) will perform format translations between Microsoft Exchange and MSMail and interface with the appropriate message transfer agents (MTAs). The MSMail Connector also includes the MSMail Connector PostOffice, which is a temporary message store that holds messages that are in transition between MSMail and Microsoft Exchange.

If you have Microsoft- and UNIX-based e-mail systems, then you can use the Internet Mail Connector (IMC) shipped with Microsoft Exchange for coexistence. UNIX-based e-mail systems typically use SMTP or POP3 Protocol. POP3 is short for Post Office Protocol 3. IMC supports UUENCODE and MIME for message transfers using SMTP. UUENCODE and MIME are commonly used UNIX encoding schemes. However, binhex (commonly used in Macs) is not supported. MIME mappings to file name extensions are supported, which facilitates automatic handling of mail attachments.

Synchronization of Directories

A common method of addressing e-mail to multiple recipients is through address lists, which are lists of e-mail userids. Often, users served by different e-mail systems within an organization belong to the same address list. In addition, there will be common user lists that should be the same across the different e-mail systems. Thus, the same directory list across different e-mail systems should be synchronized for updates. Common information in e-mail systems is also stored in public folders.

Directory information across e-mail systems can be kept synchronized either manually or automatically (if the e-mail system supports directory synchronization protocol).

Check with your e-mail vendor(s) for directory synchronization tools. Microsoft Exchange, for example, includes a Directory Exchange Agent (DXA) to keep an Exchange directory in synchronization with MSMail directory. The DXA acts as both a server and a requester to the MSMail system.

UNIX-based e-mail systems typically do not support directories or use proprietary directories (particularly for POP3 systems). If you are migrating from a UNIX system that uses a proprietary directory, to Microsoft Exchange, one way to transfer the directory contents would be to export or dump the directory contents and convert the contents into a format suitable for import with the directory import tool provided by Microsoft.

If you want to change naming conventions in your e-mail system, you can alter the exported data prior to import. The exported data is text data and you can use a text editor or write a program to alter the data. Once you have performed the other migration steps to let the user receive e-mail through Exchange, you need to manually erase the import files and user information in the UNIX e-mail system.

If you are migrating from one e-mail system to another, check with your e-mail vendor for directory migration tools. Microsoft supplies a Wizard, MAILMIG.EXE, that handles the migration of MSMail and Lotus' cc:Mail. The Wizard handles migrating mailboxes, messages in the mailboxes, e-mail message attachments, user's custom setup data such as Personal Address Book entries, etc. The Wizard performs the migration in a two-step process. In the first step, it exports the data to three types of files called the packing list, primary intermediate, and secondary intermediate files. The Wizard then imports the extracted data.

By separating the two steps, you can run the steps independently. For some other e-mail systems such as IBM's PROFS or DEC's All-in-One, the Wizard does not perform a complete migration, as it does for cc:Mail. Instead, Microsoft provides *source extractors* that extract the e-mail migration data. You can then manually run the import step using the Wizard. For e-mail systems not supported by Microsoft, you can still migrate by writing your own source extractor. Your source extractor should manually extract the data required for migration and format that data in the format suitable for import by the migration wizard. You may have to manually migrate data in public folders.

Sometimes, the source of your e-mail directory may not be another e-mail directory. You may want to use the list of valid network operating system users. For example, if you are setting up a new e-mail system and want to authorize current network operating system users, you may be able to export the names from the network operating system and import them into your e-mail system. Microsoft includes a directory import feature in the Exchange product that lets network user account information be extracted from a NetWare server or Banyan VINES server (besides Windows NT server).

e-Mail Security

As e-mail is used to conduct regular business information exchange, the need for securing the e-mail messages has become paramount. Newer e-mail systems include features such as encryption and digital signatures to ensure e-mail security.

Universal Mail Client

One way to mitigate e-mail coexistence and migration issues is to have e-mail clients that can interface with a number of different e-mail service providers at the back end. If you are coexisting e-mail systems, the Universal mail client can receive e-mail from a number of different service providers. If you are performing a migration, your users can be accessing e-mail using one provider before migration. After migration, the client can be reconfigured to access another e-mail provider.

For example, the Windows messaging client (formerly called the exchange client) supports what Microsoft calls *Universal Inbox*. This client can be configured to receive e-mail from a number of mail sources such as CompuServe Mail, Microsoft Mail, Exchange server, Internet mail, etc. The connection between the client and the mail source could be a regular office LAN/WAN or a dialup connection (for access from home or while traveling). Windows NT dialup networking support is normally required for dialup connections.

Having looked at some e-mail migration and coexistence tools in general, let us take a look at specific products from Digital for the heterogeneous e-mail environments.

MailWorks and MAILBus 400

MailWorks and MAILBus are two products from Digital for heterogeneous e-mail integration.

Figure 12.2 shows how the products fit in a heterogeneous e-mail solution.

Digital provides MailWorks and MAILBus 400, an X.400 mail backbone that interconnects all clients and servers that support X.400. Microsoft also offers an X.400 connector for integrating Exchange with X.400 backbones. Digital X.500 directory services further integrate the UNIX and Windows NT environments.

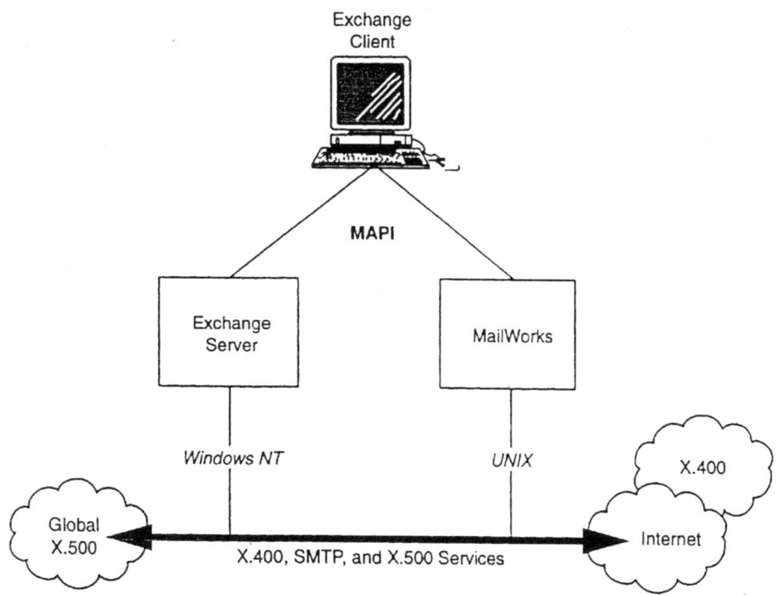

FIGURE 12.2 e-mail integration products from Digital.

MAILBus 400 Software

Digital MAILBus 400 software provides X.400 backbone functionality to UNIX and Windows NT systems. MAILBus 400 automatically recognizes File Transfer Body Parts and presents them to other X.400 servers in the manner expected by those servers. In other words, MAILBus 400 ensures that all components of messages arrive in a form that the end-user can read.

A backbone server can help manage the administration of mail transport agents (MTAs). For example, with the Digital MAILBus 400 backbone services, the administrator notifies the backbone node of a change to the MTA listing, and the backbone node then handles all of the communication among the different systems. Because the backbone server acts as a single repository of current MTA information, replication of that information on each MTA is not necessary. This feature makes it easy to set up and manage a large X.400 installation.

MAILBus 400 uses X.400 as its native backbone transport, but, like Exchange Server, can accommodate SMTP via an SMTP gateway. It thus provides efficient, reliable, high-performance backbone transport and a variety of gateways to foreign mail systems.

Using MAILBus 400, an organization can implement an X.400 backbone with the knowledge that people can exchange messages by using either the X.400 protocol or SMTP, whichever is more appropriate to the application. For example, a company may choose to use X.400 between its Exchange Servers, while transmitting SMTP to the rest of the Internet. Digital has the skill and the capability to help companies decide which of these two backbone technologies is appropriate for them, and to build integration between Exchange Server and other mail systems by using either approach.

PMDF Mailbus 400

For additional X.400 functionality, Digital partners with Innosoft International, Inc. Innosoft's PMDF 400 module provides a direct connection between the Digital Mailbus 400 message transfer agent and the messaging environments that PMDF supports.

Digital X.500 Directory Services

X.500 provides a global address book of names and electronic mail addresses for multivendor messaging systems. X.500 can store employee data (including characteristic attributes) in a single directory. You can use the X.500 Directory Service to create a vendor-independent, enterprise-wide directory service. The product supports the CCITT and ISO X.500 standard for vendor-independent directory service protocols. It is ideally suited for multivendor environments and applications that require distributed access and management.

The X.500 Directory Server software functions as an information store for OSI or TCP/IP networks. Using software clients supplied by Digital (or other X.500 software providers), X.500 Directory Server can access this information regardless of where it resides in the network.

For data consistency, MAILBus 400 stores routing information in the DEC X.500 Directory Service. The directory service provides a shared database of information that requires no manual synchronization. This lowers the cost of ownership by reducing management overhead.

MailWorks for UNIX software lets users access mail addresses from X.500, thus providing access to an enterprise-wide directory of names and electronic mail addresses.

X.500 Directory Service synchronization enables the automated and bidirectional exchange of any electronic directory information, for example, cc:mail and Microsoft Mail, in a multivendor environment.

Administrative and Planning Aspects of e-Mail Migration

Besides the technical aspects of e-mail migration such as the tools and utilities, there are a number of administrative and planning aspects of e-mail migration. These include the following:

- Planning for the migration. This is best accomplished by forming an e-mail migration team with members from the administrator, user groups, and executive oversight.
- User training prior to migration. The training material should include an "equivalent function" list that shows the most commonly used e-mail functions in the current system and how the same functions can be accomplished in the new system. Another tool commonly used and very useful in educating users and reducing user support required is a list of anticipated questions with answers (commonly called FAQs).
- Helpdesk support after the migration. Users tend to have the most number of questions and problems immediately following the migration. A helpdesk should be set up (or an existing one should be beefed up to meet the increased demand).
- e-mail userids and distribution lists should be named as close as possible to the names in the current e-mail system. But if you have been having naming problems, migration of e-mail systems is a good time to adopt a new convention.
- Migration should be attempted in batches and the first few batches should be computer-savvy users. These users are more likely to identify problems and are easier to handle from a helpdesk. Of course, within a set of computer-savvy users, you want to pick the groups that are not facing critical deadlines.
- Every step in the migration plan should anticipate problems and each problem should have solutions to complete the migration and fall-back contingency plans for irrecoverable errors that prevent successful migration.
- In a phased migration, plan to reuse the hardware resources since they are freed up when users are migrated off the e-mail system.

TABLE 12.1
TCP/IP Command and Utilities in Windows NT

TCP/IP Command/Utility	Description
arp	Utility to modify IP-to-Ethernet and Token Ring address translation tables to fix routing problems
finger	Displays information about a user on a remote system
ftp	File transfer program to transfer files, commonly used to download files from the Internet
hostname	Displays the current computer's host name
ipconfig	Displays TCP/IP settings in effect
lpq	Displays a remote print queue status (the remote computer should be running the lpd service)
lpr	Print on a computer which has an LPD server running
nbtstat	Displays protocol statistics and connections (uses NetBIOS)
netstat	Displays connections and protocol statistics
ping	Test connection to another TCP/IP node
rcp	Copies files between Windows NT and any computer running the remote shell daemon (RSHD); optionally, you can include subdirectories and files within them
rexec	Transfer a command for execution to another computer (which runs the RSH service)
route	Permits update of network routing tables
telnet	Emulate the local computer to be a terminal for a remote computer. See Chapter 6.
tftp	Transfer files to and from a remote computer (running the tftp service)
tracert	Traces the route to a given destination node

INTERNET FUNCTIONS IN UNIX AND WINDOWS NT

Besides e-mail, which was covered earlier in the chapter, there are other Internet-related functions commonly used. Such functions include FTP, Newsgroups, Telnet, World Wide Web (WWW) and WWW browsers, etc. If you are migrating from one environment to another (e.g., from UNIX to Windows NT), then you need to know what the equivalent functions are in the new environment.

TCP/IP Commands and Utilities

Prior to the advent of Windows NT, most Internet applications were developed in the UNIX environment. UNIX had included the Internet-related communication functions, TCP/IP commands, and utilities support for a long time. Windows NT also includes the same functions, either built-in or through third parties.

Windows NT includes the built-in TCP/IP commands and utilities shown in Table 12.1.

Windows NT also includes the following built-in Internet Functions at the server level:

- Gopher
- HTTP Support
- WAIS Server/Toolkit

Besides the built-in functions, NT Internet Functions available through third parties include:

- Archie
- Web Browsers such as Netscape and Mosaic (besides Microsoft's own Internet Explorer)

World Wide Web

The point-and-click convenience of the hyperlinks and the World Wide Web have become so popular that the phrase World Wide Web (WWW) is now used synonymously with Internet. The most common software for accessing the WWW is the browser. Since browsers are available for different platforms, if you migrate from one environment to another, you have to get the browser for your environment. Applications written using HTML, CGI, Perl, etc., in one environment (e.g., the UNIX environment) can be ported to another (e.g., the Windows NT environment), and this is addressed in Chapter 3. The user interface of browsers across environments is fairly standard and you can adjust from one to another with relative ease.

13 Solution Selection Factors and Guidelines

INTRODUCTION

Organizations evaluating migration and coexistence solutions across heterogeneous environments should consider a number of different factors. The factors can be broadly grouped as follows:

- Industry-wide factors
- Enterprise-specific factors
- Solution-specific factors

Let us look at each of the factors in detail.

INDUSTRY FACTORS

Microsoft Windows is established on the desktop. The familiarity of the interface, coupled with the likelihood of the Windows interface being present predominantly in the increasing home computer market, assures that the bulk of new shrink-wrapped applications will be Windows based. New enterprise applications are being developed predominantly as distributed client/server applications, while legacy applications are somewhat slowly removed from the mainframe. There are many mission-critical applications on UNIX, and UNIX is still a proven and good candidate for expanding current enterprise applications as well as new ones. Windows NT seems to be gaining market share at the expense of NetWare and to some extent UNIX. Given the above, organizations with legacy and other non-Windows-based applications are looking at Windows-based solutions not only for the desktop, but for enterprise applications as well. An organization has to decide how these and other factors (not directly related to UNIX/Windows NT migration coexistence and not covered in the book) apply to their situation.

ENTERPRISE FACTORS

The factors listed below differ between enterprises and would influence the selection of migration/coexistence solutions.

- The existing UNIX install base, including in-house developed and commercial off-the-shelf (COTS) packages. If the install base is small, the organization may prefer to use a porting tool and attempt to move toward a homogeneous environment. If the install base is large, the organization may prefer to leave the current application environment as is and add Windows using a solution like Windows in an X-terminal.
- Investment, skills, and availability of current in-house information systems staff. The skills to be considered include both system development and system administration skills. An existing homogeneous UNIX skill base may prompt an organization to build Windows skills prior to adopting Windows in the organization for mission-critical work.

- The need for office automation tools for different classes of users may prompt an organization to provide Windows applications for office users, and UNIX and Windows applications to others.
- Protection of existing legacy applications investment should be considered.
- Cost/benefit trade-offs between savings from a homogeneous environment and cost of moving applications and retraining must be considered.

Often, strategy decisions regarding migration and coexistence are made at the enterprise level. The primary factors leading to migration or coexistence choices are the same as that of homogeneous and heterogeneous environments. The following summarizes the advantages and disadvantages of migration and coexistence approaches.

Migration

Advantages include:

- Improved productivity through interface consistency
- Reduced system administration costs
- Reduced network administration costs
- Easier exchange of documents and data within the organization
- Possible to include all the functionality of the new environment
- Possible to achieve better performance

Disadvantages include:

- Costs of moving to a homogeneous environment
- Cost of maintaining a homogeneous environment
- Possibility of lock-in to one or more vendors
- Extensive retraining of users using different systems

Coexistence

Advantages include:

- You can pick the most cost-effective solution at any given point.
- The natural evolution is toward coexistence in heterogeneous environments.
- There are no additional costs involved in trying to move to another environment.
- In many cases, it is faster to make an application available to heterogeneous clients than porting.
- Up-front costs tend to be smaller than porting.

Disadvantages include:

- Interface inconsistency problems
- Need to perform system administration for multiple environments
- Need to connect and bridge different types of networks
- Exchange of documents and data is difficult and often requires format translations and loss of data fidelity
- Long-term costs of maintaining multiple environments may be more than the upfront cost of migrating and the lower cost of maintaining a nearly homogeneous environment

- Application performance for heterogeneous clients may not be the same as that of the clients the application was designed for

Build vs. Buy

Another enterprise-level factor that applies across migration and coexistence solutions is the build vs. buy decision. This, of course, is applicable to more than just migration and coexistence solutions. Some of the solutions we have discussed in the book, such as manual porting between environments and using tools based on advanced object technologies, require a skill level that may not be available internally to many organizations.

There are many firms that provide migration and coexistence services. These services include planning, evaluation, and implementation. Some of the companies that provide these services include DEC, Tandem, etc.

Solution-Specific Factors

There is a set of factors that applies to all migration/coexistence solutions, such as EUI differences, workstation resources, and standards. There are also factors that are unique to a given migration/coexistence solution. Let us look at both sets of factors in this section.

EUI Differences

It is virtually impossible that every mouse click, every keyboard stroke or combination, every function key, etc., will produce identical responses between the native Windows interface and a simulated one. The Graphical User Interface (GUI) approach in the UNIX environment, while trying to give a "comparable look-and-feel" to Windows, attempts to provide functionality superior to Windows. The differences in the way the interfaces behave could be annoying to the user if it becomes necessary to routinely switch back and forth between UNIX and Windows applications.

Workstation Resources

If both UNIX and Windows applications exist on the desktop, the resources required at the workstation (e.g., memory, disk space, etc.) increase compared to having applications of only one type. This factor may particularly trouble laptop users and those applications that require significant processing at the workstation, i.e., "fat" clients.

Standards

Many organizations, particularly in the government or under contract with it, want systems that are compliant with open system standards. The different flavors not withstanding, UNIX is more open than NT, although there are aspects of NT that are open. The WIN32 is a published API, and NT runs on multiple processor families, including Intel, PowerPC, and Alpha. However, Microsoft still controls the API and the only practical support for the API comes from Microsoft's operating systems. In fact, some of the migration/coexistence solution vendors have agreements with Microsoft that provide them access, among other things, to Microsoft source code. There have been some recent efforts to standardize the WIN32 API, the results of which remain to be seen. In the UNIX world, one can think of POSIX applications without having a specific vendor in mind. Organizations are taking a serious look at NT and the possibility that the desktop success of Windows will spill over to servers with NT and they want to be prepared. Although Windows NT is POSIX compliant, the POSIX subsystem is implemented as a separate subsystem within NT and is not really suited for developing POSIX applications. For example, the POSIX subsystem in NT lacks GUI support (includes only character support), and it is unlikely that future versions of NT will be UNIX 95 (and follow on) compliant.

Factors Related to X-Servers

X-servers let a Windows machine access UNIX applications. The factors relating to X-servers that you should consider include:

- No modifications are required in the UNIX applications.
- X-server is a Windows application and behaves like any other Windows application and includes features such as cut-and-paste, etc.
- The setup involves installing the X-server software and establishing connectivity to the UNIX server. As such, it is typically faster than other means of making UNIX applications available on Windows NT, such as porting.

Factors Related to Porting

Porting source code is applicable only if you have the source. This rules out most COTS products and old applications for which you no longer have all the sources.

Manual Porting

The biggest advantage of manual porting is that once you have accomplished the port, you no longer need the source in the environment you are porting from. The biggest downside is that it takes time and effort to accomplish manual porting. Manual porting is appropriate under the following conditions:

- Your application is small enough that manual porting can be accomplished within a reasonable time and with reasonable effort.
- Manual porting makes better business sense than other ways of making the application available in the ported to environment, such as tool-based porting or emulation.
- Your application has a long enough life expectancy that it is likely to be used as is without requiring replacement or a rewrite in the near future. If the application is close to its life expectancy, you may be better off rewriting or replacing the application.
- Once you manually port the application, you can realize significant savings in the porting-from environment through reduced usage (or no usage) of that environment.
- You have access to in-depth programming skills in both environments. If you do not have the skills internally, you may need help from third parties. For example, if you are porting a UNIX application to Windows NT, you need programming skills in both UNIX and Windows NT.

Tool-Based Porting

Your business application may have been developed from scratch, purchased as a package, or purchased as a package and modifications made to fit your environment. If you bought a package, then you need to check with the package vendor to see if they offer a version that runs in the environment you are interested in. You should also check if the vendor offers porting assistance, in particular for the custom modifications you may have. An in-house application would be an appropriate porting candidate under the following conditions:

- The application has a long useful expected life.

- The current development and maintenance programmer skill base dealing with the application would require a big learning curve for a new environment.
- The benefits of making the application work in the new environment outweigh leaving the application as is or rewriting it.
- The application size is large enough to gain some benefits when ported, but not so large that it would make porting a long, error-prone, and risky process.

There are some business benefits that can be derived by porting:

- The biggest benefit of porting is that it permits a stepping-stone approach to a potentially complex migration from one environment to another.
- Porting permits your system administrators and their custom utilities to immediately transition and be productive in the new environment.
- Porting permits you to continue to use your development and maintenance skills while you transition to the new environment.
- Depending on your applications, you may be able to get the applications working in the new environment with little effort.
- Your end-users can start using your existing applications in the new environment without having to relearn the applications.
- You can take advantage of unique features available in the new environment as a post porting step, but this may introduce divergence in the source between your sources in the old and new environments.
- If you need to run your applications in multiple environments, then porting is one way to keep a common source across environments.
- Keeping a common source is much more cost effective for development and maintenance than individual source libraries for different environments.

The disadvantages of porting are:

- You still need to keep and maintain the original source. Tool-based porting does not mean one-way migration.
- There may be annoying differences in end-user interfaces. For example, certain Windows GUI elements such as pop-up menus and window repainting operate differently from X/Motif widgets. The reverse is true as well. Some UNIX features may not be supported in Windows NT. For a user who has both a native application and a ported application, it may be annoying to go back and forth between applications where the end-user interface is not consistent. You may feel this annoyance if you run an old DOS application under Windows and you are unable to use your mouse.

If as a manager you are wondering how serious a porting problem you have, then check your code against for the following list of things that makes it easy to port:

- Code in which end-user interface handling and business logic handling are isolated
- Code in which vendor extensions to standards are isolated
- Code in which dependencies on a specific operating system are isolated (particularly true for UNIX with its many flavors)
- Overall program flow is separated into logical, modular blocks

Most of the porting today is between UNIX and Windows NT, although there are some others such as OS/2 to Windows NT. Factors for and against UNIX are given below.

UNIX is preferred by some customers for the following reasons:

- Proven in mission-critical applications
- Proven high-end availability
- Proven scalability
- Proven performance
- Proven integrity
- User familiarity with current UNIX production applications

Some factors for not considering UNIX include:

- UNIX, though it is supposed to be open, may still require considerable effort to move from one vendor to another.
- UNIX workstations are typically more expensive than PCs, and UNIX versions of software are also typically more expensive than a Windows version of the same or equivalent software.
- Users might prefer Windows-based Office products and prefer to have one simple consistent desktop.

If the customer has a Windows NT application (that was bought or developed as a test application) and would like to deploy it as a production application with other production applications on UNIX, then porting from Windows NT to UNIX is an option. Depending on factors such as the size of the application and the available skill set, this option may be preferable to rewriting the application in UNIX.

Factors Related to Cross-Platform Development

If you are developing applications and want to able to run your application without being tied to a specific environment, then cross-platform development is a solution. You cannot take an existing application and run it through any cross-platform development tool to achieve the ability to execute across platforms. You need a porting tool to do that. But for new applications, you can use 4 GL or object-oriented frameworks to enable you to execute across platforms. If you are using a third-party API or tool for cross-platform development, keep in mind that you may become dependent on the vendor for your applications. Also, watch out for royalty fees (for these and other migration and coexistence solutions), and factor the fees into your overall evaluation.

Factors Related to Emulators

The biggest advantage of emulators is that they enable applications to execute in another environment without the need for having the source (such as shrink-wrapped applications). The biggest drawback it that emulation invariably has a performance penalty (which may or may not be acceptable or may be expensive to fix). Emulation also has the user interface consistency problem mentioned earlier in this chapter.

SOLUTION SELECTION GUIDELINES

We looked at a number of different solutions for migration and coexistence between heterogeneous systems. Before we look at some guidelines in using the solutions, let us look at an administrative or procedural solution that is sometimes overlooked.

TABLE 13.1
Applications Guidelines and Applicable Solutions

Application Guideline	Applicable Solutions
Application source not available (e.g., shrink wrapped applications or old applications)	Porting solutions that need source code cannot be used
Performance	Native applications, in general, tend to have better performance than emulated solutions due to the absence of extra steps at run time
Supported applications	Although most solutions try to ensure support for the most popular Windows applications, some DOS applications and applications using certain Windows modes and device drivers do not work with some solutions.
Application data interchange	Windows applications running in another environment normally have DDE and OLE support, although the same may not be true for interchange between Windows and UNIX applications on the same desktop (clipboard interchange may still be possible)
Application location	In some solutions, it is executed on a server like NT and accessed by clients on a network; in others, the application gets executed at the client. In the former case, costs associated with installing and maintaining a server need to be included in the overall solution cost
Networking support	Varies between solutions, although most try to provide TCP/IP and NetWare support

You should include procedural solutions for review when you are evaluating migration and coexistence solutions. For example, consider the need to make Windows-based desktop office products available to a predominantly production UNIX-application user set with only occasional need for Windows applications. A procedural solution would be to set up a stand-alone Windows system or a pool of Windows systems for common use rather than enabling Windows applications on the desktop of each production user. Organizations that have tried this approach sometimes note a loss of productivity when people have to interrupt their work and train of thought and physically move to another location and return to their regular desk to continue their work.

Alternatively, you can also consider providing two machines. While this may save the trouble of people having to move from their seats, there are footprint problems to be considered. In many instances, the desktops do not have enough space to accommodate two machines. In addition, the use of two machines also increases power consumption and the need for maintenance. The primary advantage of the administrative approach is that you do not have to invest in a migration and coexistence solution. This approach works best when the users spend a very small fraction of their time in one environment compared to their work time in the production environments.

If applications are working well and the only issue is connectivity between different types of servers for file services, print services, etc., client interoperability tools would help. Table 13.1 lists the application guidelines and applicable solutions.

Consideration of the above factors and guidelines should help customers narrow their migration/coexistence solution choices and make a more informed selection of their migration/coexistence solutions.

Heterogeneous System Administration Considerations

When you have multiple environments, you can make it easy for the end-user if the system and network administrators of the different environments collaborate to ensure consistency. The following are some areas for consistency:

- Ensure that the password conventions (length, allowed characters, expiration duration, etc.) are the same between the different environments as much as possible. (This is in case you are unable to establish a common logon across environments.)
- Establish common group names across the different environments.
- Establish a common response center/helpdesk. If users can report by e-mail, try to have one e-mail ID for system and network support regardless of the user's environment. The same should also be true for help hotlines and help through intranet Web addresses, etc.
- Provide cross-permissions between administrators. There will always be an instance when an administrator of one environment is available to handle a user's problem and knows what to do, but is unable to help because the administrator does not have the right access.
- Provide cross-training for a minimal set of administration activities across environments for the administrators.

Selecting and implementing a migration and coexistence solution is a choice that organizations must make based on their circumstances and requirements. The good news is that there are a variety of approaches and products supporting these approaches for you to choose from. Each organization has to look at each of the factors mentioned, evaluate how these factors apply to their situation, and select an approach that is consistent with short- and long-term goals of the organization. This book lists the factors that should be considered. It also lists the different approaches that can be taken.

Once an approach is selected, a detailed requirements list should be prepared and the different products that support the approach should be evaluated against the requirements. This book includes brief descriptions of many of the products and also includes supplemental information in the CD as well as online and other contact information for the product vendors.

Appendix A
Additional Information

Migration/Coexistence Products and Vendor Contact Information

Product(s)	Chapter Reference	Product Vendor
Access NFS for Windows NT RhaPC-d	3	Intergraph Corporation One Madison Industrial Park Huntsville, AL 35894-0014 (800) 291-9909 (205) 730-2000 e-mail: nfs_info@ingr.com http://www.intergraph.com
Allegris	4	Intersolv http://www.intersolv.com
Amadeus		Amadeus Software Research amadeus-info@amadeus.com
ApplixBuilder, ApplixWare		Applix, Inc. http://www.applix.com
BEA Jolt BEA TUXEDO	4	BEA Systems http://www.beasys.com
Best/1		BGS Systems http://www.bgs.com best1@bgs.com
Chameleon NFS32	8	NetManage, Inc. 10725 N. De Anza Blvd. Cupertino, CA 95014 (408) 973-7171 Fax: (408) 257-6405 http://www.netmanage.com
DCE Services for Windows NT	4	Digital Equipment Corporation http://www.digital.com
DISCOVER	3	Software Emancipation http://www.setech.com
eXalt-X	5	Intergraph http://www.intergraph.com

Migration/Coexistence Products and Vendor Contact Information *(continued)*

Product(s)	Chapter Reference	Product Vendor
eXceed for Windows NT eXceed for Windows NT SDK NFS Maestro for Windows NT	6, 8	Hummingbird Communications, Ltd. 1 Sparks Avenue North York, Ontario M2H 2W1 Canada (416) 496-2200 Fax: (416) 496-2207 +41 22 733 18 58 e-mail: sales@hummingbird.com http://www.hummingbird.com
eXcursion	3	Digital Equipment Corporation http://www.digital.com
Explora	7	National Computing Devices http://www.ncd.com
Foundation Design/1		Andersen Consulting http://www.andersenconsulting.com
HP 500 Applications Server	5	Hewlett-Packard http://www.hp.com
InterDrive	8	FTP Software http://www.ftp.com
MainWin Studio	3	MainSoft Corporation 1270 Oakmead Pkwy., Suite 310 Sunnyvale, CA 94086 (800) 624-6946 (408) 774-3400 e-mail: info@mainsoft.com http://www.mainsoft.com
MKS Toolkit for Windows NT	9	Mortice Kern Systems, Inc. 185 Columbia Street, West Waterloo, Ontario Canada N2L 5Z5 (800) 265-2797 (519) 884-2251 +44 171 624 0100 Fax: (519) 884-8861 e-mail: sales@mks.com http://www.mks.com
NTerprise	5	Exodus Technologies http://www.exodustech.com

Migration/Coexistence Products and Vendor Contact Information *(continued)*

Product(s)	Chapter Reference	Product Vendor
NTrigue (for Windows NT)	5, 7	Insignia Solutions, Inc. 2200 Lawson Lane Santa Clara, CA 95054 (408) 327-6000 Fax: (408) 327-6105 +44 131 458 6849 Fax: +44 131 451 6981 e-mail: info@isltd.insignia.com http://www.insignia.com
N*u*TCRACKER, N*u*TCRACKER X-Server	3	DataFocus, Inc. 12450 Fair Lake Circle, Suite 400 Fairfax, VA 22033-3831 (800) 637-8034; (703) 631-6770 Fax: (703) 818-1532 e-mail: nutcracker@datafocus.com http://www.datafocus.com
OmniGuard		Axent Technologies http://www.axent.com
Omni SQL Gateway	4	Sybase http://www.sybase.com
OpenNT	3	Softway Systems, Inc. 185 Berry Street, Suite 5514 San Francisco, CA 94107 (415) 896-0708; Fax: (415) 896-0709 (800) 438-8649 e-mail: OPENNT@softway.com http://www.softway.com/opennt/
PATHWORKS	8	Digital Equipment Corporation http://www.digital.com/info/pathworks
PC-DCE	4	Gradient Technologies http://www.gradient.com
PC-Xware for Windows 3.1, Windows NT, and Windows 95, WinCenter Pro	6	Network Computing Devices, Inc. 350 North Bernardo Avenue Mountain View, CA 94043 (800) 600-5099 (415) 694-0650 e-mailinfo@ncd.com (WinCenter Pro) e-mail: info@pcx.ncd.com(PC-Xware) http://www.ncd.com

Migration/Coexistence Products and Vendor Contact Information *(continued)*

Product(s)	Chapter Reference	Product Vendor
Portage	3	Consensys Computers, Inc. 35 Riviera Drive, Unit 9 Markham, ON, Canada L3R 8N4 (800) 388-1896; (905) 940-2900 Fax: (905) 940-2903 e-mail: sales@consensys.com http://www.consensys.com
Reflection X for Windows NT, Reflection Z (VT420) for Windows NT	6	Walker, Richer and Quinn (WRQ), Inc. 1500 Dexter Ave. N., PO Box 31876 Seattle, WA 98103-1876 (800) 926-3896; (206) 217-7100 +31 70 375 1100 e-mail: sales@wrq.com http://www.wrq.com
Street Talk	11	Banyan Systems http://www.banyan.com
Systems Toolkit	4	Object Space http://www.objectspace.com
SNA Client for UNIX	4	Parker Software http://www.parkersoftware.com
SoftWindows	7	Insignia Solutions http://www.insignia.com
UnixWare NetWare Services	11	Santa Cruz Operations http://www.sco.com
ViewPoint	7	Boundless Technologies http://www.boundless.com
VisiODBC Driver Sets, SDK	3	Visigenic http://www.visigenic.com
WABI	7	Sun Microsystems http://www.sun.com
Willows Toolkit	3	Willows Software http://www.willows.com
Wind/U	3	Bristol Technology, Inc. 241 Ethan Allen Hwy. Ridgefield, CT 06877 (203) 438-6969; Fax: (203) 438-5013 e-mail: info@bristol.com http://www.bristol.com
WinDD	5	Tektronix http://www.tek.com

Migration/Coexistence Products and Vendor Contact Information *(continued)*

Product(s)	Chapter Reference	Product Vendor
WinTED	5	TriTeal http://triteal.com
WinTerm	7	Wyse Technology http://www.wyse.com
XoftWare for Windows NT	6	NetManage http://www.netmanage.com
XVision	6	Santa Cruz Operations http://www.sco.com
XVT Development Solution for C++, C, Windows NT (DSC ++)	4	XVT Software, Inc. 9900 Pearl East Circle Boulder, CO 80301 (800) 678-7988; (303) 443-0969 http://www.xvt.com/xvt
zApp	4	Rogue Wave Software http://www.roguewave.com

NEWSGROUPS

Newsgroups where the subject matter of this book are discussed from time to time include:

- comp.os.netware.connectivity
- comp.os.netware.misc
- comp.os.ms-windows.nt
- comp.os.ms-windows.nt.admin.misc
- comp.os.ms-windows.nt.admin.networking
- comp.os.ms-windows.nt.misc
- comp.os.ms-windows.programmer.win32
- comp.windows.ms.programmer.win32
- comp.os.ms-windows.nt.setup
- comp.os.ms-windows.nt.software.backoffice
- comp.os.ms-windows.nt.software.compatibility
- comp.unix.admin
- comp.unix.questions

- comp.unix.osf.osf1
- comp.unix.osf.misc

ONLINE SERVICES FORUMS AND SOFTWARE

	Microsoft Forums
CompuServe Forums	go winnt — Windows NT forums go msl — Microsoft software library go mskb — Microsoft Knowledge Base go WIN32 — 32-bit developer's forum go microsoft — General Microsoft forum
	DIGITAL Forums
CompuServe Software	go decpci (Topic #15 is WIN NT/ALPHA DEV) MSWIN32 (files include iftpd.zip and mftpd.zip)
America Online	goto microsoft
Microsoft Network	GO WORD: MSNTS

White Papers

A number of companies have produced white papers on different aspects of Windows NT, UNIX, and NetWare migration and coexistence.

The following white papers are available from Microsoft. You can download them from ftp://ftp.microsoft.com/bussys/winnt/winnt-docs/papers.

File Name	Description
DSMNGD.EXE	Microsoft Directory Service Manager for NetWare
FPNW_REV.EXE	Microsoft File and Print Services for NetWare
NT4UNIX.EXE	Microsoft Windows NT from a Unix Point of View
Nwipnts.exe	Microsoft Windows NT Server 3.5: Integration of Windows NT Server DHCP and WINS into a Novell NetWare IP Environment
UNIXINT.EXE	Windows-family Integration with UNIX Systems
WISE.EXE	Windows Interface Source Environment (WISE) Integrating Windows solutions with UNIX and Macintosh systems in the Enterprise
DCE.EXE	The Microsoft Strategy for Distributed Computing and DCE Services
DHCPWINS.EXE	Microsoft Windows NT Server 3.5: Dynamic Host Configuration Protocol and Windows Internet Naming Service
DNSWP.EXE	DNS and Microsoft Windows NT 4.0
DS_STRAT.EXE	Microsoft Directory Services Strategy
SERVMAC.EXE	Microsoft Windows NT Server 3.51: Services for the Macintosh
TCPIPIMP.EXE	Microsoft Windows NT 3.5/3.51: TCP/IP Implementation
TCPIPIMP2.DOC	Microsoft Windows NT 3.5/3.51/4.0: TCP/IP Implementation TCP/IP Protocol Stack and Services, Version 2.0

All .exe documents found in this directory are self-extracting zipped .doc files created in Microsoft Word for Windows 6.0.

If you do not have Microsoft Word or a compatible word processor you can use the free Microsoft Word Viewer on Windows platforms to view and print this document.

You will find the free word viewer at ftp.microsoft.com/softlib/mslfiles/wordvu.exe. And for Windows 95, at ftp.microsoft.com/softlib/mslfiles/wd95view.exe

Digital — White papers covering Windows NT and UNIX are available from Digital at http://www.windowsNT.digital.com and http:\\www.unix.digital.com. White papers are also available from many of the other vendors mentioned in this book at their Web addresses.

COURSES

Porting NetView Applications from UNIX to Microsoft Windows NT, offered by Digital Equipment Corporation.

Porting Applications from UNIX to Microsoft Windows NT, offered by Digital Equipment Corporation. Provides a technical overview of the issues involved in porting from UNIX to Windows NT systems. Course number: EY–P868EQPL0–W3.

JMH Associates

Windows NT and Win32 Programming for UNIX Programmers, covers programming in the Win32 environment for programmers who are familiar with UNIX programming. Contact jmhart@world.std.com.

Solomon Software Technologies

Windows NT for UNIX Programmers, provides in-depth coverage of the Windows NT system and products, with some detailed treatment of implementation and design issues. For information, contact 71561.3603@compuserv.com.

Demopoulos Associates

Windows NT and DIGITAL UNIX: A Technical Comparison, covers the architectural and functional similarities and differences of the two operating systems. Contact ted@osf.org.

FTP SITES

FTP Site	Files Available
ftp.microsoft.com	Microsoft support files, patches, drivers, for Windows NT, Windows 95, etc.
rhino.microsoft.com	Windows NT TCP/IP applications, information
ftp.cica.indiana.edu	Windows NT shareware and freeware
sunsite.unc.edu	Shareware and freeware, including Windows
ftp.uu.net	Code samples and development information Microsoft information in /vendor/microsoft
ftp.iastate.edu	Utilities-Check /pub/nt[cpu-type]/ for ftpdserv.zip and others

BOOKS

Windows NT 4 Advanced Programming by Raj Rajagopal and Subodh Monica, Osborne/McGraw-Hill. Provides programming concepts and examples for a number of Windows Technologies, including OLE2, ActiveX, Advanced GUI, OpenGL, TAPI, ODBC, DAO, Internet programming, WinSock 2, GDI, etc.

Windows NT Answer Book by Jim Groves. Microsoft Press. ISBN 1-55615-562-X. Contains the most commonly asked questions with answers.

Inside Windows NT by Helen Custer. Microsoft Press. ISBN 1-55615-481-X. Covers the internal architecture and implementation of Windows NT.

Migrating to Windows NT by Randall C. Kennedy. Brady Publishing. ISBN 1-56686-103-9. Primarily discusses migration from DOS and Windows and covers how Windows NT emulates those environments.

Distributing Applications Across DCE and Windows NT. O'Reilly & Associates, Inc. Explains how to use the Microsoft DCE-compatible RPC and DCE implementations based on the OSF DCE to build DCE-based applications.

The Windows NT Resource Kit in three volumes from Microsoft Press:
- *Windows NT Resource Guide.* ISBN 1-55615-598-0.
- *Windows NT Messages.* ISBN 1-55615-600-6.
- *Optimizing Windows NT.* ISBN 1-55615-619-7.

Cross-Platform Development Using Visual C++ by Chane Cullens and Ken Blackwell. M&T Books. ISBN 1-55851-428-7. Describes how to use Visual C++ to create applications for Windows, Windows NT, UNIX, and Macintosh platforms.

Win32 System Services: The Heart of Windows NT by Marshall Brain. Prentice Hall. ISBN 0-13-097825-6. Describes the Win32 APIs and provides examples.

Application Programming for Windows NT by William H.Murray. Osborne McGraw-Hill. ISBN 0078819334.

Windows NT 4 Programming from the Ground Up by Herbert Schildt, Osborne/McGraw-Hill. Introductory programming book for Windows NT.

RPC for NT by Guy Eddon. R&D Publications, distributed by Prentice Hall. ISBN 0131002236.

Networking Windows NT 3.51 by John D. Ruley. Wiley. ISBN 0471127051.

ORGANIZATIONS

Organizations involved with topics covered in this book include:

Organization	Web Address
USENIX - Technical and Professional Association	http://www.usenix.org
UNIFORUM	http://www.uniforum.org
Open Group	http://www.og.org
Object Management Group	http://www.omg.org
Open Software Foundation	http://www.osf.org
UNICODE	http://www.unicode.org

Appendix B Glossary

A

access right The permission granted to a process to manipulate a particular object in a particular way (e.g., by calling a service). Different object types support different access rights.

application programming interface (API) A set of routines that an application program uses to request and carry out lower-level services performed by the operating system.

asynchronous I/O A method many of the processes in Windows NT use to optimize their performance. When an application initiates an I/O operation, the I/O Manager accepts the request but does not block the application's execution while the I/O operation is being performed. Instead, the application is allowed to continue doing work. Most I/O devices are very slow in comparison to a computer's processor, so an application can do a lot of work while waiting for an I/O operation to complete. See also *synchronous I/O*.

audit policy Defines the type of security events that are logged for a domain or for an individual computer; determines what Windows NT will do when the security log becomes full.

auditing The ability to detect and record security-related events, particularly any attempts to create, access, or delete objects. Windows NT uses *Security IDs (SIDs)* to record which process performed the action.

authentication A security step performed by the Remote Access Server (RAS), before logon validation, to verify that the user had permission for remote access. See also *validation*.

B

batch program An ASCII file (unformatted text file) that contains one or more commands in the command language for Windows NT. A batch program's filename has a .BAT or .CMD extension. When you type the filename at the command prompt, the commands are processed sequentially.

C

character based A mode of operation in which all information is displayed as text characters. This is the mode in which MS-DOS-based and OS/2 version 1.2 applications are displayed under Windows NT. Also called character mode, alphanumeric mode, or text mode.

client A computer that accesses shared network resources provided by another computer (called a server). For the X Window System of UNIX the client/server relationship is reversed. Under the X Window System, this client definition becomes the server definition. See also *server*.

computer name A unique name of up to 15 uppercase characters that identifies a computer to the network. The name cannot be the same as any other computer or domain name in the network, and it cannot contain spaces.

D

Data Link Control (DLC) A protocol interface device driver in Windows NT, traditionally used to provide connectivity to IBM mainframes and also used to provide connectivity to local area network printers directly attached to the network.

default profile See *system default profile, user default profile.*

demand paging Refers to a method by which data is moved in pages from physical memory to a temporary paging file on disk. As the data is needed by a process, it is paged back into physical memory.

device A generic term for a computer subsystem such as a printer, serial port, or disk drive. A device frequently requires its own controlling software called a *device driver.*

device driver A software component that allows the computer to transmit and receive information to and from a specific device. For example, a printer driver translates computer data into a form understood by a particular printer. Although a device may be installed on your system, Windows NT cannot recognize the device until you have installed and configured the appropriate driver.

directory services The defining element of distributed computing, and, ultimately, a logical name space capable of including all system resources regardless of type. The goal is a blending in which the directory and the network become synonymous.

disk caching A method used by a file system to improve performance. Instead of reading and writing directly to the disk, frequently used files are temporarily stored in a cache in memory, and reads and writes to those files are performed in memory. Reading and writing to memory is much faster than reading and writing to disk.

distributed application An application that has two parts — a front-end to run on the client computer and a back-end to run on the server. In distributed computing, the goal is to divide the computing task into two sections. The front-end requires minimal resources and runs on the client's workstation. The back-end requires large amounts of data, number crunching, or specialized hardware and runs on the server. Recently, there has been much discussion in the industry about a three-tier model for distributed computing. That model separates the business logic contained in both sides of the two-tier model into a third, distinct layer. The business logic layer sits between the front-end user interface layer and the back-end database layer. It typically resides on a server platform that may or may not be the same as the one the database is on. The three-tier model arose as a solution to the limits faced by software developers trying to express complex business logic with the two-tier model.

DLC See *Data Link Control.*

DLL See *dynamic-link library.*

domain For Windows NT Server, a networked set of workstations and servers that share a Security Accounts Manager (SAM) database and that can be administered as a group. A user with an account in a particular network domain can log onto and access his or her account from any system in the domain. See also *SAM database.*

domain controller For a Windows NT Server domain, the server that authenticates domain logons and maintains the security policy and the master database for a domain. Both servers and domain controllers are capable of validating a user's logon; however, password changes must be made by contacting the domain controller. See also *server.*

domain database See *SAM database.*

domain name The name by which a Windows NT domain is known to the network.

Domain Name System (DNS) A hierarchical name service for TCP/IP hosts (sometimes referred to as the BIND service in BSD Unix). The network administrator configures the DNS with a list of *hostnames* and IP addresses, allowing users of workstations configured to query the DNS to specify the remote systems by *hostnames* rather than IP addresses. DNS domains should not be confused with Windows NT *domains.*

dynamic-link library (DLL) An *application programming interface (API)* routine that user-mode applications access through ordinary procedure calls. The code for the API routine is not included in the user's executable image. Instead, the operating system automatically modifies the executable image to point to DLL procedures at run time.

E

environment subsystems User-mode protected servers that run and support programs from different operating systems environments. Examples of these subsystems are the Win32 subsystem, the POSIX subsystem, and the OS/2 subsystem. See also *integral subsystem.*

environment variable A string consisting of environment information, such as a drive, path, or filename, associated with a symbolic name that can be used by Windows NT. You use the System option in Control Panel or the **set** command to define environment variables.

event Any significant occurrence in the system or in an application that requires users to be notified or an entry to be added to a log.

Event Log service Records events in the system, security, and application logs.

Executive module The Kernel-mode module that provides basic operating system services to the environment subsystems. It includes several components; each manages a particular set of system services. One component, the Security Reference Monitor, works together with the protected subsystems to provide a pervasive security model for the system.

extensibility Indicates the modular design of Windows NT, which provides for the flexibility of adding future modules at several levels within the operating system.

F

FAT file system A file system based on a file allocation table maintained by the operating system to keep track of the status of various segments of disk space used for file storage.

fault tolerance The ability of a computer and an operating system to respond gracefully to catastrophic events such as power outage or hardware failure. Usually, fault tolerance implies the ability to either continue the system's operation without loss of data or to shut the system down and restart it, recovering all processing that was in progress when the fault occurred.

file sharing The ability for Windows NT Workstation or Windows NT Server to share parts (or all) of its local file system(s) with remote computers.

file system In an operating system, the overall structure in which files are named, stored, and organized.

FTP service File transfer protocol service, which offers file transfer services to remote systems supporting this protocol. FTP supports a host of commands allowing bidirectional transfer of binary and ASCII files between systems.

Fully Qualified Domain Name (FQDN) In TCP/IP, *hostnames* with their *domain names* appended to them. For example, a host with hostname *tsunami* and domain name *microsoft.com* had an FQDN of *tsunami.microsoft.com.*

G

global account For Windows NT Server, a normal user account in a user's home domain. If there are multiple domains in the network, it is best if each user in the network has only one user account, in only one domain, and each user's access to other domains is accomplished through the establishment of domain trust relationships.

group In User Manager, an account containing other accounts called members. The permissions and rights granted to a group are also provided to its members, making groups a convenient way to grant common capabilities to collections of user accounts.

H

Hardware Abstraction Layer (HAL) Virtualizes hardware interfaces, making the hardware dependencies transparent to the rest of the operating system. This allows Windows NT to be portable from one hardware platform to another.

home directory A directory that is accessible to the user and contains files and programs for that user. A home directory can be assigned to an individual user or can be shared by many users.

host table The HOSTS or LMHOSTS file that contains lists of known IP addresses.

hostname A TCP/IP command that returns the local workstation's *hostname* used for authentication by TCP/IP utilities. This value is the workstation's *computer name* by default, but it can be changed.

I

integral subsystem A subsystem such as the Security subsystem that affects the entire Windows NT operating system. See also *environment subsystems*.

interprocess communication (IPC) The exchange of data between one thread or process and another, either within the same computer or across a network. Common IPC mechanisms include pipes, named pipes, semaphores, shared memory, queues, signals, mailboxes, and sockets.

K

kernel The portion of Windows NT that manages the processor.

Kernel module The core of the layered architecture of Windows NT that manages the most basic operations of Windows NT. The Kernel is responsible for thread dispatching, multiprocessor synchronization, hardware exception handling, and the implementation of low-level, hardware-dependent functions.

L

LLC Logical link control, in the Data Link layer of the networking model.

local printer A printer that is directly connected to one of the ports on your computer.

local procedure call (LPC) An optimized message-passing facility that allows one thread or process to communicate with another thread or process on the same computer. The Windows NT=protected subsystems use LPC to communicate with each other and with their client processes. LPC is a variation of the remote procedure call (RPC) facility, optimized for local use. Compare with *remote procedure call.*

locale The national and cultural environment in which a system or program is running. The locale determines the language used for messages and menus, the sorting order of strings, the keyboard layout, and date and time formatting conventions.

logon authentication Refers to the validation of a user, either locally or in a domain. At logon time, the user specifies his or her name, password, and the intended logon *domain.* The workstation then contacts the *domain controllers* for the domain, which verify the user's logon credentials.

LPC See *local procedure call.*

M

MAC Media access control, in the Data Link layer of the networking model.

mandatory user profile For Windows NT Server, a user profile created by an administrator and assigned to one or more users. A mandatory user profile cannot be changed by the user and remains the same from one logon session to the next. See also *personal user profile, user profile.*

MS-DOS-based application An application designed to run with MS-DOS and which therefore may not be able to take full advantage of all of the features of Windows NT.

N

named pipe An interprocess communication mechanism that allows one process to send data to another local or remote process. Windows NT named pipes are not the same as UNIX named pipes.

NBF transport protocol NetBEUI Frame protocol. A descendant of the NetBEUI protocol, which is a Transport layer protocol, not the programming interface NetBIOS.

NDIS See *Network driver interface specification.*

NetBEUI transport NetBIOS (Network Basic Input/Output System) Extended User Interface. The primary local area network transport protocol in Windows NT.

NetBIOS interface A programming interface that allows I/O requests to be sent to and received from a remote computer. It hides networking hardware for applications.

network device driver Software that coordinates communication between the network adapter card and the computer's hardware and other software, controlling the physical function of the network adapter cards.

network driver interface specification (NDIS) An interface in Windows NT for network card drivers that provides transport independence, because all transport drivers call the NDIS interface to access network cards.

NTFS (Windows NT file system) An advanced file system designed specifically for use with the Windows NT operating system. NTFS supports file system recovery and extremely large storage media, in addition to other advantages. It also supports object-oriented applications by treating all files as objects with user-defined and system-defined attributes.

O

object type Includes a system-defined data type, a list of operations that can be performed upon it (such as wait, create, or cancel), and a set of object attributes. Object Manager is the part of the Windows NT Executive that provides uniform rules for retention, naming, and security of objects.

OLE A way to transfer and share information between applications.

P

packet A unit of information transmitted as a whole from one device to another on a network.

page A fixed-size block in memory.

partition A portion of a physical disk that functions as though it were a physically separate unit.

permission A rule associated with an object (usually a directory, file, or printer) in order to regulate which users can have access to the object and in what manner. See also *right.*

personal user profile For Windows NT Server, a user profile created by an administrator and assigned to one user. A personal user profile retains changes the user makes to the per-user settings of Windows NT and reimplements the newest settings each time that the user logs on at any Windows NT workstation. See also *mandatory user profile, user profile.*

port A connection or socket used to connect a device to a computer, such as a printer, monitor, or modem. Information is sent from the computer to the device through a cable.

portability Windows NT runs on both CISC and RISC processors. CISC includes computers running Intel 80386 or higher processors. RISC includes computers with MIPS R4000 or Digital Alpha AXP processors.

print device Refers to the actual hardware device that produces printed output.

print processor A dynamic link library that interprets data types. It receives information from the spooler and sends the interpreted information to the graphics engine.

printer In Windows NT, refers to the software interface between the application and the print device.

protocol A set of rules and conventions by which two computers pass messages across a network. Networking software usually implements multiple levels of protocols layered one on top of another.

provider The component that allows a computer running Windows NT to communicate with the network. Windows NT includes a provider for the Windows NT-based network; other providers are supplied by the alternate networks' vendors.

R

redirector Networking software that accepts I/O requests for remote files, named pipes, or mailslots and then sends (*redirects*) them to a network service on another computer. Redirectors are implemented as file system drivers in Windows NT.

remote administration Administration of one computer by an administrator located at another computer and connected to the first computer across the network.

remote procedure call (RPC) A message-passing facility that allows a distributed application to call services available on various computers in a network. Used during remote administration of computers. RPC provides a procedural view, rather than a transport-centered view, of networked operations. Compare with *local procedure call.*

resource Any part of a computer system or a network, such as a disk drive, or memory, that can be allotted to a program or a process while it is running.

right Authorizes a user to perform certain actions on the system. Rights apply to the system as a whole and are different from *permissions*, which apply to specific objects. (Sometimes called a *privilege.*)

RISC-based computer A computer based on a RISC (reduced instruction set) microprocessor, such as a Digital Alpha AXP, MIPS R4000, or IBM/Motorola PowerPC. Compare with *x86-based computer.*

router TCP/IP gateways — computers with two or more network adapters that are running some type of IP routing software: each adapter is connected to a different physical network.

RPC See *remote procedure call.*

S

SAM See *Security Accounts Manager.*

SAM database The database of security information that includes user account names and passwords and the settings of the security policies.

scalability Scalability depends on the overall architecture of the entire application server. The three critical components of a scalable system are: operating system, application software, and hardware. No one element by itself is sufficient to guarantee scalability. High-performance server hardware is designed to scale to multiple processors, providing specific functionality to ease disk and memory bottlenecks. Applications and operating systems, in turn, must be able to take advantage of multiple CPUs. All three components are equally important.

Schedule service Supports and is required for use of the **at** command, which can schedule commands and programs to run on a computer at a specified date and time.

Security Accounts Manager (SAM) A Windows NT protected subsystem that maintains the SAM database and provides an API for accessing the database.

security ID (SID) A unique name that identifies a logged-on user to the security system of Windows NT. A security ID can identify either an individual user or a group of users.

server A LAN-based computer running administrative software that controls access to all or part of the network and its resources. A computer acting as a server makes resources available to computers acting as workstations on the network. For the X Window System of UNIX, the client/server relationship is reversed. Under the X Window System, this server definition becomes the client definition. See also *client*.

Server service A service in Windows NT that supplies an API for managing the Windows NT-based network software. Provides RPC support, and file, print, and named pipe sharing.

service A process that performs a specific system function and often provides an API for other processes to call. Services in Windows NT are RPC enabled, meaning that their API routines can be called from remote computers.

session A connection that two applications on different computers establish, use, and end. The session layer performs name recognition and the functions needed to allow two applications to communicate over the network.

socket Provides an end point to a connection; two sockets form a complete path. A socket works as a bidirectional pipe for incoming and outgoing data between networked computers. The Windows Sockets API is a networking API tailored for use by Windows-based applications.

standards Windows NT provides support for many standards, some of which are: AppleTalk, Apple File Protocol, C2, Connection-oriented Transport Protocol (Class 4), Connectionless Network Protocol (CLNP), Domain Name Service (DNS), Dynamic Host Configuration Protocol (DHCP), Ethernet, Fiber Distributed Data Interface (FDDI), FIPS 151-2, Frame Relay, IEEE 802.x, IEEE 1003.1, IPX/SPX, Integrated Services Digital Network (ISDN), ISO 8073, ISO 8473, ISO 8208, ISO 8314, ISO 8802, ISO 9660, ISO 9945-1, ISO 10646, ITU FAX Standards, ITU Modem Standards, NetWare Core Protocol (NCP), OpenGL™, OSI, POSIX, Point-to-Point Protocol (PPP), Personal Computer Memory Card International (PCMCIA), Serial Line Interface Protocol (SLIP), Simple Network Management Protocol (SNMP), Token Ring, TCP/IP, Unicode, and X.25.

synchronous I/O The simplest way to perform I/O, by synchronizing the execution of applications with completion of the I/O operations that they request. When an application performs an I/O operation, the application's processing is blocked. When the I/O operation is complete, the application is allowed to continue processing. See also *asynchronous I/O*.

system default profile For Windows NT Server, the user profile that is loaded when Windows NT is running and no user is logged on. When the Welcome dialog box is visible, the system default profile is loaded. See also *user default profile, user profile*.

T

TDI See *Transport Driver Interface*.

Telnet service The service that provides basic terminal emulation to remote systems supporting the Telnet protocol over TCP/IP.

text file A file containing only letters, numbers, and symbols. A text file contains no formatting information, except possibly linefeeds and carriage returns. Text files are also known as flat files and ASCII files.

thread An executable entity that belongs to a single process, comprising a program counter, a user-mode stack, a kernel-mode stack, and a set of register values. All threads in a process have equal access to the processor's address space, object handles, and other resources. In Windows NT, threads are implemented as objects.

Transport Driver Interface (TDI) In the networking model, a common interface for network components that communicate at the session layer.

transport protocol Defines how data should be presented to the next receiving layer in the networking model and packages the data accordingly. It passes data to the network adapter card driver through the *NDIS* Interface, and to the *redirector* through the *Transport Driver Interface*.

trust relationship Trust relationships are links between domains that enable pass-through authentication, in which a user has only one user account in one domain, yet can access the entire network. A trusting domain honors the logon authentications of a trusted domain.

U

Unicode A fixed-width, 16-bit character encoding standard capable of representing all of the world's scripts.

user account Consists of all the information that defines a user to Windows NT. This includes the username and password required for the user to log on, the groups in which the user account has membership, and the rights and permissions the user has for using the system and accessing its resources. See also *group*.

user default profile For Windows NT Server, the user profile that is loaded by a server when a user's assigned profile cannot be accessed for any reason, when a user without an assigned profile logs on to the computer for the first time, or when a user logs on the Guest account. See also *system default profile, user profile*.

user mode A nonprivileged processor mode in which application code runs.

user profile Configuration information retained on a user-by-user basis. The information includes all the per-user settings of Windows NT, such as the desktop arrangement, personal program groups and the program items in those groups, screen colors, screen savers, network connections, printer connections, mouse settings, window size and position, and more. When a user logs on, the user's profile is loaded, and the user's environment in Windows NT is configured according to that profile.

user right See *right*.

username A unique name identifying a user account to Windows NT. An account's username cannot be identical to any other group name or username of its own domain or workstation. See also *user account*.

V

validation Authorization check of a user's logon information. When a user logs on to an account on a Windows NT Workstation computer, the authentication is performed by that workstation. When a user logs on to an account on a Windows NT Server domain, that authentication may be performed by any server of that domain. See also *trust relationship*.

virtual DOS machine (VDM) A Windows NT protected subsystem that supplies a complete environment for MS-DOS and a console in which to run applications for MS-DOS or 16-bit Windows. A VDM is a Win32 application that establishes a complete virtual x86 (that is, 80386 or higher) computer running MS-DOS. Any number of VDMs can run simultaneously.

virtual memory Space on a hard disk that Windows NT uses as if it were actually memory. Windows NT does this through the use of paging files. The benefit of using virtual memory is that you can run more applications at one time than your system's physical memory would otherwise allow. The drawbacks are the disk space required for the virtual-memory paging file and the decreased execution speed when swapping is required.

volume A partition or collection of partitions that have been formatted for use by a file system.

W

Win32 API A 32-bit application programming interface for Windows NT. It updates earlier versions of the Windows API with sophisticated operating system capabilities, security, and API routines for displaying text-based applications in a window.

Windows on Win32 (WOW) A Windows NT protected subsystem that runs within a VDM process. It provides an environment for 16-bit Windows capable of running any number of applications for 16-bit Windows under Windows NT.

Windows Sockets An IPC mechanism based on the WinSock specification and compatible with the Berkeley Sockets IPC under UNIX. The WinSock specification allows hardware and software vendors to design systems and applications that can access virtually any type of underlying network, including TCP/IP, IPX/SPX, OSI, ATM networks, wireless networks, and telephone networks.

workstation In general, a powerful computer having considerable calculating and graphics capability. For Windows NT, computers running the Windows NT Workstation operating system are called workstations, as distinguished from computers running Windows NT Server, which are called servers. See also *server, domain controller.*

Workstation service A service for Windows NT that supplies user-mode API routines to manage the Windows NT redirector. Provides network connections and communications.

WOW The subsystem for running Windows for MS-DOS under Windows NT; sometimes also called Win16 or Win32.

X

x86-based computer A computer using a microprocessor equivalent to an Intel 80386 or higher chip. Compare with a *RISC-based computer.*

Index

A

B

C

J

K

L

M

N

O

P

R

S

T

U

V

W

X

Z